UNITED NATIONS INTERREGIONAL CRIME AND JUSTICE RESEARCH INSTITUTE

ESSAYS ON CRIME
AND DEVELOPMENT

edited by

Uglješa Zvekić

Publication No. 36
Rome, July 1990

CONTENTS

5

PREFACE

United Nations interest in the "development and crime issue" has been steadily increasing for some time and, although there is a lack of a clear perspective, the Organization's involvement in the ongoing debate indicates a recognition of its importance for Member States and the international criminal justice community, in particular. The significance of this involvement should be seen in the context of a critique addressed to development administrators and the academic community, both of whom, although for different reasons, have for a long time respectively overlooked the importance of crime in their analysis of development and the importance of developmental conditions in the analysis of crime and criminal justice. In addition, it should be noted that for many years debate on the issues concentrated on the developing world. The growing international interdependence and the growing internationalization of certain forms of crime and reactions to crime, almost dictate the widening of the locus of the debate to include both developed and developing countries. At the same time, a sharpening of the focus of the debate on different developmental environments and related national and transnational problems of crime, is evidently also needed.

This collection of essays addresses some of the relevant issues in an illustrative rather than systematic manner. It makes part of UNICRI's systematic efforts to promote debate and research on development and crime, through the organization of panels and seminars, the conduction of national and comparative studies on the topic, and the dissemination of information. The volume contains a number of contributions presented at a panel session organized by the Institute in the context of the Tenth International Congress on Criminology (Hamburg, 4-10 September 1988). It also contains some

7

contributions submitted for inclusion in the monographic section of the International Review of Sociology.

My gratitude goes to the contributors, to the International Review of Sociology, to the United Nations Development Programme and to the Crime Prevention and Criminal Justice Branch, Centre for Social Development and Humanitarian Affairs, United Nations Office at Vienna, for their consent to present the essays in this volume.

Ugo Leone
Director

INTRODUCTORY NOTES

Today it is almost a truism to state that there is a relationship between crime and development. In other words, processes of social transformation are in some determined way connected with changes in the levels and forms of crime and/or reactions to crime, and the criminal question is interrelated with issues of development. Both the researcher and the criminal justice administrator are faced with an increasing concern for the alleged crime generating influences of development, and for crime prevention/controlling industries and costs, which are in turn influenced in some way by the former processes. Even to the lay person, the connection appears, if not quite clear, at least rather worrisome. In some places, and with striking effect, the belief in inevitable progress as society develops seems to be seriously challenged by the growth in crime and its human, material and administrative costs. For many, crime and development are so closely interrelated that there is nothing more logical (or natural) than to look at them in a causative, or at least highly associative manner.

The essays in this volume address the topic of crime and development from various perspectives, at different levels and with different foci. Yet, some important recurrent themes can be identified.

An overview of a number of theoretical and empirical studies on crime and development *(Queloz)* shows that there is no universal theoretical framework which successfully identifies and predicts processes of development which have a bearing on criminal behaviour, and/or reactions to it. There is no global theory of social change or crime. The studies carried out have provided ample illustrative evidence regarding the existence of connections between the two

9

phenomena, but they are rather inconclusive and even contradictory as to the nature, type and direction of these connections. Furthermore, it has been shown that the dogmatic imposition of a particular theory leads only to a partial explanation. In this sense, what is required on the one hand is a more flexible theoretical framework, and on the other, more research with precise temporal and spatial locations. This point is further taken up by *Burnham* in the context of a critical review of developments in criminology, showing a strong skepticism towards a global theory of crime and social change, and macroscopic quantitative research. It is argued that research in crime and development should focus on specific contexts and issues reflecting concerns which so far have been left at too general a level of explanation, involving the undifferentiated use of the notion of crime. As to the former criticism, a trend towards a sharpening of the focus has been noted, and the holistic approach has been found wanting. On the other hand, the focus has shifted to differentiated crime categories, and more recently, to the operation of the criminal justice system. Another important development concerns an increasing use of the state or legal definition of crime in crime and development research, which surely represents a return to the traditional legal-criminological orientation.

A review of the place of the crime and development topic within the context of the quinquennial United Nations Congresses on the Prevention of Crime and the Treatment of Offenders results in similar conclusions *(Leone and Zvekić)*. It is also noted that the United Nations has devoted more attention to the problem of development than it has to that of crime, and in a certain sense, promoted the social development approach recently criticized in criminology. Within the UN perspective, the critical role of the criminal justice system in particular has been rather neglected. Although the United Nations Congresses have never articulated a conceptually clear approach to the issue, they have begun to recognize

10

the importance of placing it within the precise context of the concrete socio-economic, political, legal and cultural milieu of each particular system under consideration.

The crime and development topic is characterized not only by the lack of global theories for both crime and development, but also by the inadequacy of dominant criminological theories to provide updated and culturally-relevant explanations.

One of the issues which requires particular theoretical attention is that of paradigmatic assumptions underlying the colloquial and criminal justice rhetoric in which the connection between crime and development seems to sit quite well. This is not to deny that attempts have been made to question this connection, but these have been rather rare in comparison with the attempts made to highlight it. There is nothing strange in this since the source of the interest in crime and development lies in the perennial concern of social thought with order and change and with the role of respect for and breach of norms. The two are then intrinsically linked in an orderly framework. Yet the rhetoric is not so simple: while recognizing the connection between crime and development, it finds it somewhat unintentional. The blame to a very large extent lies with the notion of development rather than with that of crime, since development was for a long time perceived almost exclusively in terms of progress. With the recognition of development as a highly questionable notion from the perspective of progressive achievement, crime is increasingly gaining the position of a predictable phenomenon. But again, more often than not, it is perceived as a negative and pervasive effect of development, or at best, as a consequence of disorderly change. In the developmental rhetoric, disorderly change is referred to as unbalanced development; indeed some essays in this volume refer to the notion of unbalanced development to explain the increase in crime. Many studies on crime and development have concluded, alas not always on the basis of conclusive

11

evidence, that an increase in crime results from unbalanced development. Of course, the notion of unbalanced de-velopment presupposes that development is, or at least, can be orderly. Such is not the case. Evidence presented in this volume, together with other historical and social evidence, show convincingly that development is not an orderly process, at least in an overwhelming number of cases, exceptions to this being extremely rare. Leading theories of development, and most notably that of modernization, are also based on the assumption of orderly, and thus repetitive, patterns of change. Even the dependency and the world system theories fit into the paradigm of orderly change: uneven development is a consequence of the imposition of economic and social arrangements by the dominant powers in the international division of labour. If it were not for this intervention, genuine development would be an orderly process. Moreover, the assumption of order also underlies the leading theories on crime (social disorganization, anomie, cultural conflict, differential association, etc.). Crime and development rhetoric is thus an overtly order-centred rhetoric. To the social scientist, the developmental specialist and the criminal justice administrator, an order-centred paradigm forms the point of reference.

Another inadequacy concerns the cultural relevance and methodological limits of criminological approaches which have emerged from developed societies and attempt to appreciate and explain the criminal question faced by developing societies *(Houchon)*. In this connection, two processes are discussed by several contributors. The first is related to the level of primary criminalization based on the heritage of colonial legislation, which leads to the criminalization of former rights by turning them into offences. *Adeyemi* points out that certain forms of behaviour which were considered legitimate in some of the traditional societies in Africa became criminalized with the imposition of colonial criminal justice systems. This process also concerns the operation of the criminal justice system in the developing world and, in particular, the cultural and political significance of the informal control system to which we shall return later.

The second process concerns the widespread internationalization of crime. The matter of the shifting of illegality from developed to developing countries through the operation of multinational corporations is discussed by *Newman, Carranza* and *Baxi*. It appears that the amount of loss and damage resulting from corporate crime is much greater than that arising out of common criminality. Furthermore, the shifting of illegality is facilitated by the unique multinational status of such companies and the tolerance of some governments in developing countries to such types of behaviour.

Drug-related illegal activities also exemplify the process of the internationalization of crime. *Shelley* notes that certain similarities in crime patterns between developed and developing countries are the result of increased economic and political interdependence. These similarities are a visible consequence of international drug trafficking, although there are other factors that bring about the abovementioned similarities in crime patterns, such as migration, terrorist crime, sophisticated economic and corporate crime, Third World debt, etc., Yet, it is the drug phenomenon more than any other factor that epitomizes the increasingly complex relationship between the developing and developed countries. Drug trafficking has some specific features which link developed and developing countries in an on-going, illicit, economic and political relationship in three different ways: volume of trade, the resemblance to the classical pattern of corporations and the tolerance of local leaders towards certain forms of behaviour.

The issue of tolerating certain forms of criminal behaviour and repressing others is highlighted by *Baxi* in his consideration of the crime and development issue in India. *De facto* decriminalization of what is considered progressive criminality (acts that appear to promote developmental goals) and *de jure* criminalization of regressive criminality (acts which appear to retard the rationality of industrial and economic capitalist development) reflect the contradictions which emerged in the process of development and the differing positions of the state executive power and the criminal justice apparatus towards them. A tolerant attitude towards certain types of crime is at times state sponsored, and at other times the result of consensus among the dominant interests of society and the state. The privileging of organized crime, for example, influences the practice of democratic policy and the uncontrolled use of force in maintaining law and order. While serving the interest of the state in the short run, it undermines the legitimacy of state power and the rule of law in society. The privileging of certain types of criminal conduct occurs often through the by-passing of the system of justice, providing amnesty for certain offenders, the repressive use of force when dealing with revolutionary, secessionist and regional/ethnic movements, and corruption involving privileged civil servants. *Baxi* shows that the issue of crime and development should be focused on the dialectical relationship between structural changes in society and the state's articulation of responses to different forms of crime. In fact, both *Baxi* and *Houchon* call for the examination of the crime and development issue within the context of a relationship between the criminal question and the formation of the state. Thus, the practices of state formation and the particular ways in which the criminal justice system is used to tolerate certain types of criminal behaviour and repress others only highlights the complexity of the relationship between crime and development. In other words, it is not only the relationship between the processes of socio-economic change and criminal behaviour, but rather the relationship between the processes of social change, state formative practices and the state's use of the criminal justice system that is of importance to the maintenance of the state's own power and control over the direction of development.

Any explanation of crime and development should take full account of blocked opportunities and marginalization, which traditional theories take as signs of risks, danger and predelinquency. Marginalization as related to development and crime should be examined in the context of social, economic and political history and the ways in which the structures of inequality and exploitation turn into (the structures of) criminalization. *Newman* discusses the problem of poverty as part of an ongoing process of separation of the "underclass" from the rest of the society. It has long been recognized that while the burden of crime effects all citizens, it is differentially distributed almost entirely along the principal line of social stratification. It affects different social strata and groups in society in an uneven way and in such a manner that the socially victimized become increasingly prone to crime as well as to criminal justice victimization. Using the evidence provided through the United Nations crime surveys, he suggests that the cost of crime is felt most by the underclass in the national context, and by the least developed and developing countries in the international context. While property crime rates in developed countries are generally recognized to be much higher than those in developing countries, their impact is cushioned by the higher levels of economic and social support capacities of developed countries. The same protection is not afforded by the economies of developing countries or the weaker economic and social capacity of the lower social strata. *Newman* concludes that the price the developing countries may be expected to pay is that the cost of crime will be shifted more and more towards the lower strata within their societies. "Crime thus is not a cost of development at all but rather development promises to cushion the impact of crime and diminish considerably its cost to any country that is fortunate to be included in the world's economic growth."

Savona looks at the issue of organized crime as an aspect of the internationalization of the criminal question. The rationalization of criminality is no longer confined to the traditional forms of organized crime, such as trafficking in arms and drugs, but has become increasingly linked with common criminality. The response of the criminal justice system is mainly inadequate or tardy. It is noted that when the criminal justice system adopts certain strategies, organized crime is quick to change its own strategy. The rationalization of crime thus requires an increased rationalization of the criminal justice system. Both *Savona* and *Carranza* point out that the criminal justice system perspective and *modus operandi* are based on outdated criminological theories and visions of crime and obsolete strategies for dealing with the criminal question, resulting in a reduced capacity to confront emerging criminal phenomena.

While *Houchon* questions the use of criminological approaches which have emerged from developed societies in confronting the criminal question in developing societies, *Carranza* utilizes the range of classical criminological theories to explain the relationship between development and crime in Latin America, as does *Adeyemi* in relation to Africa. However, they point out that these criminological theories should not be taken at their face value, but rather their explanatory potential should be examined in relation to empirical concrete realities. *Carranza*, for example, within the political-economy/dependency framework, analyzes the consequences of capitalist peripheral development on crime. It is noted that there has been an increase in conventional crimes as well as in new forms of crime. The quantitative increase is mainly in relation to property crime, which accounts for almost 60% of the total crime structure in Latin America and can be explained by the theory of deprivation and Merton's theory of differential access to legitimate means. Similarly, *Adeyemi* albeit within the modernization framework, uses a number of classical theories to explain the relationship between development and crime in Nigeria. As a result, in the absence of a global theory of crime, it is suggested that certain classical theories of criminal behaviour may help explain particular types of relationship between some processes of development and forms of crime.

Queloz notes that quite a few studies on crime and development have neglected, or rather have given little attention to, changes in social and crime-control structures and policies in terms of their effect on crime. This brings us to the issue of formal and informal control, another issue which merits much more attention than has so far been given to it in studies on crime and development. The dominant and conventional view was that development is accompanied by an increase in formal control and a decrease in informal control mechanisms. This view, as highlighted in essays by *Adeyemi* and *Masamba*, requires critical re-examination. *Adeyemi* points out that the formal system of crime control in Africa is based on its colonial heritage (the same point is made by *Houchon*) and emphasizes the different cultural types on which the imported and traditional control systems are based. The formal criminal justice systems received in Africa under the colonial regimes are based on an individualistic culture, while, on the other hand, African culture is, in general, a communal culture. Conflicts and crisis in the operation of the criminal justice system are thus to be expected, as is the inefficiency of the formal system. As previously noted, primary criminalization exemplifies well the possible sources of conflict and low level of confidence in the state-centred criminal justice system. The costs of the maintenance and development of the formal criminal justice system and its inability to function properly, even when judged within its own functional parameters of success, contribute further to its crisis. Dispute settlement outside the formal justice system is widely spread and has a lot to do with the explanation of the dark figure. It is argued that more culturally acceptable and relevant methods of tension-

17

management in society and in criminal justice would close the gap between the professional state-centred and imposed criminal justice and *modus operandi* on the one hand, and societal visions and practices of crime control on the other. In addition, this would make the criminal justice system more efficient and more legitimate. The informal, traditional system of control based on strong communal and kinship bonds, a supporting belief system and sanctions underwent transformation as a result of development. Indeed, this lead to the weakening of the traditional control system. Yet, the system proved to be highly adaptive and innovative, enlarging its jurisdiction to include membership roles based on para-synomy relations and modernizing its own tension- management structure. *Masamba* shows that contrary to the conventional (and distorted) view of the informal system as having a simple structure, it is made up of a developed network of roles and rules. It has proved to be adjustable to new social conditions, exemplifying the capacities of collectivities to manage problematic situations without resort to the formal criminal justice system. The point being made is that informal control plays an important role in some developing environments. Development of the criminal justice system should not necessarily mean its formalization in terms of a higher degree of state-centredness and intervention. Rather it should move towards culturally-relevant development. It appears that the cultural and structural bases and the very operation of the informal control system act as a "cushion" between certain problematic and criminalized situations and the criminal justice system's reaction. Therefore, while, as *Newman* points out, economic and social wealth cushions the effects and costs of crime in developed countries, the communal system of care, responsibility and dispute settlement would appear to posses a similar potential for developing societies.

In a comparative examination of the crime rate in several Arabic societies, *Souryal* points out that Saudi Arabia has quite a low crime rate despite intensive socio-economic development. Such a result, it is claimed, cannot be explained by the severity of punishment nor by the homogeneity of the Saudi population; rather it is the combination of socio-religious rules and their application. The application depends not only on the role of the government, but also on that of the cultural/spiritual community. Both roles are amalgamated and mutually reinforce each other.

Three essays in this volume present empirical results on the development and crime relationship. *Carranza* and *Adeyemi* concur that the development process in Latin America and Africa has been curtailed by the inability of these countries to accumulate capital. In Latin America there has not only been an increase in property and economic crime, particularly on the part of transnational companies, but also in terrorism, kidnapping, torture, and crimes against public and constitutional order. *Carranza* notes, as does *Shelley*, that drug trafficking is increasingly becoming the most threatening criminal industry in the region.

The criminal question should be examined in the context of economic and political models of development, the international economic order and other processes producing structural violence, a rupture in the democratic system and the abuse of human rights. In Africa, and in particular in Nigeria, the decline of the rural economic sector and the absolute decline of the rural population have resulted in extremely high urban growth rates. Thus, *Adeyemi* identifies this massive, rapid urban migration and the consequent weakening of traditional social support structures as one of the main criminogenic factors. A severe and structural deterioration of the economic situation leads to poverty and other forms of marginalization and alienation. The criminogenic impact of these processes is highlighted by an increase in crime rates.

The study of crime and development in Yugoslavia is an example of a quantitative macroscopic approach, which reveals a number of the advantages and limitations encountered in using such an approach. Contrary to aggregate world data presented by *Newman*, and regional and country data presented by *Carranza* and *Adeyemi*, the preliminary results of the Yugoslav study show that neither intensive development (steep upward trends in developmental parameters) nor recession in development (a slowing down in the increase and/or downward trends) have been reflected in a significant increase or decrease in crime trends. Furthermore, it has been indicated that the determination of the relationship between crime and development has remained at approximately the same level throughout the 1966-1986 period. The prediction rate of crime trends on the basis of selected developmental parameters is consistent over time and rather high. A more detailed analysis indicated significant variations in terms of different types of crime. Thus, it is noted that property crime followed trends in development more closely than some other types of crime. During the period of intensive upward development, property crime registered a slight increase followed by a significant increase in the period of socioeconomic crisis. Economic crime, on the other hand, showed a reverse trend in the former developmental period and an increase in the period of crisis. Sexual offences, and to a certain extent, crimes against person showed stable rates, revealing their relative independence from the chosen set of developmental indicators. The general factor of development appears to be sufficient and appropriate for the analysis of general macrosocial influences on crime, particularly in relation to property and economic crime. This finding appears to support *Burnham's* argument regarding the need for a locally-focused and crime- differentiated approach. It has also been noted that all associations are of an indirect nature, indicating the need to examine a host of other factors which are not identifiable at the level of statistical analysis.

The essays in this volume raise several important issues which must be considered when examining the relationship between crime and development. Yet, there does not appear to have been any major "breakthrough" in studies on crime and development. In this sense, much remains to be done. However, the further development of criminology united with, rather than divorced from, issues of social structure and change can make an important contribution to the understanding of the crime and development issue. The volume demonstrates the importance of structural analysis, while bearing in mind the increasing risk of making incorrect assumptions about the stability of structures and orderly change in the context of rapid transition. It also highlights a need for the sharpening of the focus and locus of investigation, but again with caution and recognition of the fact that processes of political and economic interdependence and the internationalization of crime (and reaction to it) must be increasingly put into the right perspective: neither overemphasizing nor underestimating their effects. The study of crime and development indeed requires that particular attention be paid to the operation of the criminal justice system, both formally and informally. This directs the analysis towards the values and goals of viable cultural, political and economic systems. The increasing interdependence and overlapping of local and global phenomena, and indeed different local aspects, makes the discourse on crime and development even more complex and thus more challenging.

Uglješa Zvekić
Editor

CHANGEMENTS SOCIAUX, CRIMINALITE ET CONTROLE DU CRIME

A propos de leur interdépendance et des enseignements fournis par la recherche

Nicolas Queloz *

Introduction

Les crises économiques, politiques, sociales, tout autant que les révolutions technologiques, secouent de spasmes fréquents la société mondiale, sans épargner aucune région ni aucune société nationale, entraînant leur lot de changements de structures, de valeurs, de mentalités et de comportements. Aussi les éléments à observer sous la rubrique "Changements sociaux, criminalité et contrôle du crime" ne manquent-ils pas. "Les sciences sociales sont nées, pourrait-on dire, du malheur des hommes ... En bref, les difficultés et les crises que connaît une société contribuent à faire émerger une réflexion et l'alimentent."[1]

Par ailleurs, en ce domaine, le grand problème des chercheurs est tout autant (si ce n'est plus) d'ordre méthodologique: comment cerner ces changements et les évaluer sous tous leurs aspects, en respectant les nuances, les rythmes, les formes, la nature ou encore le sens ou la direction, afin de parvenir à analyser et expliquer (au moins partiellement) les effets qu'ils peuvent exercer sur les comportements humains? "On peut, et même on doit, se placer à plusieurs points de vue ... Parmi toutes les choses qui changent il y a une grande variété de types de changement ou mieux de

---

* Chaire de travail social, Université de Fribourg, Suisse.

modalités du changement ... Nous avons en effet une idée tout intuitive du changement social; nous croyons le comprendre alors que nous avons seulement une expérience très confuse que les choses bougent ici et là!"[2] Il faudrait savoir, notamment, si elles bougent toujours et partout de la même façon?

Changements sociaux, criminalité et contrôle du crime: présentation des concepts

Dans le domaine de la criminologie, ces vingt dernières années, on a pris coutume de voir apparaître le thème "Développement et criminalité" ou "Crime and Development" aussi bien dans des congrès ou conférences internationales (p. ex. 4ème Congrès des Nations Unies pour la prévention du crime et le traitement des délinquants, Kyoto, 1970, consacré à "Criminalité et développement"), que dans la littérature et la recherche comparative.[3]

Pour notre part, nous préférons le concept de "changement social" à celui de "développement", essentiellement parce qu'il est plus large (et permet donc de couvrir bien plus d'éléments de la réalité sociale) et plus neutre (ou beaucoup moins chargé idéologiquement et ainsi moins exposé à des controverses).

En conséquence, en raison d'une acception plus globale et moins équivoque, nous parlons donc de "changements sociaux" et nous préconisons de considérer ainsi tous les processus de transformations politiques, économiques, sociales et culturelles qui affectent la texture et la structure d'une société ("avancée" ou non), aussi bien dans un sens positif (ou de progrès, d'innovation, d'amélioration des conditions de vie ou de santé, p. ex.) que dans un sens négatif (ou de régression, de dépérissement, de crises, de conflits [même si nous n'ignorons pas, bien au contraire, que crises et conflits peuvent aussi être créateurs et pas forcément dévastateurs], de guerres, etc.).

En ce qui concerne la criminalité, c'est d'abord, bien sûr, la criminalité enregistrée et ayant suscité une réaction sociale, soit dans sa globalité (somme des infractions aux lois pénales), soit dans ses principaux types ou variétés (infractions contre les personnes, contre les biens, contre l'Etat, criminalité économique, liée aux stupéfiants, etc.) qui doit être envisagée. Cette criminalité officielle est la forme la plus visible et la plus marquante, parce que formellement sanctionnée, des divers comportements déviants.

Mais, malgré l'absence de données fiables à leur sujet, il faut aussi tenter de prendre en considération les formes beaucoup moins apparentes de la criminalité, mais qui sont peut-être de meilleurs indicateurs des changements sociaux: comme la criminalité organisée; ou la criminalité écologique; ou encore l'arbitraire et les actes illégaux des forces de l'ordre ...; etc.

Un autre élément essentiel, mais qui n'est que rarement expressément pris en considération, c'est celui de l'ensemble des mécanismes formels et informels de contrôle social de la criminalité; ils comprennent notamment, dans la sphère la plus visible et la plus institutionnalisée, les divers aspects de la politique criminelle, des entreprises d'élaboration ou de révision des normes pénales, l'organisation des systèmes de justice pénale et les diverses interventions de leurs agences dans la prise en charge des cas de criminalité et de leurs auteurs.

L'objectif général d'une étude sur les changements sociaux, la criminalité et son contrôle, est de mettre en lumière (description) et d'analyser (interprétation) les relations réciproques entre ces ensembles de faits sociaux avec, généralement, un intérêt tout particulier voué à l'impact que les transformations au niveau des structures sociales peuvent avoir sur la fréquence et la nature de la criminalité (comme phénomène social, mais aussi comme ensemble de comportements humains) et sur l'intensité et les formes de son contrôle.

Il faut également garder à l'esprit que l'augmentation ou la diminution durable de la criminalité dans une société donnée; ou le passage marqué d'une délinquance violente à une délinquance astucieuse; ou encore le développement toujours plus étendu et sophistiqué de l'organisation du crime, constituent, chacun, un changement social en soi, tout comme les transformations des modes de prévention, de prise en charge et de traitement de la criminalité (que ce soit dans un sens progressiste ou réactionnaire) représentent un changement social certain.

Touraine[4] l'exprime en d'autres mots: "On parle constamment de déviance ou de marginalité, de folie ou de crime, c'est-à-dire de non-conformité avec une règle, une coutume, un groupe. Il faut au contraire définir les conduites de crise par la rupture d'une relation sociale et donc par la décomposition d'un système social...".

Toutefois, nous sommes d'avis, comme Barel[5], que le "vrai" changement social, ou le changement positif, c'est celui qui aboutit au déblocage social, qui permet de dépasser un vide social, une impasse, une situation bloquée, contribuant ainsi à ce qu'une société parvienne à son auto-dépassement, à son désenlisement.

Pour être tout à fait complet et précis, nous proposons (voir Fig. 1) une figure de représentation des *composantes du changement social et de leurs interactions*, les transformations ayant trait spécifiquement à la criminalité et au contrôle du crime figurant, respectivement, dans les ensembles (D) et (B) de cette représentation.

Le grand problème, pour la recherche, est de matérialiser ces diverses variables et de trouver comment les mesurer ou les cerner le plus adéquatement et de la façon la plus fiable ou réaliste possible.

En général, les tableaux de variables proposées avec leurs divers indicateurs ou modalités ont une structure qui s'articule comme les déterminismes sous-jacents aux phénomènes étudiés, et donc préalablement supposés à titre d'hypothèse (préjugé déterministe).

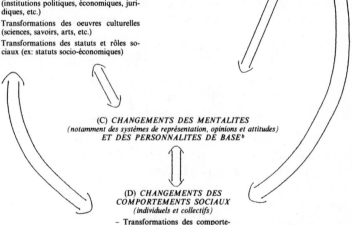

Fig. 1

Représentation des composantes du CHANGEMENT SOCIAL et de leurs interactions[a]

(A) CHANGEMENTS DES STRUCTURES SOCIALES[b]

- Transformations de la base écologique (modifications de l'environnement) et de l'aménagement du territoire (rapports zones rurales — zones urbaines; urbanisation; etc.)
- Transformations de la base démographique (modifications du nombre de la population; de sa densité; de la structure par âge, par sexe; migrations; etc.)
- Transformations des techniques et des technologies
- Transformations des modes de production, de consommation, de communication et de loisirs (industrialisation; tertiarisation; informatisation; etc.)
- Transformations des appareils organisés (institutions politiques, économiques, juridiques, etc.)
- Transformations des oeuvres culturelles (sciences, savoirs, arts, etc.)
- Transformations des statuts et rôles sociaux (ex: statuts socio-économiques)

(B) CHANGEMENTS DES VALEURS. NORMES ET REGLEMENTATIONS SOCIALES[b]

- Transformations des mécanismes de régulation sociale et de contrôle social
- Transformations des valeurs et pratiques religieuses et morales
- Transformations des modèles et pratiques éducatifs et de socialisation
- Transformations des modèles et pratiques juridiques et judiciaires

(C) CHANGEMENTS DES MENTALITES
(notamment des systèmes de représentation, opinions et attitudes)
ET DES PERSONNALITES DE BASE[b]

(D) CHANGEMENTS DES COMPORTEMENTS SOCIAUX
(individuels et collectifs)

- Transformations des comportements conformes aux normes sociales
- Transformations des comportements non-conformes aux normes sociales (déviances, délinquances, criminalité)

---

[a] Malgré sa présentation graphique, cette figure ne présuppose pas d'ordre ou de relations hiérarchiques ni chronologiques entre les ensembles (A), (B), (C) et (D).

[b] Transformations intervenant aux niveaux:
- de la (des) société(s) globale(s)
- des classes sociales
- des groupements (famille, école, groupements religieux, entreprises, groupes de pression, etc.)
- des petits groupes (formes et degrés de sociabilité).

27

Et ce sont en effet des procédés et traitements statistiques très variés (et souvent trop sophistiqués) qui sont généralement utilisés pour essayer de vérifier ces déterminismes.

La grande faiblesse de ces procédures est que toutes les facettes de la réalité qui ne sont pas (ou qu'en partie) quantifiables échappent à l'explication ou alors sont introduites dans l'interprétation "sous réserves", à titre d'hypothèses permanentes.

Nous relèverons encore simplement toutes les difficultés qui s'ajoutent à ces problèmes méthodologiques dans le cas de recherches comparatives internationales, où il s'agit, notamment, de s'entendre sur les définitions et la comparabilité des variables utilisées et de leurs nombreuses modalités.[6]

Tendances des recherches sur les relations entre changements sociaux, criminalité et contrôle du crime

D'une vaste recension que nous avons faite de la littérature de ces vingt dernières années portant sur le thème "Socio-Economic Development, Social Change and Crime"[7] il ressort que les principales variables prises en compte, outre la variable dépendante "criminalité", sont les suivantes:

— le "développement socio-économique", mesuré souvent par une multitude d'indicateurs démographiques, économiques (notamment par le produit national brut par tête, le taux d'occupation par secteurs d'activités économiques, des indicateurs de production et de consommation, etc.), des domaines de la santé, de l'éducation, des transports et communications, etc., la devise des chercheurs-statisticiens boulimiques pouvant ici se résumer à "plus l'on y mettra d'indicateurs (et de chiffres), plus ça aura de l'allure" ...;

— la "modernisation" qui, pour Shelley[8] par exemple, se définit par "industrialisation" + "urbanisation", deux variables-clés également très souvent utilisées dans les recherches et auxquelles sont fréquemment liées la "densité de population" et les "migrations" (nationales ou internes, et internationales);

— depuis le milieu des années 70, les variables "crise économique" et "chômage" ont été régulièrement introduites dans les études "changements sociaux et criminalité", de même que la variable "participation de la femme aux activités économiques";

— enfin, un plus petit nombre d'études se sont intéressées aux variables "système politique" (ou type de gouvernement: autoritaire VS démocratique; stable VS instable) et "système de contrôle social"/"système de justice pénale".

Quant au cadre de référence théorique de ces recherches (et dans la minorité des cas où il est explicitement signalé), il renvoie généralement aux modèles suivants: théorie de l'anomie (Durkheim; Merton); théorie du conflit de cultures (Sellin); théorie marxiste; théorie du lien social (Hirschi); théories de la déprivation relative et de la frustration.

D'un point de vue méthodologique, les méthodes et techniques utilisées dans les recherches de type "Développement socio-économique, changements sociaux et criminalité" sont exclusivement quantitatives: recueil d'une multitude de données statistiques officielles; analyse de séries temporelles; analyses statistiques variées (factorielle, de corrélation, de régression, etc.); analyse comparative des niveaux de développement intra- et international, etc. Rarement, et de façon très accessoire, il est fait usage de techniques plus qualitatives, telles que: interviews de notables; analyse de contenu des journaux; analyse des débats parlementaires; analyse de dossiers judiciaires; observations des auteurs sur le terrain.

Enseignements que l'on peut tirer de ces recherches

Nous soulignerons ici les quelques résultats ou conclusions stables ou confirmés qui se dégagent des études sur les changements sociaux et la criminalité.

La première leçon à mettre en exergue, qui pourra paraître décourageante aux yeux de certains, mais que, pour notre part, nous considérons comme essentielle parce qu'elle permettra peut-être enfin d'aller au-delà de vieilles murailles obstruantes et inhibantes (ou de renverser de "vieux démons"), c'est qu'il n'existe pas de modèle global à prétention universelle permettant de prédire quelles variables du changement social, et selon quel ordre de priorité, ont un impact majeur sur les comportements (conformes et non-conformes) des individus. Ceci ne rend que plus pertinente notre figure de représentation plurielle des composantes et interactions possibles entre changement social, criminalité et contrôle du crime (voir Fig. 1 supra).

L'influence des changements sociaux sur la criminalité n'est pas identique pour toutes les sociétés et les transformations sociales ponctuelles, datées et localisées, sont bien plus précieuses pour expliquer l'émergence de comportements délictueux que ne le serait un hypothétique "processus global de développement". A notre avis, ceci n'est qu'un élément supplémentaire pour critiquer l'utilisation du concept de "développement" et y préférer celui de "changement social".

Une deuxième constante des recherches analysées est que les changements sociaux ont des effets opposés sur les crimes contre les personnes et les crimes contre les biens.

Lafree et Kick,[9] par exemple, ont montré que les variables "croissance de la population", "inégalité des revenus", "niveau de développement" et "urbanisation" avaient chacune une influence inverse ou divergente sur le meurtre et sur le vol. Pour ces auteurs, ces variables socio-structurelles affectent de façon différentielle les occasions et les motivations relatives au meurtre d'une part, et au vol d'autre part. A leur avis, ceci devrait constituer un stimulus pour mener à l'avenir des études de cas nationales sur des catégories spécifiques de crimes.

D'autres recherches[10] ont également montré que la croissance économique et l'amélioration des conditions d'existence entraînent généralement une augmentation des crimes contre la propriété et une diminution des actes de violence contre les personnes. Comme pour contribuer à nuancer quelque peu ce "modèle prédictif", Mukherjee[11] a constaté qu'en Australie les crimes contre la propriété ont augmenté brusquement aussi bien en période de grave récession économique (Grande Crise des années 30) qu'au cours de la pleine euphorie conjoncturelle des années 60.

En ce qui concerne les effets des changements sociaux sur les caractéristiques de la population officiellement enregistrée pour avoir commis des délits ou des crimes, bon nombre d'études apportent des éléments relatifs aux migrants, aux femmes et aux jeunes.

A propos des migrants, si toute généralisation est impossible en raison notamment des différences liées aux genres de migration (intranationale ou internationale; économique ou politique, etc.) ou aux divers statuts légaux que peuvent avoir les migrants, on peut toutefois relever des études menées sur le thème "migration et criminalité" les quelques éléments suivants:

— la sur-criminalité des migrants (ou leur sur-représentation dans la population pénale) est loin d'être une constante dans les divers pays étudiés, et le comportement des migrants intra-nationaux est souvent plus problématique que celui des travailleurs immigrés;

— le taux de criminalité des migrants de la deuxième génération est généralement supérieur à celui de leurs parents;

— la criminalité intra-groupe (au sein des populations immigrées) est forte et très souvent réglée de façon interne.

Les résultats des recherches relatives à l'influence des changements sociaux sur la criminalité des femmes et des jeunes demeurent, quant à eux, très ambigus. Si dans "Crime and Modernization" Shelley affirmait que l'industrialisation et l'urbanisation modifiaient la nature de la population délinquante, entraînant plus de femmes et de jeunes à commettre des infractions, son avis devient plus nuancé en

1986 puisqu'elle constate que c'est la forme plus que la fréquence de leur participation à la criminalité qui a changé.

En fait, sur le thème qui nous intéresse, la majorité des études récentes sur la délinquance féminine retiennent, comme variable explicative de celle-ci, la participation de la femme aux activités économiques ou sa part dans la population économiquement active d'un pays. Mais, bien souvent, ces recherches postulent que cette variable n'est qu'intermédiaire et qu'au premier plan, c'est la question de l'émancipation, voire de la libération de la femme qui expliquerait essentiellement les changements intervenus dans la fréquence ou dans la nature de la délinquance féminine. Néanmoins, aucune évidence n'est apportée d'une relation de causalité entre l'émancipation de la femme et son comportement délictueux.

Bien que nous nous situions ici au coeur d'un phénomène de changement social et de son éventuel impact sur les comportements, la grande faiblesse de ce type de recherches est leur absence de perspective globale qui permettrait d'intégrer et de relier l'émancipation (sociale, économique, politique) de la femme à d'autres éléments du changement social: non pas seulement à l'accroissement de sa participation aux activités économiques (travail rétribué hors de la sphère domestique), car cela n'est qu'un aspect des transformations globales (dont il s'agit de tenir compte) des structures de production et d'échange de biens et de services dans une société; mais aussi: changements des normes et valeurs (évolution des moeurs, "libération sexuelle"); modifications des représentations et des pratiques d'accès à l'éducation, à la formation, à la vie publique; transformations des modèles familiaux (notamment liés à la nuptialité, à la natalité, à l'autorité domestique, à la divorcialité), etc.

Quant au thème de l'impact des transformations sociales et psychologiques sur la délinquance des jeunes, d'excellentes recherches de Leblanc menées à dix ans d'intervalle (1974 et 1985) sur des cohortes d'adolescents vivant à Montréal, ont révélé ce qui suit: malgré une détérioration des conditions de vie des familles (augmentation du chômage et du divorce), une altération de la personnalité de base des adolescents (accroissement de la méfiance, de l'anxiété, de l'émotivité et de l'insécurité), mais un resserrement du contrôle social (surtout sur les activités de loisirs), la délinquance révélée des adolescents est demeurée inchangée aussi bien quant à sa nature (non aggravation des activités délictueuses) que du point de vue de sa fréquence, en soulignant même une tendance légère à la baisse. En conséquence, il convient de conclure que "la délinquance cachée produite par les adolescents d'une décennie donnée est équivalente à celle de la décade précédente. Cette conclusion est valable pour les décennies 1960, 1970 et 1980 à Montréal... et aux Etats-Unis (...) Il en ressort que les transformations sociales et les modifications de la personnalité modale des adolescents n'altèrent pas de façon significative le niveau des activités délictueuses des mineurs".[12]

Par ailleurs, sur la base de données permettant de comparer la situation des sociétés occidentales à celle des sociétés du Tiers Monde,[13] nous dirons, de façon très synthétique, que:

— plus l'on passe des sociétés rurales intégrées aux sociétés industrielles et urbaines complexes,

— plus se pose alors de façon accrue le problème de la jeunesse ou le fait que la jeunesse soit perçue comme un problème social;

— plus se pose aussi, par conséquent, le problème du contrôle social de la jeunesse;

— et, finalement, plus se pose le problème de la délinquance juvénile, tout au moins comme thème lancinant du discours public (surtout politique et médiatique).

De façon assez étonnante, c'est précisément sur les changements intervenant au niveau politique (notamment de la politique criminelle) et des mécanismes de contrôle social (informels et légaux) des comportements délictueux, que les recherches classiques de type "changements sociaux et criminalité" ont le moins porté leur attention. Il faut certainement rattacher cet étrange oubli à la fâcheuse incommunicabilité, dans le champ de la criminologie et de la sociologie criminelle, entre les tenants des recherches étiologiques d'une part, et les fervents de l'approche du contrôle social et de la réaction sociale d'autre part.

Toujours est-il que Chirol[14] remarquait, à l'issue d'une vaste étude comparative sur le développement socio-économique et la délinquance juvénile menée en France, Hongrie, Pologne et Yougoslavie (1975): "Nous aurions dû inclure une importante variable indépendante dans notre recherche, à savoir les différences régionales relatives à l'équipement et aux ressources du système de justice pénale (y compris la police)"...

Dans son étude ethnocriminologique de l'Afrique Noire, Brillon[15] a constaté que la criminalité officiellement enregistrée est un phénomène essentiellement limité aux grandes villes, mais que les statistiques ne sont nullement le reflet de la situation et de l'évolution réelles de la criminalité. Il a démontré, en effet, que la visibilité d'un comportement délictueux au Sénégal et en Côte d'Ivoire était fonction à la fois de la distance physique (zones situées dans un rayon de 10 km d'un poste de police et de 50 km d'un tribunal) et de la distance culturelle (acculturation, "occidentalisation") par rapport aux normes et systèmes pénaux "modernes" hérités du colonialisme.

Complémentairement à cela, il faut relever l'importance que revêtent les processus de changement des normes et pratiques pénales, en particulier lorsqu'ils sont insufflés par des reformes décidées par l'Etat. Salas[16] rappelle par exemple que la période post-révolutionnaire a été suivie, à Cuba, par une intense campagne de criminalisation (répression de nouveaux délits), d'accroissement de la sévérité des peines, ainsi que de l'abaissement de l'âge de la minorité pénale. La Chine, depuis le début des années 80, a connu une véritable frénésie de la codification, adoptant une multitude de normes pénales (criminalisation de nombreux comportements auparavant non sanctionnés) et recourant à une répression accrue.[17]

Comme l'a montré Killias[18] dans son analyse comparative de 55 pays, la disponibilité des ressources économiques et financières ainsi que la forme de gouvernement ou de pouvoir politique (démocratique VS autoritaire) exercent un poids prépondérant sur la sévérité et les types de pénalités retenues. Si, à cela, vient s'ajouter une crise de légitimation du système, par suite de troubles et d'insécurité politiques, d'accroissement des inégalités sociales, ou, dans les pays capitalistes, de forte augmentation du chômage, la politique criminelle subit alors une forte inflexion répressive, voire vindicative.

Perspectives d'avenir

Dans cette dernière partie, en tenant compte des tendances et enseignements principaux que nous avons essayé de tirer des recherches récentes concernant les relations entre changements sociaux, criminalité et contrôle du crime, nous souhaitons esquisser les perspectives et contours que ces recherches pourraient prendre au cours des années à venir, essentiellement sur les plans théorique, méthodologique et des thèmes d'analyse à développer.

D'un point de vue théorique

Sur ce plan, il s'agirait à l'avenir de surmonter deux faiblesses: soit de se départir d'un trop grand dogmatisme théorique, notamment en évitant de s'enfermer dans une perspective excessivement déterministe, ou, dans certains cas, évolutionniste (trait caractéristique de la plupart des études intitulées "Développement et criminalité"); soit, ce qui est encore plus fréquent, de se donner la peine d'émerger d'un flou ou d'un brouillard théorique épais, en s'efforçant de mieux afficher et de mieux préciser ses perspectives, modèles ou références théoriques de base. Mentionner au passage, et en vrac, une intense "situation d'anomie", des signes évidents de "désintégration sociale", de "conflits de cultures" et de "frustration", relève davantage de la vulgate scientifique que d'un solide cadre de références théoriques.

Par ailleurs, dans le domaine de la sociologie du changement social, des auteurs tels que Mendras, Forse[19] ou Boudon[20] ont clairement souligné qu'il n'existe pas de théories générales ou globales du changement social. "On ne peut construire de théories du changement social *stricto sensu*... qu'à propos de processus sociaux partiels et locaux, datés et situés." Par conséquent, il ne peut y avoir "de théories scientifiques du changement social que partielles et locales".[21] Ci-dessus, au chapitre des "enseignements", nous avons mis en évidence cette même leçon à tirer des recherches sur les relations entre changement social et criminalité: il n'existe pas de théorie générale et universelle permettant de prédire quelles modalités essentielles du changement social, et selon quel enchaînement, favoriseraient les comportements criminels.

D'ailleurs, il s'agit de rappeler que la relation "changement social-criminalité-contrôle du crime" n'est pas à sens unique, mais qu'il y a une véritable inter-relation ou interaction entre ces phénomènes, que l'on peut d'ailleurs résumer à une interrelation de changement sociaux (cf Fig. 1): pensons simplement au mouvement réactif classique consistant à réviser le code pénal ou à "moderniser" l'équipement policier ou l'appareil répressif d'un pays pour répondre à l'apparition ou à la recrudescence d'actes jugés "socialement inacceptables".

Ainsi, sur le plan théorique, même si nous ne la considérons pas comme la seule approche à adopter pour les recherches ayant trait au thème qui nous intéresse ici, nous reconnaissons plusieurs mérités à la perspective interactionniste et stratégique proposée notamment par Mendras/-Forse, Boudon ou Barel. Ses principaux axiomes sont les suivants:

— on ne peut expliquer un phénomène ou un ensemble de phénomènes sociaux qu'en les situant au niveau d'un système précisément localisé dans le temps et dans l'espace;

— les phénomènes sociaux (p. ex. le changement social ou la criminalité) sont conçus comme le produit des actions individuelles ou des comportements des agents (individus, groupes, institutions) du système considéré;

— les phénomènes globaux observés ne résultent pas directement de la volonté des agents mais des effets d'agrégation de leurs décisions, qui entraînent des résultats indéterminés et parfois paradoxaux (ou contraires aux objectifs ou décisions des agents, "effets pervers").

"Autrement dit, puisqu'il n'y a pas de théorie globale du changement, il convient de s'attacher à l'étude de microprocessus, qui peuvent d'ailleurs avoir une valeur paradigmatique plus large. Une deuxième caractéristique de cette approche réside dans ce qu'il est convenu d'appeler "l'individualisme méthodologique": le changement social, même au niveau macrosociologique, n'est intelligible que si l'analyse descend jusqu'aux agents ou acteurs sociaux les plus élémentaires composant les systèmes auxquels on s'intéresse." [22]

Parmi les avantages de cette perspective, nous relèverons les deux suivants, proches de notre intérêt thématique: elle permet d'abord de bien appréhender les relations dialectiques ou à double sens (ou en "looping") entre les composantes du changement social, au nombre dèsquelles figurent notamment les transformations touchant aux structures sociales, à la criminalité et à son contrôle. Ensuite, dans cette approche, on peut concevoir les conflits, la déviance et la délinquance, non pas seulement comme des transgressions et des comportements socialement négatifs et nuisibles, mais aussi comme des innovations, des situations créatrices et porteuses de changements. "Plus la société change, plus se créent des situations nouvelles dans lesquelles les acteurs doivent inventer des conduites, et les conflits servent à ajuster entre elles les conduites d'acteurs aux intérêts contradictoires".[23]

D'un point de vue méthodologique et des thèmes
de recherche à développer

Sur le plan de la méthode et des techniques utilisées, les recherches de type "changements sociaux, criminalité et contrôle du crime" auront à se diversifier considérablement, sous peine de gâtisme et de stérilité. Le choix d'une multitude de variables et d'indicateurs pour leur seul mérite d'être à caractère numérique et de se prêter ainsi aisément à une (in) digestion par l'ordinateur et au petit jeu des manipulations statistiques sera bientôt, nous l'espérons, d'une époque révolue.

D'autre part, une longue série de contradictions engendrées par ces recherches auront à être levées. Ainsi, plutôt que d'ambitieuses recherches quantitatives à visée comparative entre les grandes régions du globe, beaucoup trop complexes et rarement porteuses de riches enseignements, nous soutenons vigoureusement l'idée d'intensifier les études de cas nationales ou limitées aux pays voisins, ou culturellement proches, d'une même région (pays arabes, Amérique latine, Afrique Noire, p. ex.), et portant à la fois sur diverses catégories spécifiques de crimes et sur les mécanismes et pratiques concrets et quotidiens de contrôle social, de criminalisation et de réaction sociale face aux comportements et individus délinquants.

Une proposition extrêmement judicieuse de Houchon[24] est d'analyser dans leur interdépendance des phénomènes sociaux morphologiquement proches (les uns relevant plus spécifiquement des changements socio-économiques, les autres de la criminalité et de son contrôle), comme par exemple: la marginalisation de la jeunesse et la délinquance juvénile; le "squatting" et l'économie informelle en milieu urbain et les tactiques policières de raffles et de ratissages, etc.

D'autre part, des études de type socio-historique (menées par des historiens, économistes, politologues, sociologues, criminologues), soit existent déjà et pourraient être mieux exploitées, soit devraient être complétées et développées dans une perspective interdisciplinaire.

Quant aux thèmes de recherche encore à explorer sous la rubrique "Changements sociaux, criminalité et contrôle du crime", nous y voyons notamment:

(a) Au plan des changements sociaux: l'intérêt ne devra plus se centrer uniquement sur les transformations de structures, (ensemble (A), Fig. 1) mais désormais se porter aussi plus attentivement sur les changements de valeurs et de modèles sociaux (ensemble (B), Fig. 1; p. ex. évolution des moeurs, des us et coutumes, des modes de socialisation et des modèles familiaux), ainsi que sur les transformations des mentalités collectives et des personnalités de base (ensemble (C), Fig. 1).

(b) Au plan des comportements, individus et organisations criminels: si l'attention s'est beaucoup focalisée sur l'opposition "crimes contre les personnes" VS "crimes contre les biens", bon nombre d'autres catégories de crimes nécessitent des études plus poussées sous l'angle de leur inter-relations avec les changements de société: des plus communes et banales, comme la criminalité routière qui prend des proportions extrêmement massives; aux plus souterraines, mais extrêmement néfastes socialement, comme p. ex.: criminalité organisée; criminalité économique; criminalité écologique; trafics de drogues; crimes politiques; actes terroristes; mais aussi actes de violence étatique, génocides, tortures, procédures extra-légales et arbitraires, trop souvent justifiées au nom de "la Loi et de l'Ordre" ou de la "Raison d'Etat"...

(c) Au plan des processus de contrôle social à la fois socialisateurs et re-socialisateurs: complémentairement à l'interrogation sur les phénomènes d'émergence et de mise en oeuvre concrète des valeurs, normes, pratiques et agences de socialisation, de ré-éducation et d'exclusion sociales, il s'agira notamment d'analyser de façon plus approfondie et systématique:

— comment et pourquoi les phénomènes dits de "modernisation" (d'"industrialisation" et d'"urbanisation") entraînent le passage du contrôle social de la sphère informelle et inorganisée à la sphère formelle et organisée: analyses socio-historiques de l'emprise et du développement croissants de l'appareil d'Etat, mais aussi, et de plus en plus, de systèmes de sécurité et de justice privées, parallèlement à la désintégration et à la perte d'influence des solidarités locales et de la sphère communautaire ("société civile")?

— Quelles influences les changements sociaux ont-ils pratiquement sur la socialisation des jeunes générations, aussi bien dans les sociétés industrielles ou post-industrielles que dans celles du Tiers-Monde? Des recherches longitudinales, portant sur des cohortes d'enfants et d'adolescents tout au long de leur phase d'éducation et de conform(is)ation[25] devront être intensifiées.

En Europe occidentale, p. ex., la crise économique et le chômage ont favorisé, dès le milieu des années 70, un retour des modèles de socialisation de type "discipline (re)productrice" et, au niveau de la justice pour mineurs et des instances de resocialisation, la résurgence des théories répressives (dites "néo-classiques"). Et pourtant, note Walgrave,[26] "... nous savons très bien que si nous allons très loin dans cette direction, nous contribuons à long terme à un monde socialement invivable, où la solidarité pour autrui, l'autonomie personnelle, les relations affectives et amicales se perdraient. (...) Eduquer c'est aussi contribuer à un idéal de société. Cet idéal n'est pas clair du tout, et les outils socialisateurs pour l'atteindre le sont encore moins" ...

En conclusion, nous sommes d'avis que l'un des défis majeurs de la criminologie des années 90 sera, non pas de tenter de répondre directement et servilement aux "impératifs de la lutte anti-criminelle", mais, bien plus, d'améliorer et d'affiner ses cadres de référence et ses modèles théoriques et méthodologiques, et de mener des recherches ainsi plus précises, mieux étayées et plus rigoureuses, ce qui, en fin de compte(s) (ou de façon médiate), contribuera certainement, de manière plus efficace et plus sensée, à de meilleures politiques de contrôle du crime.

Références et notes

[1] C. Bachman et J. Simonin, *Changer au quotidien*, Une introduction au travail social. Paris, Etudes vivantes, Tome 1, 1981, p. 19.

[2] R. Ledrut, *La révolution cachée*, Paris, Casterman, 1979, p. 175.

[3] *Annales Internationales de Criminologie*, 1986, Vol. 24, consacré aux relations entre développement économique et criminalité.

[4] A. Touraine, *Pour la sociologie*, Paris, Seuil, 1974, p. 62.

[5] Y. Barel, La société, le sens, l'indécidable. In *Actions et recherches sociales*, 1987, No. 4, pp. 31-40.

[6] Pour des développements à ce sujet, voir p. ex. "Recherches comparatives internationales", *Annales de Vaucresson*, 1985, No. 22.

[7] United Nations, United Nations Social Defence Research Institute (UNSDRI), "Socio-Economic Development, Social Change and Crime. Review of the Literature" by N. Queloz, A. Replinski, T. Kubo, *Project Document on Crime and Development*, Rome, April 1988.

[8] L. I. Shelley, "Crime and Modernization Reexamined", *Annales internationales de criminologie*, 1986, Vol. 24, pp. 7-21.

[9] G. D. Lafree and E. L. Kick, "Cross-National Effects of Developmental, Distributional and Demographic Variables on Crime: A Review and Analysis", *Annales internationales de criminologie*, 1986, Vol. 24, pp. 213-235.

[10] G. Rahav, "National Development and Crime Rates", *Annales de Vaucresson*, 1985, No. 22, pp. 35-52.

[11] S. K. Mukherjee, "Economic Development and Crime: A Case of Burglary", *Annales internationales de criminologie*, 1986, Vol. 24, pp. 237-254.

[12] M. Leblanc, "L'impact des transformations sociales et psychologiques sur la délinquance cachée des adolescents", in *Changement de société et délinquance juvénile*, ACCO, Leuven, Vol. 1, 1987, pp. 193-213.

[13] C. A. Hartjen and S. Priyadarsini, *Delinquency in India*, New Brunswick, N. J., Rutgers University Press, 1984; N. Queloz, "Jeunesse et délinquance: une relation ambigué, aussi bien en Suisse que dans un pays du Tiers-Monde", in J. Schuh, Ed., *Jugend und Delinquenz - Jeunesse et delinquance*, Gusch, Verlag Ruegger, 1988, pp. 285-335; N. Queloz, "La justice des mineurs dans l'optique récente des Nations Unies et la question de son développement en Afrique", *Revue internationale de criminologie et de police technique*, 1988, No. 1, pp. 33-48.

[14] Y. Chirol et al., *Delinquance juvenile et développement socio-économique,* La Haye/Paris, Mouton, 1975.

[15] Y. Brillon, *Ethnocriminologie de l'Afrique Noire*, Paris, Librairie Vrin, 1980.

[16] L. Salas, Crime in Post-Revolutionary Cuba, *Annales internationales de criminologie*, 1986, Vol. 24, pp. 83-109.

[17] Y. Zhaohui, "New Crimes Emerging in the Process of China's Development and the Strategic Policies and Measures to be Taken", *UNAFEI Report*, Tokyo, No. 30, Dec. 1986, pp. 53-66.

[18] M. Killias, "Power Concentration, Legitimation Crisis and Penal Severity: a Comparative Perspective", *Annales internationales de criminologie*, 1986, Vol. 24, pp. 181-211.

[19] H. Mendras et M. Forse, *Le changement social. Tendances et paradigmes*, Paris, A. Colin, 1983.

[20] R. Boudon, *La place du désordre. Critique des theories du changement social*, Paris, PUF, 1984.

[21] *Op. cit.*, pp. 219-220.

[22] H. Mendras et M. Forse, *op. cit.*, p. 140.

[23] *Op. cit.*, p. 237.

[24] G. Houchon, "Criminalités, criminalisations et changements sociaux en Afrique au sud du Sahara: Leurres et lueurs", *Revue internationale de sociologie*, 1989, No. 3.

[25] M. Leblanc, *op. cit.*

[26] L. Walgrave, "Changements sociaux: changements dans la problématique, les conceptions et les politiques envers la délinquance juvénile", in *Changement de société et délinquance juvénile*, ACCO, Leuven, Vol. 1, 1987, pp. 11-22.

CRIME, DEVELOPMENT AND CONTEMPORARY CRIMINOLOGY

*Robin W. Burnham **

Introduction

A new realistic criminology is spreading rapidly through the research and policy planning arms of an increasing number of governments. It is now the received wisdom in such countries that crime is here to stay, that it defies neat, or comprehensive, explanation as much as it defies measures to reduce or eliminate it, that the focus of attention should be on machinery and policies adopted by governments and administrations in response to crime, and that crime prevention can be shown to be effective only in a limited and clearly defined context.

There has been, if not a revolution, then a major change in the philosophy of science of criminology in the last 20 years. The gist of that basic change might be described as an acceptance of the following propositions:

> (i) that the general concept of "crime" is much more complex, and in policy-making much less useful, than had been assumed before.

> (ii) that explanations in causal terms at a general level are therefore extremely difficult and subject to refutation. Recent aetiological research efforts in the U.S.A. do seem to bear, perhaps, more promise than other studies; but these new studies require such great

* Social Affairs Officer, Crime Prevention and Criminal Justice Branch, Centre for Social Development and Humanitarian Affairs (CSDHA), United Nations Office at Vienna.

resources (in the millions of dollars), have such a long lead-time (at the very least, five years), and could well be so culture-specific, that they are of only marginal interest to developing countries for the forseeable future.

(iii) that the primary concern of applied criminology should be to study crime within a specific category and location, and above all the effects and effectiveness of the societal response to it. Criminology in that tradition has become, to a significant extent, the sociology of criminal justice.

(iv) that broad scope, wide-ranging studies of criminality are now regarded increasingly with suspicion, and correlations of reported crime rates with socio-economic parameters are now seen as, at best, pointers to possible influencial factors, rather than statements of truth. Most of such little good evidence as exists seems to suggest that development is indeed probably criminogenic.[1]

(v) that the complex question of "aggregation of data" is part of the central difficulty, and the problem of which data can and cannot be aggregated, and the focus of that aggregation, is one of the main scientific questions of the moment.

One major conceptual change has been in the way in which the word "crime" is used and understood. In the earlier tradition, it was assumed that something called "crime" existed, as a distinctive logical and ontological category of which all the individual components had some unique qualities in common. In contrast, some 20 years ago the idea crystallised that the only thing which all acts labelled "crime" have in common is that they are breaches of the law of the country concerned. Other than that, there is nothing conceptually or descriptively linking the acts which make

44

up different categories of offence, except perhaps for "disrespect for the law", and even that need not be true for all crimes.

Crime has often and traditionally been referred to as a sickness or a disease. The criminologists, who introduced the new paradigm 20 years ago took the logic of that metaphor much further and pointed out that there is very little in common between having a broken leg, a cancer or cholera. What these illnesses have in common is that they require a response by trained people, and that the organizational infrastructure of that response, but not the response itself, will be similar. The misleading impression given by that common infrastructure is very important in this analysis.

Likewise there is nothing in common in terms of the behavioural sciences between an armed robbery, embezzlement, a sexual assault or the operations of organized crime syndicates, except that they are against the law, and have victims.[2] Indeed, "crime without victims" do not share even that much in common. The implications of those distinctions are that discussions of crime as a coherent, unitary phenomenon are scientifically unsound and so for practical purposes misleading. We can talk usefully about only quite narrowly defined categories of crime, and only with a clear cut assumption of the temporal and special environment in which they occur. "Crime" as a scientific concept is very "slippery", although the concept is an integral and indispensable part of everyday speech.

The drift of criminology over the last 20 years, therefore, has become more specific in nature and more focused in its object of study. Even the relationship between "crime" and something else, such as unemployment, bad housing, poverty or whatever, has been narrowed and sharpened in focus. For instance, some relationship may be established between the incidence of bank robbery and changing rates of employment in one community at one time; and some relationship may be established between the rate of petty theft and changes in the demographic profile in another community at the same (or different) time. It makes no sense to try to add these different categories together in an attempt to build some grand general theory of "crime".

Recent social science methodology has been much affected by the recognition that the unfocused aggregation of data, especially from different sectors, is likely to produce results which may look impressive but which are of doubtful scientific value. For instance, some contemporary research has made significant progress by differentiating between the rates of participation of different social groups in criminal activity and the frequency of offences by participants. The former shows considerable differences between the different groups, the latter very little; i.e. members of group A are much more likely to participate in criminal activity than members of group B, but once they do participate, there is little discernable difference between the behaviours of members of the different groups. Likewise, a useful distinction has been found between not only the criminal and non-criminal, but between high-rate and low-rate offenders. Crime prevention schemes focus on the first category; the operations of the criminal justice system are related more to the second. Coincidentally with the move to the more narrow and specific field of study, there has been a growing distrust of comparing data from different categories of events, and a growing awareness of the way in which important differences in the variables under study can be masked by a comprehensive lumping together of the data. The sweeping and the broad-scope are now considered suspect, almost useless, unless done with great care, in great depth, and therefore at great expense. The "holistic" approach to the study of crime and crime prevention has been found wanting, and is now generally rejected. That has been a major change over the last ten to fifteen years in most criminological schools of thought.

In those studies which have been undertaken recently on the relationship between crime and some socio-economic factor, two traits have become increasingly noticeable. The first is local precision. Data are collected and analysed in separate small, controlled environments, and the analysis of the results compared across the different sites, crime types etc. The data are not aggregated into "crime" and "employment" (or whatever) in general. It is accepted that the only meaningful level of analysis is a change in the rate of crime type x in comparison with certain specified changes in the employment patterns in a small sub-national, spatial unit.

The second trait is that the dependent variable is quite often a measure of the activities of some part of the criminal justice system, rather than the rate of recorded crime: for instance, the size of the prison population. A recent study[3], concluded that the relationship between crime and unemployment may not be consistent over time (and that becomes even clearer when specific types of crime, not "crime" as a whole are considered), or in different social environments, but above all is probably not the same as the relationship between criminal justice policies and unemployment. None of those important differences could have emerged if a strategy of wide-scope data aggregation had been adopted.

In another study,[4] testing a technique for distinguishing universal categories of deviance from types of deviant behaviour limited to particular areas or cultures, the author went about as far as it is possible to go in aggregating data derived from different sources while retaining control over data and their interpretation. Even so, the most important, and rigorous, results were obtained with the data which were compiled separately and locally by on-site researchers. They would have been impossible to derive from centrally-controlled secondary data.

The same kind of methodological problems which have forced a much more modest set of ambitions on criminological research with respect to crime and socio-economic explanations of crime, have applied also in the study of the formal societal reaction to crime, namely the machinery of criminal justice. The last twenty years have seen the gradual adoption of a systemic approach to the study and analysis of the workings of the main agencies of criminal justice, namely the police, prosecution, the courts and the prison or correctional services, complemented by a variety of non-institutional agencies, so that the term "criminal justice system" for the whole is now widely accepted, and within that approach considerable attention has been focused on the relationship between the component agencies.

The criminal justice system operates in an environment not only of society at large, but of the other sector of society. These other sectors include both the other main agencies of the public service, such as education, health and employment agencies, and also such parts of the private sector as major employers. Some important agencies belong to both sectors, such as the media and the trade unions. Just as, in the 1960's, hopes were high that a sufficiently imaginative and broad-scope approach would throw explanatory light on the major problems of the relationship of "crime" to the rest of the socio-economic nexus, so more recently there has been enthusiasm for a comprehensive approach to the relationship between the sectors which would permit some major breakthrough in social planning and the improvement of the social tapestry. So far, the results, in those cases where the necessary data are readily available to evaluate such progress, are almost equally disappointing. It seems that the explanation may be similar, deriving from the fact that the processes of modelling the phenomenon under study is much more complex than was previously thought, and that the more complex the relationships studied, the less focused the analysis. In short, it is all a lot more difficult, scientifically, than we thought twenty years ago.

Finally in this short review of the scaling-down of expectations over the last twenty years, a note on the self-perception of the discipline of criminology may be appropriate. In the 1960's, there were many debates as to whether criminology was truly a sub-division of law, psychology or sociology, with several smaller disciplines claiming some recognition. There now seems to be general agreement that criminology is a mixed discipline, a combination of many fields, with operational and evaluation research techniques and concepts coming increasingly to the fore. Many of the newer generation of leading criminologists have come from the "harder" sciences, especially the applied sciences such as engineering, in addition to the traditional disciplines of law, sociology and psychology. The characteristic that most contemporary criminologists have in common is that they are eclectic, and the more disciplines and perspectives in which they have some competence, and from which they can draw, the better. The current state may be described as the process of building the basis of a new discipline, guided by the traditions of science. The term "multi-disciplinary" is now tautology when applied to the sharply focused topics which make up most of contemporary criminology. If it is used in the more old-fashioned sense of trying to include consideration of a wide range of factors drawn from different fields of study, it will probably and rightly be perceived as outmoded. Harsher critics would say that, like "holistic", it is methodologically discredited or meaningless.

It may seem paradoxical that these contemporary and truly multi-disciplinary criminologists have been a major force in the re-assertion of the primacy of the law in criminology and criminal justice science, and the subsequent relegation of the "social development" approach. As trained scientists, they perceive that the law is the critical factor in defining what counts as crime.

Such scientists also pointed out that the meaningful measurement of improvements in and to the quality of life in respect of, or resulting from, specific forms of crime prevention, or the prevention of specific forms of crime (not the same thing) was so difficult as to be almost without policy value. That is not to say that the improvements are without value. I have never heard that argued. Rather, the value has to be taken on trust, as common sense dictates, unless someone is prepared to invest a lot of resources in the research. The evaluation of the impact can be done only using primary data, generated for the purpose. That entails time and money.

Scholars coming from such backgrounds and bringing new vision, have been among the leading proponents of the arguments that improvements to the quality of life, better nutrition, education, employment etc. should not be justi-fied on the grounds of side-effects, such as projected crime prevention, but simply as good in themselves. There are two grounds for such arguments. The first is that if these measures are advocated on the grounds that they produce certain desirable consequences, such as a reduction in "crime", they will be discredited if it is shown that the consequences do not happen: and, as argued above, it is extremely difficult to prove any clear-cut results. An absence of demonstrated positive results can easily be interpreted as a failure, and so be used against further support for the original measures. Indeed, such advocacy can be counter-productive, because the current level of knowledge about the relative pay-off from different investments in this area is very low. The second argument is that, among the reasons for improvements to the quality of life, such as substituting nutrition for mal-nutrition, education for illiteracy, health for illness and so on, crime prevention or reduction comes very low down on the list, and should do so. The main reason for getting rid of those evils is that they are evils, causes of unhappiness to those who suffer from them. The fact that those sufferers may then "pass on" a proportion of their unhappiness to others (e.g. the relatively prosperous) is, in proportion, secondary.

These arguments, are not concerned to show that governments or ther other agencies should not seek to improve the quality of life of their citizens; or whether that will reduce the level of criminality.[5] They do imply that it is very difficult to measure the degree by which it reduces criminality, and so it should be done for quite other reasons. Common sense and human experience suggest that crimes of need, if not crimes of greed, will be reduced by improving the quality of life, and that is a good thing.

The law is, I have argued, the central feature of the concept of crime. Contemporary criminologists, whatever their scientific background would emphasize that. They may criticize the way lawyers think, or practice their profession, or the way the function of the law is conceived and operationalised; but they do not deny the primacy of law. The criminal justice system is the main manifestation of the law in practical terms: the way in which it works determines what the law appears to be to most citizens. Recent research has revealed many problems with the way the law is put into practice, not least the enormous amount of public money spent on it. The criminal justice system is, in most countries, a major consumer of public resources. In many countries it is a growing consumer.

It is obviously, and generally agreed to be, true that in the complex and interdependent world of today, what happens in one sector influences what happens in another, as a fact of life. But that does not mean that sometimes what happens within a sector is not the most important. In criminal justice, at least, what happens within the sector (including the interactions between the agencies) is arguably more important than the details of the relationships with the other sectors. No-one, I believe, would say that no notice should be taken of other sectors: but to give those relationships primacy is to lose contact with the fact that crime and criminal justice, are primarily matters deriving from the law, how it works in practice, and how it and its implementations could and should be improved. "Inter-sectoral" as a kind of "buzz-word" tends to appear with "multidisciplinary". They are both words belonging to the public relations aspects of criminology in the early 1970's, not the realistic rigorous criminology of today.

Perhaps the terminology of interdisciplinary and multi-sectoral was promoted because it sounds positive, promising and hopeful. People always prefer to hear the optimistic rather than the pessimistic, and there is no doubt that contemporary criminology is much more pessimistic than the older version. But presumably that which is "true", i.e. is supported by evidence, should be promoted rather than that which is comfortable and comforting. The promise of the older version made it, in its time, very attractive to managers and officials, especially those in politically sensitive positions, who need to be seen to be doing something effective, and who do not have a lot of resources to throw at their problems. It is noteworthy that sceptical criminal justice system managers and professionals were usually unimpressed by the earlier, optimistic approach, but are increasingly supportive of the contemporary realistic school.

The optimistic approach therefore, should be discarded, at least for the forseeable future, because for scientific reasons there cannot be a useful product, and not just for reasons of lack of resources to carry out such a programme at the international level. The existing data, or data likely to be obtained in the near future, are insufficient and inappropriate for that type of research. There are far too many variables to be controlled to allow for any more than the most vague conclusions, in which there can be only limited confidence. The most moderate critic would say that such an exercise could not be done currently by any inter-governmental body. The most rigorous might say that it cannot be done, except over a period of several years, and at great cost; and even then, for the reasons of scientific logic reviewed earlier, the likelihood of a policy-relevant product is very low.

Conclusions

To summarize, I have tried to argue that:

(i) Applied criminology at the national level in many countries has changed in the last two decades and the international approach seems not to be changing with it, but perhaps even to be going in the opposite direction.

(ii) That national change started in a few places, but has spread and is spreading. Following the usual human experience of new ideas taking root first with the relatively young, there are many older criminologists in many countries who are unaware of the change, or reject it: but currently they seem to be a dying breed because the change is based on the replacement of more romantic, but more primitive science by a better scientific paradigm.

(iii) The "social development" approach to crime prevention and criminal justice has come to be seen in the broad sense as marginal to the CPCJB, because:

(a) Criminologists are not against social development: they see it as something helpful, but as very difficult to analyse, and so requiring a great investment of effort and resources with the possibility of a very modest gain. The goals of social development should be pursued for their own sake as a matter of priority. If there is, as most people believe, a spin-off effect of a reduction in crime, that is a bonus.

(b) The prevention of a disease and the treatment if contracted are usually very different: as they are also very different for different diseases. The differences more important than the superficial similarities. Social development is concerned with making the world better: the main instruments of crime prevention, the criminal law and the criminal justice system, are concerned with stopping the world getting worse, and that is a very different type of operation.

(c) As in some forms of medicine, there are no current grounds for optimism: like AIDS, there is no forseeable good news, but that does not mean we should stop trying, on the one hand, or indulge in wishful thinking on the other. One criminological friend suggested that a strategy of crime prevention based on attempting to overcome evil in the world is parallel to a strategy for containing AIDS based on decrying the fact that human beings have sexual drives.

(d) If concern with what is desirable, a better world, becomes dominant over what is feasible, we are likely to attempt worthy things which are beyond us. In the long run, no-one will gain. In that respect, the implications and limitations deriving from the fact that most international work has to use almost entirely secondary data, have not been sufficiently taken into account.

(iv) The international criminal justice research community would probably find it a good investment to use some of its limited resources, of both money and expertise, in re-evaluating its priorities and feasibilities in line with these emerging national trends. It is not a matter of re-inventing the wheel; of re-designing one, because "roundness" is now seen as having a different shape from that usually accepted, especially at the international level, some years ago.

Notes

[1] For reasons for that are complex, and although I am willing to discuss them at length with anyone interested, it would make this already long paper far too long to do so here.

[2] The generality of the concept of victim has been an important part of the rise of victimology as a fast growing branch of criminology.

[3] S. Box, *Recession, Crime and Punishment*, B. and N. Imports, 1987, illustrates this point well. Box uses a range of data from local to national, and national data from two countries, but in a very careful way, to avoid misleading or unjustified aggregations of data. His results are relevant to this paper in two respects. First, he shows that the use of imprisonment in the United Kingdom, and to a lesser extent in the United States, has increased in close correlation with an increase in unemployment, and that a statistically disproportionate share of that increase in the prison population is made up of the unemployed. He is able to show also that some of that disproportionate increase is due to a change in sentencing strategy by the courts, rather than to an increase in criminal activity by that sector of the population, although such a behavioural change also occurred. Secondly, he shows that in a similar period of economic recession and unemployment in the 1930's no parallel increase in imprisonment rates or recorded crime rates took place.

[4] G. Newman, *Comparative Deviance*, Elsevier, New York, 1973.

[5] It may well not reduce the level of recorded criminality, because the crimes of the very poor are committed mostly against the very poor, and are, as such, unrecorded and unaccessible to the United Nations or any other user of secondary data.

PRIORITES ET STRATEGIES
POUR UNE CRIMINOLOGIE DU TIERS-MONDE

Guy Houchon *

Le cordiale invitation qui m'a été adressée de contribuer à ce volume portant sur la criminalité et le développement ne supprime pas pour moi l'angoissante question de la légitimité d'une intervention. Je m'explique: trois manuels couvrent le champ de la criminologie en Afrique, ils sont l'oeuvre de 3 Nord-Américains et d'un Européen. Il en va de même de la plupart des comptes rendus qui leurs sont réservés dans les revues scientifiques. De sorte qu'il existe un risque de voir "criminalité et développement" devenir un thème monopolisé par le Centre qui procède à des grandes manoeuvres dans la Périphérie. Cette situation provoque parfois, en d'autres lieux, des réactions bien informées de protestation, c'est l'"America Latina y su criminologia"[1] et des démonstrations d'autonomie, c'est la "Criminologia de la liberación"[2].

Et pourtant la retraite digne et silencieuse est une réponse simpliste devant la co-responsabilité internationale des criminologues. Qu'il suffise de citer quelques problèmes situés à leur niveau usuel d'articulation.

Au niveau de la criminalisation primaire

C'est l'héritage des législations coloniales ou le rôle des modèles législatifs d'urgence relayés par des pouvoirs qui, par les mécanismes de répression directe ou de l'hégémonie (Gramsci) étouffent dans l'ouate du consensus les tragiques

---

* Professeur, Unité de criminologie, Université Catholique de Louvain, Belgique.

inégalités de leurs formations sociales, que viennent confirmer les appareils d'Etat à travers le fonctionnement du système d'administration de la justice pénale (S.A.J.P.). On assiste parfois à des manifestations extrêmes de type obsessionnel, où l'acteur historique se conduit comme un "délinquant inquiet qui légifère"[3], mais de manière plus commune, on se trouve devant la criminalisation d'actes de résistance à un ordre nouveau que l'on s'évertue à appeler "modernisation" et qui souvent implique la transformation en marchandises de biens antérieurement inaliénables et indivisibles comme la terre et ses produits. Aussi la poursuite du vol de bois de forêt au Maroc[4] reproduit-elle le scénario rhénan des années 1840!

Dans ces conditions, la criminalisation primaire crée des catégories juridiques distinctes socialement décontextualisées.

Au niveau des formes de la criminalité on peut citer de manière non exhaustive, mais répondant au souci qui vient d'être énoncé: les recels du pillage des patrimoines nationaux, la criminalité organisée triangulaire du type drogues — armes — exportation illégale de capitaux, le crime international (non encore reconnu) d'usure de la dette[5] et l'exportation frauduleuse de déchets industriels et nucléaires.

Au niveau de la criminalisation secondaire

Le constat d'ineffectivité des institutions judiciaires comme médiatrices et productrices de l'Etat de droit me paraît central. Ineffectivité telle que, pour l'Afrique au moins, il me paraît impossible de rendre compte statistiquement du transit des flux d'arrestations policières et des chiffres de stock des populations pénitentiaires à partir d'un modèle d'interdépendance des diverses parties du S.A.J.P. Cette configuration statistique atypique traduirait une inquiétante autonomie des deux institutions précitées[6].

Certes les chiffres de la détention provisoire indiquent une plage de recouvrement qui explique une partie de la variance, puisque les travaux de Carranza ont pu montrer, d'une manière saisissante, au moins pour l'Amérique Centrale, l'influence considérable des héritages juridiques, de Common Law ou latin, en contrastant les taux de détention provisoire[7]. Mais cette hypothèse n'est peut-être pas aussi facile à confirmer en Afrique, en comparant par exemple le Nigéria et la Tunisie.

Enfin au niveau de l'exécution de la peine le rôle constant de l'emprisonnement ne cesse d'intriguer. Lors du séminaire tenu à Harare (Zimbabwe) en mars 1988 pour les Directeurs d'administration pénitentiaire africains anglophones, on ne pouvait s'empêcher de s'interroger sur la consolidation du succès de la privation de liberté par emprisonnement en Afrique, à tout le moins comme forme emblématique du pénal.[8]

Peut-être aura-t-on remarqué que les questions qui viennent d'être évoquées contiennent autant d'aspects techniques que éthiques.

Reprenons, à ce titre, la question de la légitimité en criminalisation primaire et secondaire. Le problème posé ici n'est pas tant l'effet individualisé de lois répressives que leurs effets de masse. En effet, la thèse de la criminalité instrumentale justifiée de Fanon[9] peut être diversement appréciée en termes de morale politique, mais techniquement elle n'autorise pas une approche différentielle des phénomènes criminels. La question des rapports du pénal avec celle de la formation de l'Etat, voire du concept anglo-saxon proche mais différent de Nation-building[10], peut être explorée dans deux directions dont l'antinomie pourrait être réduite:

1°) Certaines formations politiques et idéologiques (et donc pénales) sont tellement nécessaires à un système économique donné qu'elles peuvent en être considérées comme consubstantielles ou organiques.

2°) La notion d'Etat, acteur social collectif relativement autonome demande à être approfondie dans la pratique de l'exercice des fonctions pénales.

Il en résulte qu'il est tout aussi simpliste de proposer la succession d'oppression de l'Etat néo-colonial à l'Etat colonial qu'il ne l'est de légitimer la délégation de l'appareil pénal par un transfert à des élites nationales, et ce d'autant plus que la légitimité est une affaire plus processuelle que ne le laisse entendre la théorie wébérienne.

Si l'effet individualisé d'un droit pénal "politique" (ce qui est évidemment un pléonasme volontaire) peut concerner des luttes entre élites, quelle que soit leur appartenance, idéologique, ethnique ou autre, cela pose de sérieux problèmes de droits de l'Homme qui agitent, à juste titre, l'opinion internationale éclairée; l'application de ce même droit pénal crée, en dérive, des effets de masse considérables. Un grand nombre de citoyens sont criminalisés, moins bien lotis culturellement ou économiquement que des opposants, leurs comportements paraissant moins noblement motivés et étant assimilés à la criminalité dite "commune".

Un tel fonctionnement du S. A. J. P. ne peut qu'alimenter, parmi les populations ciblées, la production de phénomènes psycho-sociaux de rationalisation/verbalisation que Sykes & Matza ont identifié depuis longtemps sous le terme de "techniques de neutralisation"[11]. Ainsi se boucle un cycle qui nous conduit des formes de criminalisation aux processus criminogènes.

Face à la situation complexe qui vient d'être décrite, deux stratégies complémentaires, encore que parfois ponctuellement rivales, peuvent s'organiser.

La première est représentée par les travaux de divers organes et instituts des Nations Unies et notamment l'Institut Interrégional de Recherche des Nations Unies sur la Criminalité et la Justice (UNICRI précédemment UNSDRI). Elle vise à déterminer les priorités telles qu'elles sont déterminées par les acteurs du terrain en termes de représentations sociales de la criminalité et du S. A. J. P. L'ouvrage "Research and International Co-operation in Criminal Justice" et le rapport de recherche tri-lingue sur "L'inadaptation sociale des jeunes et les droits de l'Homme dans le contexte du développement urbain"[12] en constituent des produits très soignés, notamment sur le plan méthodologique. Menés dans le prolongement cumulatif des préoccupations d'une politique criminelle, maintenant quarantenaire, des N.U., inscrits dans un paradigme culturaliste au nom d'une "Criminologie du Tiers-Monde", leur méthodologie est volontairement dépendante d'une technologie de recherche telle qu'elle peut être pratiquée, sur le terrain, par des chercheurs autochtones.

L'option de base est nettement pragmatique. David la résume en tête d'une communication à la First Joint International Conference on Research in Crime Prevention à Riyad[13]. "Les besoins en matière de prévention de la criminalité et de justice pénale tels que ressentis (needs experienced), se manifestent principalement dans le domaine de la recherche orientée vers l'action afin de résoudre des problèmes concrets et spécifiques relatifs à la politique (criminelle) et d'adopter des activités et des programmes innovateurs pour la formation du personnel, l'échange d'information, le diagnostic intégral de la prévention de la criminalité et du traitement dans le contexte de la planification du développement, y compris le rassemblement des données et de l'information dans divers secteurs de la délinquance en rapport avec l'urbanisation, la migration, le chômage et l'industrialisation."

Cette définition des choses, s'organisant en stratégie, me paraît à la fois très rentable et comporter certains risques. Voyons d'abord ses aspects très positifs.

I *La mise au point d'indicateurs criminologiques.*

Toute une tradition orientée vers la quantification des sciences sociales ne peut être aisément renvoyée, quelle que soit la valeur de ses critiques épistémologiques. Les grandes enquêtes sur l'état de la criminalité et le fonctionnement de la justice pénale sont de plus en plus performantes. On peut souhaiter que ces données, alliées à d'autres bases d'information des N. U., soient retravaillées dans des monographies comme celle, déjà ancienne, de Wickwar, *The Place of Criminal Justice in Developmental Planning*[14]. La notion de planification intégrale (compréhensive) est précieuse.

II *La proposition d'expertise régionale et centrale.*

Il s'agit ici de valoriser les potentiels fatalement réduits de la recherche dans les pays du Tiers-Monde.

III *La notion d'intégration réciproque de la politique criminelle et de la politique de développement.*

Il s'agit d'un thème essentiel de la politique criminelle des N. U. que l'on retrouve dès que s'éclipse l'orientation clinique et pédagogique de la Commission sociale provisoire. Je n'en prendrai pour exemple que la formulation d'un rapport de ce que l'on appelait alors le Groupe consultatif d'experts en matière de prévention du crime et du traitement des délinquants à Genève en 1965. "Il est... urgent de renoncer... à une attitude, qu'elle soit celle des Gouvernements ou des milieux professionnels, où l'on considère que la criminalité est... un phénomène social isolé, du seul ressort d'un groupe restreint de spécialistes et qu'on ne doit combattre que par la sanction pénale ou des mesures de réadaptation à l'égard du délinquant"[15].

C'est à la notion de développement que je vais m'attacher pour prendre quelque distance à l'égard du courant pragmatique, sans toutefois me livrer à un vain exercice de sémantique. Remarquons seulement que si l'on se focalise sur les indicateurs précités de l'urbanisation, de la migration, de l'industrialisation et du chômage, on rencontre une série de difficultés (ce qui n'est ni étonnant, ni dirimant) que l'on résoud souvent maladroitement.

En effet, la prédiction d'une montée de la criminalité en raison de l'urbanisation (voire d'une industrialisation qui, dans les pays concernés, ne l'accompagne pas partout, ainsi par exemple les différences entre l'Afrique dans son ensemble et l'Asie du Sud-est) est un aphorisme assertorique:

1º) La variable indépendante est complexe[16].

2º) Même en se servant des criminalités légales ou apparentes comme variables dépendantes, les "croissances" présentent des vitesses et des directions très variables.

3º) Les variables intervenantes, que l'on ne prend pas toujours soin de rechercher, sont la plupart du temps puisées dans le stock de ce que Cressey a appelé la "evil causes evil fallacy"[17].

Cette approche contient le risque d'une culpabilisation implicite des populations ciblées, de leur désorganisation, de leur anomie, voire de leur pauvreté. La notion de développement n'est pas l'équivalent de celle de modernisation, sauf à rabattre la première sur un schéma strictement dualiste (avec un secteur moderne et une société traditionnelle en simultanéité a-synchronique).

Dès maintenant il vaut mieux se tourner vers une définition plus neutre. D'ailleurs, les responsables des l'UNSDRI proposent ici l'expression "changements sociaux", que l'on peut traduire par "la transformation structurelle d'un pays, recherchée de manière consciente, explicite, ordonnée, et rationnelle"[18]. Une série de travaux classiques ont été menés dans la ligne de la modernisation, que ce soient ceux de Clifford, Clinard & Abbott, Mushanga et de Shelley[19]. Comme le fait remarquer C. Sumner[20], si l'on veut mener une analyse criminologique dans cette perspective, il est nécessaire de lui adjoindre celle des "blocked opportunities". Les recherches sont alors menées dans deux directions: le phénomène urbain et une interprétation culturaliste.

Le phénomène urbain conduit à interroger prioritairement la délinquance de rue (et notamment juvénile). On délaisse ainsi la criminalité rurale ou plus exactement la criminalité perpétrée en milieu rural, notamment la victimisation de masse comme celle que l'on rencontre en Ouganda, au Mozambique, dans le Nord et l'Est du Zaïre, actuellement au Burundi. Aucun de ces phénomènes n'apparaît sur les trois administrations de l'échelle de priorité de l'enquête de l'UNSDRI[21].

La perspective culturaliste du courant de la modernisation conduit à identifier les effets et non les causes des "blocked opportunities". On se retrouve ainsi devant le multifactorialisme criminologique classique que j'ai dénoncé dans mon rapport de synthèse sur la question des priorités de recherche au Congrès de criminologie de Madrid en 1970[22]. Je me bornerai dans cet exposé à citer un seul exemple de son dysfonctionnement en criminologie juvénile africaine.

On fait généralement grand cas d'un facteur classique de délinquance comme celui de la dissociation familiale. Or, la mobilité conjugale est une donnée démographique constante et donc normale de la vie sociale africaine. On a en effet pu calculer, en ne retenant que le facteur de mortalité, que la probabilité pour une femme mariée à 18 ans à un homme de 25 ans de vivre toute sa période féconde avec le même partenaire était de 29%. Autrement dit, en excluant toutes les autres causes de rupture d'union, un peu plus du 1/4 des couples peuvent espérer passer ensemble toute la période du 18e au 50e anniversaire de la femme[23]. D'autres exemples empruntés notamment aux migrations des milieux ruraux vers les villes pourraient montrer qu'ils sont souvent traités d'une manière telle que l'on s'écarte de ce qui me paraît devoir être une position à la fois théorique et opérationnelle centrale. Toute criminologie (comme discipline de savoir et d'action) qui n'engage pas prioritairement à l'aplanissement des inégalités d'avoir ou de pouvoir est inévitablement conduite au correctionalisme[24]. La déviance est identifiée à une pathologie dont les facteurs morbides sont des "facteurs criminogènes". Ceux-ci sont généralement situés, non pas au niveau de la structure sociale, mais dans une ou plusieurs sous-cultures, pour venir se fixer électivement chez des individus dont la personnalité est fragile, non prédisposée.

Dans ces conditions, les symptômes de la marginalisation sont traités comme des indicateurs de risque, de dangerosité, de pré-délinquance. Le dispositif intellectuel est alors en place pour qu'une amplification sociale de la déviance se transforme en grave problème social exigeant un dispositif (pénologique) considérable. Toute recherche de type alternatif est mise à l'échec, soit par rejet, soit par accumulation d'effets pervers.

C'est ce risque d'impasse qui me conduit à proposer la deuxième stratégie, à titre complémentaire: celle que les sociologues d'expression française appellent la construction de l'objet[25].

Dans cette perspective, je voudrais attirer l'attention sur deux courants dans le recherche en sciences sociales africaine: l'histoire sociale et l'anthropologie de la marginalisation en milieu urbain.

A côté d'une histoire du pénal et notamment de la prison relativement bien développée avec des travaux comme ceux de Seidman pour le Ghana, de Shivjii et de Williams pour l'Afrique de l'Est[26], s'organise un courant d'histoire populaire[27][28] se développant dans le cadre de l'histoire politique et sociale, qui s'attache à l'examen des structures d'inégalités et d'exploitation. On établit ainsi des séquences de types sociaux et de mouvements sociaux à travers le temps et leurs rapports avec la paysannerie et, plus tard, le prolétariat semi-urbain et urbain. On peut ainsi examiner l'accueil fait à certaines formes de violence, de banditisme, de fanatisme religieux syncrétique à la violence institutionnelle. Le caractère diachronique des séries autorise une fructueuse décentration à l'égard de la période coloniale, qui ne revêt plus cette position archétypique et permet ainsi que s'établissent un avant et un après dans la violence populaire réactionnelle accompagnée de diverses formes de conscience sociale[29].

Bien que certains historiens et sociologues africanistes hésitent de moins en moins à utiliser le concept de classe sociale, il me paraît prudent de nous arrêter à son seuil tant qu'une analyse exhaustive n'en aura pas été communément reçue.

Je laisserai momentanément sans exposé les recherches d'anthropologie urbaine, ayant publié sur cette question il y a quelques années déjà un travail de synthèse sur la marginalité dans les pays du Tiers-Monde dans une étude différentielle du squatting et de l'économie informelle dans leurs perspectives criminologiques[30].

Ce que j'ai voulu proposer pour une criminologie du Tiers-Monde (label qui demanderait un exposé justificatif en soi) n'est pas une opposition stérile entre deux images réductrices d'un courant pragmatique aveugle, complice des forces d'oppression et d'un courant théorique éthéré, sans retombée dans les pratiques sociales. Les priorités de recherche ne peuvent se confondre avec les urgences (même légitimes). En l'absence d'une construction d'objet, le criminologue que d'aucuns s'évertuent à appeler expert (acteur de l'éphémère) se trouve dans une situation absurde. On le place à une coupure (au temps zéro de l'immédiat) d'un ensemble processuel (interactions entre criminalisations primaires, criminalisations secondaires et criminogénèse) en lui demandant d'aider à planifier. Je ne livre pas ici une expression de criminologue dans un fauteuil (armchair criminologist), même si je puis avouer l'avoir éprouvée sur le terrain, vertigineusement...

Références et Notes

[1] R. Del Olmo, *America Latina y su criminologia*, Siglo veintiuno editores, Mexico, 1981.

[2] L. Anyiar de Castro, *Criminología de la liberación*, Ed. University Zulia, Maracaibo, 1987.

[3] I. Sow, "Contrepoints, Le pouvoir de tuer", *Politique Africaine*, September 1982, No. II: 7, p. 75.

[4] F. Rezaka, *Contrôle social et pratiques de renvoi en milieu berbère*, Mémoire de licence en Criminologie, U. C. L., Louvain-la-Neuve, September 1984, pp. 2-15.

[5] J. Vega Vega, "The International Crime of Usury: The Third World Foreign Debt", *Crime and Trial Justice*, No. 30, pp. 45-59.

[6] G. Houchon, "Marginalité urbaine et système pénal, ces formes parallèles de régulations urbaines", Groupe de recherche villes et citadins du Tiers-monde, Document Provisoire, mai 1987, GLYSI, Université, Lyon, No. 11, pp. 117-127.

[7] E. Carranza et al., *El preso sin condena en América Latina y el Caribe*, ILANUD, San José, Costa Rica, 1983.

[8] G. Houchon, "Contemporary trends in penology and their influences on the African penal system," The paper was presented at the Seminar for Chiefs of Penitentary Administrations in African Countries, Harare, Zimbabwe, March 1988.

[9] F. Fanon, *Les damnés de la terre*, Maspero, Paris, 1966, spec. p. 225, et sv.

[10] C. Mahabir, *Crime and Nation-building in the Caribbean, the Legacy of Legal Barriers*, Sclenkman, Cambridge, Mass., 1985; J. Opolot, *Criminal Justice and Nation-building in Africa*, University Press of America, Washington, 1976.

[11] G. M. Sykes and D. Matza, "Techniques of neutralization: A theory of delinquency", *American Social Review*, 1957, No. 22, pp. 664-670.

[12] U. Zvekic and A. Mattei, *Research and International Co-operation in Criminal Justice*. Survey on Needs and Priorities of Developing Countries, UNSDRI, Publication No. 29, Rome, 1987; *L'inadaptation sociale des jeunes et les Droits de l'Homme dans le contexte du développement urbain*, UNSDRI, Publication No. 22, Fratelli Palombi, Rome, 1984.

[13] P. David, Position paper, *First Joint International Conference on Research in Crime Prevention*, Riyadh, Saudi Arabia, January 1984, UNSDRI, Publication No. 26, Rome, 1985, p. 205.

[14] W. Wickwar, "The Place of Criminal Justice in Developmental Planning", Monographs of the United Nations Crime Prevention and Criminal Justice Section, New York, New York University Press, 1977.

[15] Nations Unies Doc., E/CN/S/3/88, Genèva, Decembre 1965.

[16] V. par ex.: Cf. W. Bradshaw, "Urbanization and Underdevelopment: A global study of modernization, urbanization and economic dependency", *American Social Review*, 1987, No. 52, pp. 224-239; C. O. Lerche, "Economic Influences on Popular Disturbance in Nigeria", *Journal of Asian and African Studies*, 1980, No. XV: 3-4, pp. 193-202.

[17] D. Cressey, *Delinquency, Crime and Differential Association*, Martins Nijhoff, The Hague, 1964, p. 40.

[18] K. Griffin, *Underdevelopment in Spanish America*, 1969, cité par C. Mahabir (cote 10).

[19] W. Clifford, *An Intertroduction to African Criminology*, Nairobi, O. U. P., 1979; M. B. Clinard and D. J. Abbott, *Crime in Developing Countries*, Wiley, New York, 1973; T. M. Mushanga, *Crime and Deviance*, Kampala, Uganda, East Africa Literature Bureau, 1976; L. I. Shelley, *Crime and Modernization: The Impact of Industrialization and Urbanization on Crime*, Southern Illinois University Press, Carbondale and Edwardsville, 1981, v. toutefois du même auteur "Crime and Modernization Reconsidered", *Annales Internationales de Criminologie*, 1986, No. 24 1 et 2, pp. 7-22.

[20] C. Sumner, *Crime, Justice and Development*, Cambridge Studies in Criminology, Heineman, London, 1982.

[21] v. cote 12.

[22] v. G. Houchon, "Les ordres de priorité en recherche criminologique", Memoria de VI Congreso Internacional de Criminología, 1973, Vo. 1, Madrid, pp. 361-410.

[23] G. Houchon, "Marginalité urbaine et système pénal en milieu africaine. Recherche d'un profil bas dans le contrôle social formel", *Revue Internationale de Criminologie et de Police Technique*, 1987, No. 4, pp. 375-384.

[24] G. Boehringer, "African Criminology: Towards the Necessary Dialogue", *East African Law Journal*, 1975, No. XI: 1, pp. 81-106.

[25] P. Bourdieu et. al., *Le métier de sociologue*, Mouton-Bordas, Paris, 1968, p. 217 et sv.

[26] R. B. Seidman, "The Ghana Penal System: An Historical Perspective", *University of Ghana Law Review*, 1966, III: 2, pp. 89-121; D. Williams, "The Role of Prisons in Tanzania: An Historical Perspective", *Crime and Social Justice*, Sumner 1980, pp. 27-40; I. G. Shivji, Semi-Proletarian Labour and the Use of Penal Sanctions in the Labour of Colonial Tanganyika (1920-1930) in C. Sumner, Ed. cote 20.

[27] D. Crumney, Ed., *Bandity, Rebellion and Social Protest in Africa*, J. Currey, London, 1986.

[28] Adde. O. Marenin, "The Anini Saga: Armed Robbery and the Reproduction of Ideology in Nigeria", *The Journal of Modern African Theory*, 1987, No. 25: 2, pp. 259-281.

[29] Adapté d'après D. Crumney, cote 27, p. 3.

[30] G. Houchon, "La théorie de la marginalité urbaine dans le Tiers-monde, etude différentielle du squatting et de l'économie informelle dans leurs aspects criminologiques", *Psychopathologie Africaine*, Paris-Dakar, C. N. R. S., 1987, No. 7, pp. 181-229.

CRIME AND THE HUMAN CONDITION *

Graeme Newman **

The poverty-crime link

Introduction

Research in countries in many parts of the world has demonstrated that crime is more prevalent in the poor and lower classes — and this research finding holds whether conducted in Europe, Asia or the Americas.[1] But there is much disagreement in the criminal justice literature concerning the *interpretation* of this relationship. Because the majority of research studies rely on officially reported crime statistics, the critics argue that the interpretation of the crime/poverty link is biased by a definition of crime that "favors" the better off. Indeed, they point out, crimes of the powerful, such as corporations and governments, are rarely recorded in official statistics. This criticism applies especially to the case of victims who suffer violent deaths (such as from pollution, marketing of unsafe products) by the more powerful in society, which are rarely reported as the result of "violent crime."[2]

A more useful way to look at this problem is to consider which strata of society may suffer more from crime, the

---

* The paper was originally prepared on behalf of the Crime Prevention and Criminal Justice Branch.

It was commissioned by the United Nations Development Programme (UNDP), with whose permission it is being reproduced. The views expressed are those of the author and do not necessarily represent the views of UNDP.

** Professor, School of Criminal Justice, SUNY at Albany, USA.

context within which this victimization and crime occur, and to consider how victimization and crime are related to each other. Whether the poor commit more or less crime than the rich is less of a question when it comes to considering the human condition. It is more important to consider the context of life within which this crime may occur, and who may suffer.

This approach suggests an additional criticism of traditional research on the poverty/crime link: their definition of "poverty" is vague, and most often non-existent. In fact poverty is more often defined as "lower class." We will suggest in this essay that the poor actually constitute a "class" below the lower class, and that this idea provides insight into the relationship between poverty and crime at the global level.

The Poor as an Underclass

Most often, the lowest group of a society consists of either (1) those who have congregated in one area over several generations or (2) those who are "temporarily" congregated in a particular area as a result of many factors including natural disasters, rapid socioeconomic change, industrialization, family disorganization etc. Neighbourhoods of the poor are characterized by a moving population, slums, breakdowns in family life, disease, grossly inadequate sanitation etc. Increasingly, it is becoming apparent that these neighbuorhoods — shanty towns, slums, they have many different names — are most typified by a lack of adequate housing. In short, most of this "class" is homeless.

A number of researchers have recently argued that the lower echelons of society — the homeless — have become more and more split off from the rest of society over the last two decades. Although most of this research has been conducted in developed countries, particularly the United

States, there is good reason to think that the same process is occurring in the developing countries of the world, as we shall see below. While this finding has come of something of a shock to developed societies of the west, it is not so surprising to some eastern societies, where the very lowest class — often termed a "caste" — has held a thoroughly split-off position for many generations[3]. They constitute an underclass.

The underclass is inhabited by what Wilson and others have described as "the truly disadvantaged."[4] While there is much controversy concerning how the underclass should be identified and defined, there is little disagreement that in most societies such a class exists, though its condition may vary relative to the particular economic and political structure of the country. The underclass may be divided into additional strata:

1. Upper level: must spend more than 70% of income on housing, may be employed or unemployed.

2. Middle level: Temporarily homeless (less than a year). Usually unemployed.

3. Permanently homeless, may or may not be employed.

4. As development increases, a tendency for the homeless and underclass to gravitate to the fringes of cities, and establish squatter and slum settlements.

It has been estimated that as of 1987, 1 billion people have inadequate shelter (one fifth of the world's population), and 100 million people have no shelter at all. This figure can only be a rough estimate, though, and it is probably higher.[5] For, because these persons have no "fixed address" they cannot be counted easily. It is probably reasonable to conclude, however, after the extensive research in the United States over the past decade, that the number of homeless in developed countries is increasing.[6] Reports from developing countries would also suggest that the numbers

71

are increasing, particularly in countries which have experienced rapid industrial growth, with concomitant rapid urbanization and migration from rural to city. The size of slum areas in large cities in Asia, Africa and Middle East, and Latin America has increased over the last two decades[7].

It may also be argued that the patterning of the homeless is different across countries according to level of development, although some argue that the pattern is the same: that crowded cities produce the same homeless population the world over: "It is a world-wide phenomenon, be it in India, Ghana, Zambia, China, Britain or America"[8]. While there is virtually no research from an international perspective on this question, we can compare some individual research projects on particular cities.

Table 1

Homeless in Various Cities by Selected Socio-Demographic Characteristics

Characteristic	Ibadan	Pune	U.S.
Race/caste	n.a.	56% Hindu lowest caste	New York City: 55% Black, 24% Hispanic , 38% Black total U.S.
No Education	35%	50%	Ohio: 36% (no high school graduation)
Gender	n.a.	n.a.	53% female 68% male (N.Y.C.)
Families	n.a.	n.a.	55% (N.Y.C.)
Average Age	40	n.a.	40 (N.Y.C.). Ohio 30 total U.S.: 40
Employed	19%	80%	25% (Ohio)
Been in Jail	n.a.	n.a.	58% (Ohio)
Been in Mental Institution	10% deformed beggars	n.a.	2.5% (U.S.) 30% Albany, N.Y.

Tables 1 and 2 provide a rough overview of research findings from studies in the United States[9], Nigeria[10] and India[11].

Table 2

Self Reported Cause of Homelessness

Financial (evicted, lost job etc.)	33%	n.a.	37% Ohio 45% New York
Personal	38%	n.a.	21% (Ohio)
Natural Disaster	26%	24%	2.5% (N.Y.C.)
Drugs/alcohol	n.a.	n.a.	3-4% New York/Ohio

We may make the following observations based on Table 1, concerning the social and demographic background of the underclass:

1. The average age of the underclass in all cities studied is roughly 40, although there is a recent trend in parts of the US for the average age to decrease somewhat, as there is an increase in homeless teenagers and families.

2. If we interpret "caste" in a general way, i.e. as referring to powerless groups of either religious or ethnic distinction we see that the underclass is made up of such individuals — whether in the West or East, as shown by the racial proportion of homeless in the U.S. (which far exceeds the proportion of Blacks and Hispanics in the U.S. population) or the lowest Hindu caste of India.[12]

3. The studies of Eastern cities and homeless did not report the proportions of males as against females. Since most were referred to as having moved to the cities in search of work, it is likely that the proportions are not substantially different from those of the U.S. In the U.S. the male proportion is only slightly higher than the female: which certainly questions the myth that the underclass of

America is populated by male skid row bums. This is further supported from Table 2, where we find that alcohol and drugs are reported to play a minor role in precipitating homelessness.

The most impressive finding, however is revealed in Table 2, which displays the proportions of respondents who gave reasons as to why they were homeless. Clearly, the predominant cause is financial: whether losing a job, housing too dear for the wages received, evicted etc. There is a large body of research which supports this finding.[13]

If we accept the statements of these homeless persons at face value, it would suggest that their destitute condition is not caused by personal failure, but by the economic and environmental context in which they live.[14] This context is that of *development*: the global modernization of all countries through financial and industrial development. While this process is occurring in all countries, including the western "developed" countries, it is thought that development has a much more direct and devastating effect on the lesser developed countries. In fact, it is possible to identify a group of countries which in themselves form an "underclass."

The World's Poor: The Least Developed Countries

In the studies reviewed in the previous section, it was found that in India and Nigeria a high proportion of individuals was homeless as a result of a natural disaster, whereas in the U. S. this was the explanation of only a very small proportion. The homeless of the less developed countries are far more victimized by disasters because of their country's lack of economic and capital resources.

An examination of some recent disasters befalling developing and developed countries proves this point. For example, while the earthquake in San Francisco of October 17, 1989 caused considerable loss of life, an earthquake of similar magnitude in a developing country, without the wealth available to build strong earthquake resistant structures, caused loss of life and damage far greater than that experienced in the U.S. This is born out by the much greater destruction and injury caused by the earthquake of similar magnitude in Armenia in December 1988. And the earthquake in Northern China two days after the San Francisco quake brought far greater destruction.

The point to be understood is that development provides a greater cushion against disasters, whether natural or man-made (e.g. crime). We will return to this important point again below. The well worn statistic of the world's starving population bears repeating, however. According to the World Commission on Environment and Economic Development, an estimated 60 million people died between 1984 and 1987 of diarrheal diseases as a result of unsafe drinking water and malnutrition — most of them children.[15] The majority of these individuals lived in the least developed countries of the world, countries characterized by fragile and dependent economies, more than a quarter of the newborn dying at birth, less than 1% of GNP devoted to health care, a disease ridden population, increases in illiteracy, severe lack of even minimally educated man-power. Sometimes almost a majority of their populations live in conditions which in the West would be described as "homeless." [16] Many of these countries had also experienced reverses in economic development, again strikingly similar to the situation of the underclass within countries: the gap between the developed countries and the truly poor countries is widening further and further.

In sum, we have identified two processes at work:

(1) An essentially economic process within both developed and developing countries, which works towards increasing the economic well-being of more people within those countries, but at the severe expense of the truly poverty stricken. An underclass is emerging within these countries.

75

(2) A world wide economic process is producing an underclass of least developed countries, whose "development" is in many respects backwards. They have been left out of the promised prosperity of development. They are at the periphery of the world's economy.

It remains now to examine the link between these two processes and crime.

Development and crime

The relationship between development and crime is very complex from the international perspective. Much research has demonstrated that property crime increases with increased development[17], although findings for other types of crime are less conclusive[18]. We may examine these complexities both from a monocultural point of view, and an international perspective.

A Monocultural Study: the UNICRI project in Yugoslavia

In a current monocultural study being conducted by the United Nations Interregional Crime and Justice Research Institute, the complexities of the development/crime relationship have been underscorred[19]. In an intensive study of crime and a wide range of development factors for the periods 1973, 1980 and 1986 in Yugoslavia, UNICRI found that neither intensive development nor slowdowns in development were directly related to relative increases or decreases in crime respectively. In general, it was hypothesized that criminal justice phenomena may be, to a certain degree, independent of the process of development. The study did find, however, somewhat in line with the earlier U. N. macro study of crime trends (1st and 2nd world crime surveys) that property crime increased during periods of economic development. In contrast, violent crime decreased, and other types of crime remained roughly the same, with fraud increasing during economic down-turn. As

UNICRI concludes, "the interrelation between development and crime is neither universal nor unidirectional."

The International Perspective

In this section, we shall re-examine the findings reported in the U. N. First and Second world crime surveys. These data have been collected by the United Nations Crime Prevention and Criminal Justice Branch over the past 15 years. They represent the most reliable and valid data available on international crime statistics. However, because of the difficulties and complexities in both collecting the data and constructing general crime categories that held across the many different criminal justice systems of the world, we urge caution in their interpretation. On the other hand, through the application of modern statistical techniques, it has been possible to improve the validity and breadth of the statistics, as we shall see below.

The data of the first and second world crime surveys provide a unique opportunity to examine the relationship between development and crime. As we noted above, much literature is unclear as to whether there is a relationship between development and crime. Furthermore, it is usually assumed (though rarely stated) that the increase in crime that results from economic development, occurs among the poor, since it is the poverty class that is most often the direct product of economic development. In this section, we will examine the relationship between development and crime, using a new method of data analysis that considerably enhances the data of the 1st and 2nd world crime surveys.[20] These data cover the years 1970 to 1980. Unfortunately, the data for the 3rd world crime survey are not yet collated, so it is not possible to go beyond 1980. Preliminary investigation, however, suggests that the trends observed in the present analysis have continued through to 1985.

In general, the 1st and 2nd world crime surveys demonstrate that as development increases (as measured by Gross Domestic Product *per capita*) so also does property crime. This was demonstrated in the first report to the U.N. General Assembly[21], and in our re-analysis it is also supported, as can be seen in Figure 1. However, as can be seen in Figure 2, the relationship for violent crime is the reverse: the less developed countries tend also to experience higher violent crime rates (also a finding in the original report). This relationship between development and the two broad crime types has been supported by a number of analyses using the U.N. World Crime Survey Data, and using a variety of measures of "development" (e.g. proportion of population engaged in agriculture, level of education, illiteracy rate etc.).[22]

We can see from Figures 1 and 2 that the rate of theft for developed countries is several times higher than the developing countries, and shows no sign of slowing down — the gap continues to grow.[23] However, for assault, the developing countries show a much higher rate which may be increasing more rapidly than the developed countries.

Figure 1

Assaults per 100,000 Pop.
World Crime Surveys, 1970-1980

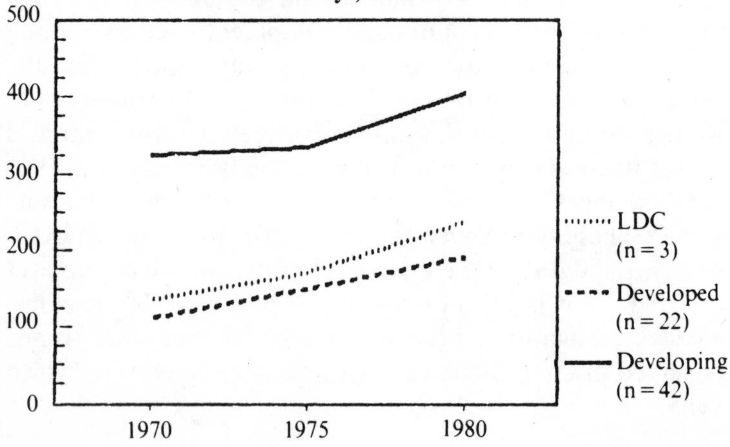

.... LDC
(n = 3)

- - - Developed
(n = 22)

—— Developing
(n = 42)

Figure 2

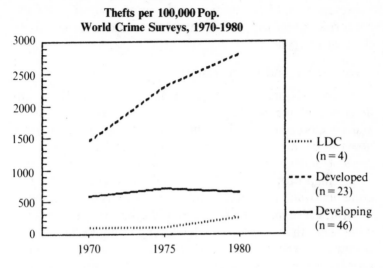

**Thefts per 100,000 Pop.
World Crime Surveys, 1970-1980**

It will be noted that we have included data on the least developed countries for which, unfortunately, even using our new techniques, we were able only to obtain data on a small number of countries. These countries were selected from the list of least developed countries reported by UNCTAD in their 1987 report on the condition of least developed countries.[24] Our expectation was that, if the findings within countries are such that the truly disadvantaged are getting worse and worse off, then we may also find that this pattern is reflected on an international scale, if we think of least developed countries as the truly disadvantaged. Figures 1 and 2 do not bear out this hypothesis. We can see that the violent crime rate for the LDCs is similar to that of the developed countries, and the property crime rate for the LDCs is considerably less than the developed countries, though slightly higher than the developing countries. How do we explain these findings?

79

We think that this apparent anomaly shields other processes at work, in particular the impact of crime on the countries concerned. This led us to an additional analysis of the cost of crime.

Development and the cost of crime

In this section, we wish to suggest that the relationship described above between violent and property crime types and development may be somewhat misleading, or at least needs to be interpreted against the complex backdrop of the concept of development. For example, in Sweden, which has a very high property crime rate, one doubts that this rate of crime has quite the impact on Swedish society, since Sweden has a much higher level of social and economic supports for its citizens than the typical developing country. Developed countries, while they appear to have in general very high property crime rates, actually may feel these crimes less, simply because there is much more economic support and affluence within which the crimes are experienced.

For example, if a brick is dropped in a small puddle of water, the impact will be considerable. However, if several bricks are dropped into a large pond, the impact will barely be measurable. We suggest that this may be a more accurate way of interpreting the trends and relationships between property and violent crimes to development. We have therefore prepared two additional graphs in which we have computed a "cost index" of the crime rates. This index has been calculated by expressing the crime rate per 100,000 persons as a percentage of the gross domestic product *per capita*. In this way we are able to take into account the size of the "pond" (the country's economic output) compared to the "brick" (the particular crime rate). Figures 3 and 4 demonstrate the outcome of this analysis.

It can be seen immediately that the impact of both types of crime — assault and theft are felt much more by the developing countries rather than the developed countries.

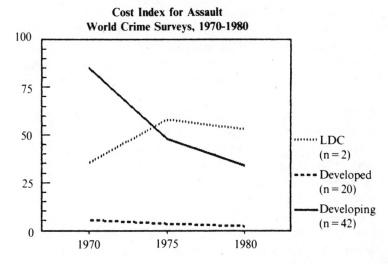

Figure 3

**Cost Index for Assault
World Crime Surveys, 1970-1980**

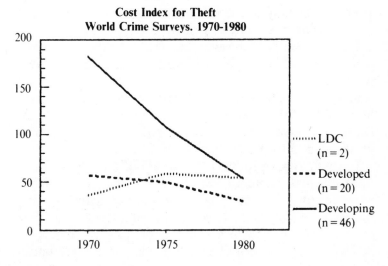

Figure 4

**Cost Index for Theft
World Crime Surveys. 1970-1980**

Furthermore, the apparent difference between the developed and developing countries in terms of property crime has disappeared. The impact of property crime is greater on developing countries than developed countries, even though the latter have actual property crime rates many times higher than developing countries.

An interesting conclusion may now be made from these findings. Instead of the usual conclusion that the "price of development is an increased crime rate" we should more accurately conclude that as development increases, the impact of crime may be less, even though the rates themselves increase.

We should add of course, that these are conclusions made for aggregate data, and should not be applied to one particular country. While the observations may hold for the group of countries, they may not hold for any particular country. Indeed, as we saw above, the monocultural study conducted by UNICRI suggests that the relationship between development and crime in one particular country (Yugoslavia) may not agree with the general hypothesis of an increasing crime rate caused by development.

Figures 3 and 4 however, also raise further important considerations. While the cost index has declined considerably over the 10 year period, particularly for the developing countries, the situation of the least developed countries is more serious. The explanation for this finding, we think, lies in the increasing process of sedimentation of social problems into the underclass.

It would appear, for example, from our review of data on the truly disadvantaged and homeless, that in developed countries, increases in crime rates are essentially increases that have affected the lower strata of the societies concerned. The expected "price" that developing countries may be expected to pay for increases in economic development is, therefore, that the growth in crime will be shifted more and more to the lower strata of their societies. This is cause for considerable alarm, because it suggests that as development continues, the lower strata become more and more cut off from the broader society. It is this class that absorbs the major impact of the increase in crime. In other words, as development continues, a clearly identifiable underclass emerges. In some countries, this underclass has existed for centuries, in others for a lesser time. But in those where the underclass has existed for centuries, the hope has been that with development, this underclass would be assisted to achieve more economic independence. Our data would suggest that the reverse is the case. There is little doubt that the relationship between poverty and crime will continue to deepen, with more and more crime focussed on the underclass, yet a more general lack of impact of crime felt by the wider society.

On the global level, this hypothesis is supported, if only from a small number of countries. But the trend is impressive. We can see from Figures 3 and 4 that whereas the cost of both property and violent crime has shown a significant decline over the past decade for developing countries, this is not the case for the least developed countries. In fact, there is good reason to believe that the reverse process is emerging: that the cost of crime is increasing for least developed countries (LDCs), and this applies for both property and violent crime. This is most significant given the picture presented in Figures 1 and 2 where the LDCs appeared to be suffering less from the crime problem. But when one takes into account the context in which the crime occurs, we argue that the impact of crime is potentially far greater for LDCs.

In conclusion, while the "price" of development may be various increases in types of crime, particularly property crime, it also brings with it a decrease in violent crime, and more significantly because of the increased quality of life, particularly economic well-being, the costs of crime are far outweighed by the other benefits of development. The

83

exception to this process is that the ultimate costs are born by the underclass in each society, the class of people least able to withstand it.

If we consider that the impact of crime is felt less by broader society in developed countries, yet that substantial crime increases occur at the bottom levels of society — the underclass, a process of social definition of criminality may set in. This process may be described as follows.

While in fact the majority of people who are economically well off are basically free from the threat of crime, it is apparent that a sizable proportion of such people are frightened of being victimized, even when crime that is depicted on the media is most often depicted as a result of disorganization among the poor. What we are suggesting here, then, is that for the majority of people, crime is not a significant factor in affecting their quality of life in an absolute sense. Rather, the more it affects the poorer people, and is depicted this way in the media, the more the poorer classes are seen as "foreign" or "despicable" and "alien." By this process the poorer classes are thus shunned and separated from society, ignored, even as they sleep out doors and beg in the open. Their victimization is virtually transformed into their criminality.

In 18th century England these people were called "the dangerous classes." They have names of various kinds in many, if not all, the world's countries still today, and are becoming more and more identified and defined as "a problem." The stereotype of such people is that they are drug addicts, lunatics, alcoholics, lazy people who will not work, and would rather beg. They are seen as people who deserve their lot in life (for whatever the cultural reason: whether through a caste/religious system, or through a western "work ethic" principle).

Of course, this mythology is just that. We saw in the earlier sections that the essential make-up of the underclass was not of criminals or lunatics, but of people who have been victimized by the economic system of which they are no longer a part. However there are some ways in which crime is patterned in the underclass, both in terms of their being victims of crime and perpetrators of crime.

Crime and the underclass

Very little is known about the extent or type of crime among the underclass, that is, the homeless. Most research is limited to the collection of a small amount of data, as shown in Table 1, where it has been found that roughly 50% of the homeless in the United States have been in jail or prison. However, none of the research indicates why the individuals had been in jail — it is entirely possible that many commit small crimes in order to gain shelter, especially in the harsher climates. We do know from the research studies reported above, that many, particularly women and children who now constitute a considerable portion of the underclass, have fled from homes of violent abuse. The role of interpersonal and criminal violence would appear to be a strong feature in the lives of the underclass, mainly as victims. And certainly many have a history of such victimization. As has been noted by a number of researchers, the homeless are "easy victims for... drug pedlars, human assassins, armed robbers, interlopers and vagabonds"[25].

Yet research also shows that the victims of crimes by the underclass are also those, mainly, of the underclass. This is particularly so of crimes of violence, since being poor, there is little to be stolen (though in a culture of poverty, even small items can assume enormous value. Take, for example, the cigarette economies that develop in prisons where personal possessions are at a minimum). But because of the demands of survival, the young, who have not yet quite lost hope, develop considerable skills in lying, cheating, and the use of violence if necessary. This has been found among the street children of Cali, Colombia. These street children were

85

not starving, but they had to work the streets every day in order to eat well.[26] The patterning of shanty towns and urban development in Colombia is also complex problem in itself. Mohan has reported, for example, that the individuals who make up this class (or classes) are neither initially poor, do not invariably migrate from the country, and are not without skills. However, the Shanty towns described in other research nevertheless exist for individuals who, for essentially financial reasons, cannot find adequate housing. Very often, such shanty towns grow up in areas of a city that have been neglected, and the homeless from other parts of the city, or from other large cities in the same country, will migrate to this area[27].

The homeless are essentially defenseless when sleeping on the streets. A recent example of a killer stalking the streets of Calcutta randomly killing the homeless as they sleep on the sidewalk and in doorways,[28] highlights the terrible state of fear these individuals must live in every night of their lives.

It is apparent that violent crime is going to be a major problem in the underclass, since they have fewer possessions, so that small items take on massive value. The cultures of violence that arise out of conditions of sheer scarcity have been observed and catalogued in many diverse parts of the world, from the Middle East nomadic tribes to the juvenile gangs of Los Angeles.[29]

In many underclass societies, the youth, still energetic, not completely without hope, adopt rebellious solutions to their predicament, and develop unique ways of acting and structuring meaning into their lives. Thus, the strong macho tendencies of youthful street gangs: possessions are meagre, but identities and impressions can be manipulated extensively. Many youth gangs therefore develop macho-violent ways of acting, and will prey on those least able to defend themselves: the homeless, the aged etc. The violent crime of these groups can be seen largely as a direct result of the desolate cultural landscape in which these persons live and grow. The characters that they develop are infused with mythical, superhuman qualities: the wish to transcend the ghetto or slum, but the understanding that this is absolutely not possible on one's own. This desolate but fantastic cultural ethos leads to the use of violence, often seemingly "senseless" to outsiders.[30]

But it is doubtful whether the truly underclass have the energy to commit much crime, since to commit crime, after all, takes effort.[31] It is doubtful whether those whom the U. N. Commission on Environment and Development spoke: the millions who are starving and diseased, would have the energy to commit crime. However, little is known about this question. One can understand starving individuals stealing in order to survive. It is more likely that the destitute are victims of crime rather than perpetrators. It is to this question that we now turn.

The world cost of corporate crime

When industrial accidents and environmental pollution occur, it is the poverty stricken who generally bear the brunt of the damage and injury. Take the following examples reported by the World Commission on Environment and Development:

> Liquid gas tanks exploded in Mexico city killing 1,000 people and leaving thousands homeless. Those made homeless were those who were already poor, and living close by the dangerous gas tanks, unable to afford housing in a safer area.

> A leak from a pesticides factory in Bhopal, India, killed 2,000 people and injured over 200,000 more.[32]

A case can be made that the injury and destruction that result from corporate criminality is far greater than that produced by the underclass. The logic of this view is quite

87

simple: since the powerful are just that, they are able to do more damage. We hasten to state that we do not seek to indict all corporations. The majority are law abiding and provide important work and welfare for their employees. We wish only to draw attention to the possibility that the upper classes also commit crime, that crime is not the sole domain of the lower class. And that multinational corporations in particular are in a unique position to bypass the laws of many individual countries.

In the case of Bhopal, and possibly other disasters, these may have been man made due to negligence, some would say as a result of criminal negligence by corporations. In fact the catalogue of the human costs of corporate crime is only just beginning to be written. There is little doubt that as a result of this kind of white collar and corporate crime, massive numbers of lives have been lost (many more than through "traditional crime" of the underclass)[33]. In fact one U.S. study computed the amount of loss and damage from corporate crime to be 12 times that of common crime.[34] This is particularly so when corporations are able to avoid prosecution because of their unique multi-national status, and when they are able to influence governments of developing countries into allowing greater pollution and dangerous practices than would be allowed in developed countries.[35] Companies also market dangerous products, especially drugs and pesticides to developing countries,[36] products that are banned in their own country. We may also observe that it is very often the poor who are affected by these disasters — as, for example, the Bhopal tragedy which affected largely poor people who had moved into surrounding shanty towns and cheap housing close to the chemical factory.[37] The extent to which corporate crimes affect the human condition around the world is much in need of further study, and should be established as a priority.

In an effort to look a little more closely at what might be called "white collar crime" we computed the rates of fraud for developing and developed countries (there were no LDCs reporting fraud). The results of this analysis are revealed in Figures 5 and 6 where we see a similar pattern in crime trends as displayed earlier for property crime (Figure 2). It is not surprising to find the fraud rate in developed countries to be several times higher than the developing countries, and in fact growing at a more rapid rate than that of the developing countries. But once again we note the cost index in Figure 6 where the impact of fraud for developing countries is almost as great as for developed countries.

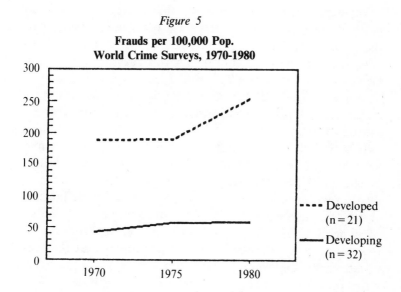

Figure 5

Frauds per 100,000 Pop.
World Crime Surveys, 1970-1980

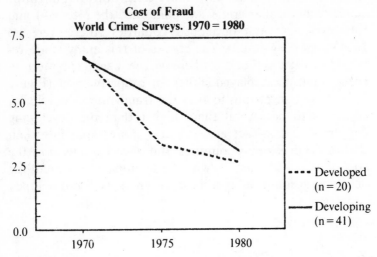

Figure 6

Cost of Fraud
World Crime Surveys. 1970 = 1980

- - - - Developed (n = 20)

——— Developing (n = 41)

We would speculate, therefore, that a high rate of fraud in developed countries impacts society much less, because of the strong and rich economic state of these countries. In contrast, in developing countries with struggling economies, even a fraud rate much lower than that of developed countries will be felt far more severely. Perhaps this is no better demonstrated in the particular case of the Philippines during the Marcos rule.

It is true that the definition of what a crime is becomes very difficult in this realm. And indeed, it is even more difficult to establish criminal procedures and effective ways of dealing with such events should they become defined as crimes[38]. There is very little effort to examine the morality of underclass compared to upper class crime from a dispassionate point of view. Some would argue that the corporate criminals should know better: especially as they have more power and therefore more choices, compared to the underclass who are virtually constrained and determined by their conditions. The fact remains that the majority of either classes does not commit crime. But it is equally apparent that whatever the different rates of crime committed by the two groups, it is the poor who are victimized by both.

It is also apparent, however, that the cost of crime is also born directly by the society which must allocate resources to policing and other aspects of criminal justice in response to crime. It is to this aspect of the cost of crime that we now turn.

The Cost of Criminal Justice

Unfortunately, usable data on expenditure by member countries on criminal justice system were not collected in the first and second world crime surveys. Data on the number of criminal justice personnel were collected, however, and these can give us a rough idea of the cost of criminal justice to countries, since it is usually personnel that are the major cost item. We can see from Figure 7 that developing countries have a comparatively high rate of policing compared to developed countries, and this is especially so in the more recent year of 1980. This is particularly perplexing when one considers that the overall crime rate of developing countries is not as high as it is for developed countries.

A semblance of an answer to this puzzle is shown in Figure 8, where we see the numbers of judges and prison officers per 100,000 pop. We can see that the number of judges in developing countries has remained pretty much the same at less than half the rate of developed countries. And while the rate of prison personnel is less than that of developed countries, it is clear that the developing countries are rapidly catching up. We may conclude, therefore, that the cost of criminal justice is considerable for developing countries, and that expenditure on personnel tends to be on those criminal justice functions which require less education and training, i.e., policing and prison officers. There are insufficient data for us to estimate the overall cost of criminal justice, since we would need data on expenditures on prisons and courts, two very expensive items.

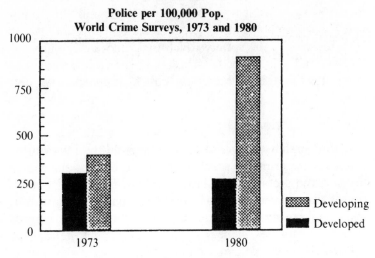

Figure 7

**Police per 100,000 Pop.
World Crime Surveys, 1973 and 1980**

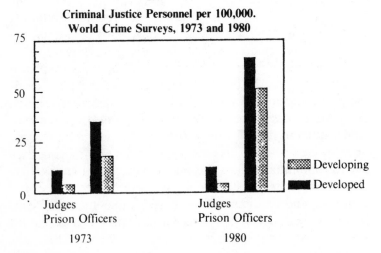

Figure 8

**Criminal Justice Personnel per 100,000.
World Crime Surveys, 1973 and 1980**

92

Conclusions and Recommendations

The process of development, crime and the sedimentation of social problems is generally the most pressing problem requiring further attention.

1. It is clear from both UNICRI's study and our own analysis, that the relationship between development and crime requires much more investigation, and the collection of much more meaningful data. Individual country studies would enhance our growing knowledge of the relationship between crime and development, and flesh out the exceptions to the global trends. Recommendations for intervention, crime prevention and assistance must depend on such individual country studies.

2. The collection of adequate data on the level of crime in least developed countries, and the assistance to these countries in the collection and assembly of such data is crucial. Without a systematic body of meaningful information, it is not possible to mount prevention strategies. Crime prevention depends essentially upon having accurate information.

3. *The sedimentation process.* There are three serious processes under way. The first is the displacement of crime from developed countries to developing countries. This is achieved through the "shifting of illegality" by multinational corporations who are able to avoid laws in one country by operating in other countries where there are no such prohibitions. The second is the process of cultural separation of the underclass from the rest of society. They are becoming more destitute, and seen as more alien. The role of the popular media needs to be carefully assessed in this regard. The third, the most widely recognized, is that the underclass — both as countries in themselves and as classes within particular societies, have become cut off from the rest of the world's economy.

4. By far the most important observation of this study is that the cost of crime, i.e. its human, social and economic impact, is felt most by the least developed countries and the developing countries. The data clearly show that, while property crime is many times higher in developed countries, it nevertheless impacts on developing countries far more because of their fragile economies. The same applies to violent crimes, in fact possibly more so, since the violent crime rate in developing countries tends to be higher than the developed countries. Thus by the same principle of the cost of crime outlined above, the developing countries must suffer the impact of violent crime enormously more.

5. The implications for developing countries therefore have to be re-thought. In this light, crime is not a cost of development at all, but rather development promises to cushion the impact of crime and diminish considerably its cost to any country that is fortunate to be included in the world's economic growth.

6. The exceptions to this observation are the Least Developed Countries. For it is here that we see repeated on a world scale what has occurred within developed countries over the last two decades: development has produced relative prosperity for most people. But it has left behind the forgotten class, the underclass, who have fallen further and further behind. We have suggested that this same process has occurred on a global scale, in that the Least Developed Countries have become the World's underclass, and thus are subject to the victimization of poverty and crime.

Addendum: Drugs and Crime

If we examine the reported drug crimes comparing developed and developing countries, we find little difference. In general, drug crimes make up only a very small percentage of all serious crime, no more than 10% since 1970[39]. It is likely, however, that their costs are considerable, particularly since much drug use appears to be related to other criminality. For example, in the United States, it has been estimated that the costs of drug abuse are $59.7 billion annually. One third of this amount is thought to be crime related[40]. A number of studies conducted in the United States, Great Britain and Australia indicate that drug users and abusers commit a large amount of both property and personal crime[41]. It is thus obvious that the relationship between illegal drugs and crime is serious.

The illegal drugs-crime connection may be divided into four categories. The first category involves the fact that the production, manufacture and sale of many drugs are criminal acts in most countries. The remaining categories are: criminal acts committed by drug traffickers in the course of distribution activities[42]; criminal acts of drug users which are designed to procure money to purchase illegal drugs[43]; and violent acts committed by drug abusers, particularly while under the influence or experiencing withdrawal symptoms[44].

The United Nations world crime survey data do not break down drug crimes into detailed categories such as these. Countries have simply reported "drug crimes" which may include both abuse and trafficking. In figure 9 we have compared the changing rates of drug crimes in major geographic regions. We can see that drug crimes reported in the Latin American countries have declined from 1975 to 1980. In contrast, the rate for Asia has remained by far the highest and has increased dramatically over the same period. The area in which drug crime remains lowest is in Europe and North America.

This picture seems to contradict the impression gained from the media concerning the serious effects of drug abuse and trafficking. However, according to the research reported above, it is very likely that much traditional crime: assault, robbery and theft may in fact be drug related, but is reported in those crime categories, rather than as drug crimes.

95

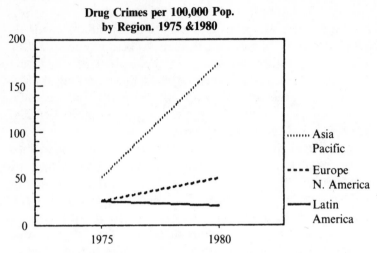

Figure 9

**Drug Crimes per 100,000 Pop.
by Region. 1975 &1980**

Asia Pacific

Europe N. America

Latin America

Some researchers believe that the nature of the illegal drug market tends to breed corruption and violence[45]. Several links have been established between organized crime and drug trafficking. In Italy, organized crime groups control a growing market in heroin and cocaine. These groups are involved in a variety of criminal activities that may be partially funded by illicit drug money. In London, cocaine use has become a symbol of status among the criminal underworld, and organized criminal groups have taken over large drug trafficking enterprises[46]. It is estimated that over half of all organized crime revenues in the United States are derived from the illicit drug business, with estimates ranging from $10 to $50 billion per year[47].

References and Notes

[1] A long line of studies supports this conclusion. See J. Braithwaite, *Inequality, Crime and Public Policy*, London, Routledge and Kegan Paul, 1979; M. Lynch and W. B. Groves, *A Primer in Radical Criminology*, New York, Harrow and Heston, 1989; R. Sampson, "Structural Sources of Variation in Rates of Offending," *Criminology*, 1985, No. 23, p. 647. In regard to violent crime see M. Wolfgang and F. Ferracuti, *The Subculture of Violence*, London, Tavistock, 1967.

[2] See section V. below.

[3] W. J. Wilson, *The Truly Disadvantaged*, Chicago, University of Chicago Press, 1987. See also for a rejoinder, C. V. Willie, *The Caste Class Controversy*, New York, General Hall, 1979.

[4] *Ibidem.*

[5] World Commission on Environment and Development, "From One Earth to One World", *Habitat*, 11: 4, 1987, pp. 9-24.

[6] A. M. Jamshid and B. Wiegand, *Homelessness in the United States*, Westport, Connecticut, Green Press, 1989.

[7] M. Bapat, "What will 'the International Year of Shelter for the Homeless' Bring for the Urban Poor?", *Habitat*, 1987, pp. 5-22, especially page 6 for a history of shanty settlements.

[8] O. A. Labeodan, "The Homeless of Ibadan", *Habitat*, 13: 1, 1989, p. 75.

[9] A. M. Jamshid and B. Wiegand, *Homelessness ...*, *op. cit.*

[10] O. A. Labeodan, "The Homeless ...", *op. cit.*, pp. 75-85.

[11] M. Bapat, "What will 'the International Year ...", *op. cit.*, pp. 5-22.

[12] The caste factor in homelessness is also supported in S. S. Srivastava, *Juvenile Vagrancy*, New York, Asia Publishing House, 1963; M. V. Moorthy, *The Beggar Problem in Bombay*, Bombay, Indian Conference on Social Work, 1959.

[13] A substantial number of studies support the finding of the economic causes of homelessness. In the United States: P. L. Masa and J. A. Hall, *Homeless Children and their Families: A Preliminary Study*, Washington D. C., Child Welfare League, 1988; K. Hopper and J. Hamburg, *The Making of America's Homeless from Skid Row to New Poor 1945-1985*, New York, Housing and Development Policy Unit, 1984 (particularly emphasizing lack of availabity of low income housing); M. Hope and J. Young, *The faces of Homelessness*, Lexington for D. C., Heath, 1986. The majority of homeless in the United States is not caused by a dramatic drop from middle class life. It is a series of steps, usually from a poor marginal position in the first place, i.e. the cause is largely economic; F. S. Redburn and T. F. Buss, *Responding to America's Homeless*, New York, Praeger, 1986; J. Erikson and C. Willhelm, *Housing and*

97

Homeless, New Brunswick, N.J., Center for Urban Policy Research, 1986; D. Salerno, K. Hopper and E. Baxter, *Hardship in the Heartland: Homelessness in Eight U.S. Cities*, New York, Community Service Society of New York, 1984. In India, S.S. Srivastava, *Juvenile Vagrancy*, New York, Asia Publishing House, 1963; M.V. Moorthy, *The Beggar Problem in Bombay*, 1959, Bombay, Indian Conference on Social Work. In London, T. Cook, *Vagrancy: Some New Perspectives*, New York, Academic Press, 1979; J. Sandford, *Down and Out in Britain*, London, Peter Owen, 1971. In Nigeria, O.F. Okediji, *The Rehabilitation of Beggars in Nigeria*, Ibadan, National Council of Social Work in Nigeria, 1972.

[14] This is clearly supported by the work of many researchers. See particularly the review of literature in T. Cook, *Vagrancy ...*, *op. cit.*

[15] World Commission on Environment and Development, "From One Earth ...", *op. cit.*

[16] United Nations, Conference on Trade and Development. *The Least Developed Countries: 1987 Report*, New York, United Nations, 1987, p. 8. This report identified some forty-member countries of the United Nations.

[17] For a review of this research see L.I. Shelley, *Modernization and Crime*. Carbondale, Illinois, Southern Illinois University Press, 1981; W.B. Groves, R. McCleary and G. Newman, "Religion, Modernization and World Crime", *Comparative Social Research*, Vol. 8, Greenwich CT. VAI Press, 1985, pp. 59-78.

[18] G. Newman and W.B. Groves "Criminal Justice and Development", *International Journal of Comparative and Applied Criminal Justice*, June 1986; W.B. Groves and G. Newman, "Islam, Religiosity and Crime". *Journal of Criminal Justice*, 1987, 15:6, pp. 495-504; G. Newman, W.B. Groves and R. McCleary, "Religion, Modernization ...", *op. cit.*

[19] U. Zvekic, "Development and Crime in Yugoslavia. Results of the Preliminary Analysis", Report, UNICRI, Rome, 1989; see also U. Zvekic, Ed., *Essays in Crime and Development*, UNICRI, 1990.

[20] This method uses two types of data enhancement: the estimation of data through a straight line method, and the estimation of data offences recorded by extrapolating from proportions apprehended to crimes recorded, since many countries have only recently begun to report crimes recorded, whereas they reported apprehensions for a longer period. Since the proportion of apprehensions to crimes recorded is generally constant, it is possible to estimate crimes recorded. An extensive amount of missing data were able to be replaced by these estimations.

[21] United Nations, "Crime Prevention and Control: Report to the Secretary General", A/32/199, 22 September 1977.

[22] G. Newman and E. Vetere, *World Crime: A Comparative Analysis.* Unpublished report to the United Nations Crime Prevention and Criminal Justice Branch, 1980. See also G. Newman and W. B. Groves, "Islam, Religiosity ...", *op. cit.*

[23] *Developing countries*: Algeria, Argentina, Bahamas, Bahrain, Barbados, Belize, Cape Verde, Chile, Colombia, Costa Rica, Cyprus, Ecuador, Egypt, El Salvador, Fiji, Guyana, India, Indonesia, Iraq, Jamaica, Kuwait, Madagascar, Malaysia, Mauritius, Morocco, Oman, Pakistan, Panamá, Perú, The Philippines, Poland, Portugal, Qatar, Senegal, Seychelles, Syngapore, Sri Lanka, Santa Lucia, Syrian Arab Republic, South Korea, Thailand, Tonga, Trinidad, Togo, Turkey, Yugoslavia, Zimbabwe.

Developed countries: Australia, Austria, Canada, Denmark, Finland, France, German Federal Republic, Greece, Ireland, Israel, Italy, Japan, The Netherlands, New Zealand, Norway, San Marino, Spain, Sweden, Switzerland, United States, United Kingdom.

Least developed countries: Bangladesh, Maldives, Nepal.

[24] United Nations, Conference on Trade and Development, *The Least Developed Countries: 1987 Report*, New York, 1987.

[25] A. G. Onibokum, "The Social Dimension of Homeless in Nigeria", paper presented to the International Conference on the Homeless, Port Harcourt, Nigeria, 19-27 November 1987.

[26] L. Aptekar, *The Street Children of Cali*, Durham, Duke University Press, 1988. By and large most studies show that homeless and beggars are roughly 60% "able bodied", the rest are handicapped either mentally or physically. See S. S. Srivastava, *Juvenile Vagrancy*, New York, Asia Publishing House, 1963; M. V. Moorthy, *The Beggar Problem ...*, *op. cit.*

[27] Cali is generaly an exception to the rule. Other studies show proportions of the urban homeless as high as 80% coming from the rural areas. Often these people come to the cities in search of better social and welfare services. S. S. Srivastava, *Op. cit.*; M. V. Moorthy, *op. cit.*

[28] The "Stone Man" who kills his victims by dropping a huge stone on their heads as they sleep, *New York Times*, October, 1989.

[29] For a review of these see P. Marongiu and G. Newman, *Vengeance: The Fight Against Injustice*, New Jersey, Littlefield Adams, 1987.

[30] See for a detailed account of this violent crime and the incredibly intense psychological feelings attached to violent crime, especially robbery, J. Katz, *Seductions of Crime: Moral and Sensual Attractions of Doing Evil*, New York, Basic, 1988.

[31] The recent attention by criminologists to rational choice and crime suggests that criminals must strive and choose in order to carry out their crimes. See D. Cornish and R. V. Clarke, *The Reasoning Criminal*, New York, Springer-Verlag, 1986.

[32] World Commission on Environment and Development, "The Global Challenge", *Habitat*, 1987, No. 11:4, pp. 9-24.

[33] There are many studies supporting this claim. See R. J. Michalowski, "Crime Control in the 1980's: A Progressive Agenda", *Crime and Social Justice*, 1983, pp. 13-24; J. Reiman, *The Rich Get Richer and the Poor Get Prison*, New York, Wiley, 1984; G. Geis, "Upperworld Crime", in A. Blumberg, Ed., *Current Perspectives on Criminal Behaviour*, New York, Knopf, 1974.

[34] R. Kramer, Corporate Criminality: The Development of an Idea", in E. Hochstedler, Ed., *Corporations as Criminals*, Beverley Hills, Sage, 1984.

[35] N. K. Karunarutne, *Transnational Corporate Deviance: Managing and Uncontrollable*. Albany, State University of New York Press, 1990 (In press).

[36] N. Frank, *Crimes Against Health and Safety*, Albany, New York, Harrow and Heston, 1985.

[37] M. J. Lynch, M. Nalla and K. Miller, "Cross-cultural Perceptions of Deviance: The Case of Bhopal", *Journal of Research in Crime Delinquency*, Vol. 26, No. 1, pp. 7-35.

[38] B. Fisse, "The Social Policy of Corporate Criminal Responsibility", *Adelaide Law Review*, 1978, No. 6, pp. 371-382.

[39] United Nations, Seventh Congress on the Prevention of Crime and the Treatment of Offenders, Milan, Italy, *New Dimensions of Criminality and Crime Prevention in the Context of Development: Challenges for the Future*, A/CONF. 121/18, 30 May 1985.

[40] H. Harwood, D. Napolitano, P. Kristiansen and J. Collins, *Economic Cost to Society of Alcohol, Drug Abuse and Mental Illness*, Research Triangle Park, North Carolina, Research Triangle, 1984.

[41] B. Johnson, P. Goldstein, E. Preble, J. Schmeidler, D. Lipton, B. Spunt and T. Miller, *Taking Care of Business: The Economics of Crime by Heroin Abusers*, Lexington, Maryland, Lexington Books, 1985; D. Nurco, J. Ball, J. Shaffer and T. E. Hanlon, "The Criminality of Narcotic Addicts", *Journal of Nervous and Mental Disease*, 1985, N. 173, pp. 94-102; I. Dobinson and P. Ward, "Heroin and Property Crime: An Australian Perspective", *Journal of Drug Issues*, 1986, No. 16, pp. 249-262; J. Inciardi, *The War On Drugs*, Palo Alto, California, Mayfield, 1986; R. Hammersley and V. Morrison, "Effects of Polydrug Use on the Criminal Activities of Heroin-users", *British Journal of Addiction*, 1987, No. 82, pp. 899-906; T. Bennett and R. Wright, "The Impact of Prescribing on the Crimes of Opiate Users", *British Journal of Addiction*, 1986, No. 81, pp. 265-273; D. M. Anglin and G. Speckart, "Narcotics Use and Crime: A Multistage, Multimethod Analysis", 1988, No. 26, pp. 197-233. A survey of state prison inmates in the United States found

that 43% were daily users of illegal drugs in the month preceding their arrest and conviction (Bureau of Justice Statistcs, 1988. "Drug Use and Crime", Washington, D. C., National Institute of Justice). A nationwide program tested the urine of arrestees in several U. S. cities determined that between 51 and 83% recently had some form of illicit drug. Moreover, between 20 and 84% of those testing positive were arrested for a violent offense (National Institute of Justice, 1989, "Drug Use Forecasting Program", Washington, D. C., National Institute of Justice).

[42] Recently, increased attention has been paid to juvenile gangs which are involved in drug trafficking. In the United States, it is posited that violence between rival drug selling gangs has caused an increase in the inner city violent crime rate (see *Juvenile Justice Bulletin*, 1988. "Juvenile Gangs: Crime and Drug Trafficking", Washington D. C., United States Department of Justice). Some researchers believe that the nature of the illegal drug market tends to breed corruption and violence. N. Weiner and M. Wolfgang, Newbury Park, California, Sage, 1989; P. Goldstein, "The Drugs Violence Nexus: A Tripartite Conceptual Framework", *Journal of Drug Issues*, 1985, No. 15, pp. 493-506.

[43] Numerous studies indicate that relatively high costs may force habitual users to commit crimes in order to afford illegal drugs. Evidence for this economic model has been found in both the United States and Australia (Johnson et al., 1985, Dobinson and Ward, 1986, Nurco et al., 1986, Nurco et al., 1985, Anglin and Speckart 1988). It also has been determined that the rate of property crime among drug abusers increases substantially during periods of active narcotic and cocaine use and decreases as use curtails. (J. Collins, R. Hubbard and J. Valley Rachel, "Expensive Drug Use and Illegal Income: A Test of Explanatory Hypotheses", *Criminology*, 1985, No. 23, pp. 743-764; D. M. Anglin, M. Douglas and G. Speckart "Narcotics Use, Property Crime and Dealing: Structural Dynamics Across the Addiction Career", *Journal of Quantitative Criminology*, 1986, No. 2, pp. 355-375; I. Dobinson and P. Ward, "Heroin and Property Crime: An Australian Perspective", *Journal of Drug Issues*, No. 16, pp. 249-262; B. Johnson, P. Goldstein, E. Preble, J. Schmeidler, D. Lipton, B. Spunt and T. Miller, *Taking Care of Business...*, *op. cit.*; Nurco et al. ..., *op. cit.*; G. Speckart and M. D. Anglin, "Narcotics Use and Crime: An Overview of Recent Research Advances", *Contemporary Drug Problems*, 1986, No. 13, pp. 741-769. In fact, heroin users are estimated to commit six times as many crimes during periods of active use compared to periods of abstention (D. Nurco, J. Ball, J. Shaffer and T. E. Hanlon, 1985, "The Criminality of ...", *op. cit.*, No. 173, pp. 94-102 and twice the number of property crimes as non-using offenders (B. Johnson, P. Goldstein, E. Preble, J. Schmeidler, D. Lipton, B. Spunt and T. Miller, *Taking Care of Business ...*, *op. cit.*).

101

⁴⁴ J. Inciardi and A. Pottieger, "Drug Use and Crime Among Two Cohorts of Women Narcotic Users: An Empirical Assessment", *Journal of Drug Issues*, 1986, No. 16, pp. 91-106.

⁴⁵ N. Weiner and M. Wolfgang, *Pathways to...*, *op. cit.*; P. Goldstein, "The Drugs Violence...*, op. cit.*, No. 15, pp. 493-506.

⁴⁶ R. Lewis, "European Markets in Cocaine", *Contemporary Crises*, 1989, No. 13, pp. 35-52; E. Nadelmann, "Drug Prohibition in the United States: Cost, Consequences and Alternatives", *Science*, 1989, No. 245, pp. 939-947.

⁴⁷ Wharton Econometric Forecasting Associates, *The Impact: Organized Crime Today*, Washington D. C., 1986, President's Commission on Organized Crime.

SOCIAL CHANGE, ORGANIZATION OF CRIME, AND CRIMINAL JUSTICE SYSTEMS

Ernesto Ugo Savona *

This paper describes certain trends in criminality, and formulates a hypothesis for its rationalization. This rationalization characterizes different types of criminality and is leading to a change in the criminal scenarios. The result of this process is a wide range of organized forms of criminality which include traditional petty, political, economic and organized crimes, often linked together by a functional interdependence.

Focus is placed mainly on the relationship between organized crime and white collar crime, and it discusses the thesis that in attempting to explain the nature of economic and organized crime those theories have failed to pay sufficient attention to recent identifiable developments in a variety of criminal behaviours. The tendency on the part of researchers and law enforcement agencies has been to address only facts consistent with the accepted wisdom about the causes and origins of organized and white-collar crime. Consequently, the theories developed were based on the ideological positions held by those concerned. One of the effects of this was the passing of laws that proved inefficient because based on legal paradigms that were already obsolete.

These new forms of criminality must be considered a continuum which includes illegal, and does not exclude legal,

---

* NIJ Fellow, National Institute of Justice, US Department of Justice, USA; Professor of Criminology, Faculty of Law, University of Trento, Italy.

activities. The enterprise paradigm is the most useful tool to understand this form of crime, and this understanding is very important for the development of new criminal policies. There is an obvious inter-relationship between present day conceptual paradigms, explicatory theories and the resultant efficacy of the criminal justice system. The author believes that the rationalization of criminality must be confronted with rationality by the criminal justice system. Only in this way will it be possible to combat this phenomenon. The absence of adequate strategies to defeat it now, will guarantee a flourishing future for the organization of criminality.

Crime trends

For the past ten years the quality and quantity of social problems we confront have been generally considered to be the result of social changes. Taking into account the diverse cultural, political and economic factors involved in social life, it is increasingly difficult to distinguish between the "national" and "international" origins and characteristics of social problems. The same may be said of criminality, the international dimensions of which are often ignored by the criminal justice systems because their main concern is to control crime at a national level. Important international dimensions must be considered and confronted if we want the criminal justice system to be more effective in their effort to control crime.

In the absence of precise data[1] and detailed research into the relationship between crime and development at macro level[2], it is possible only to describe some recent trends.

Between the 70's and the 80's there has been a worldwide increase in reported crime. Violent crimes (homicide, burglary, and assault) have almost doubled, whilst crimes against property (theft and fraud) have almost trebled[3].

Levels of reported crimes vary between developed and developing countries. Levels of reported crimes against property have increased more in the former while violent crimes have increased more in the latter.

If we look at how reported crime is composed we see that almost half of all crime in developed countries is theft, whereas theft constitutes only a quarter of crime in developing countries. In view of the restricted nature of such data we can only make some general observations from which some possible hypotheses arise.

Towards a progressive rationalization of crime?

There are certain signs of a transformation in the nature of criminality which enable one to speculate upon the existence of a process of rationalization in criminality. These transformations may be observed in a variety of countries both at national and international levels; Italy constitutes a specific example. What is this process of rationalization? It implies a complicated reorganization process on the part of criminality which is increasingly capable of controlling a vast spectrum of legal and illegal activities. Increasingly evident is the objective of economic gain, as well as the use of primarily business models of various dimensions. This process involves many diverse forms of criminality and it is possible that in coming years it will profoundly modify the nature of crime.

New developments within the process of rationalization may be seen in the functional interdependence that increasingly links the traditionally separate areas of criminality. Common crime (violence and theft), political crime, organized and economic crime are all increasingly drawn into the rationalization process. Even some forms of petty crime (e.g. drug related) appear to be, willingly or not, more and more dependent on and linked to organized crime. The reasons for this are, first, the increased availability of criminal labour and second, petty criminality constitutes a channel to for the accumulation of resources to acquire goods in the illegal market which, as such, is indirectly attached to organized criminality that operates in the highest profit sectors of the illegal market. There is also evidence of growing and strengthening ties between political terrorism, organized crime and economic crime, at national and international levels. Links between a variety of criminal organizations are essential in order to carry out their intricate business.

The functional interdependence between a variety of criminal sectors is a relatively new development which, in my opinion, must be examined. We need analytic instruments to help us understand the data concerning recent developments in criminality. The rationalization process described above indicates, unequivocally, that crime is concentrating, above all, on objectives of income generation and on achieving these objectives through increased organization. How widespread are the processes of organizational development in crime? It is clear, from investigations into organized crime in a variety of countries, that almost half the developed nations regard organized crime as a problem to be confronted and as much as a third of the whole world considers it a very serious problem.[4]

One can argue that property crime will progressively spread following a process of rationalization, which has developed out of the need to penetrate the wealthy economies and the need to overcome modern systems of control. Organization, without doubt, provides criminality with the most efficient method to overcome or to control competition in illegal markets and to maximize opportunities for the accumulation of wealth. Organization enables crime to manipulate to its advantage, the rules of economic development through the use of corruption, intimidation and violence. It is in the area of organization that the most significant developments will probably occur over the next few years, even if it isn't detectable through official statistics. To illustrate this one has only to look closely at the data on homicides in Italy to see that, apart from quantitative variations, there is an increasing tendency for them to be linked to activities of organized crime.[5] This is particularly the case in specific regions concerned with problems of homicides and organized crime.[6] Events in Sicily provide an example.[7] Of course, I do not believe that the interpretation of such examples can be applied generally to other countries. The violence of organized crime expresses itself in a variety of ways and directions. However, one may hypothesize that violent crime will increasingly become a functional part of contemporary organized crime, which binds petty crime, political crime, and economic crime. These binds are the result of the process of rationalization of crime, have become a particular problem for the criminal justice system and of great importance to criminologists and researchers of these systems. This process challenges current explicatory paradigms of particular kinds of criminality. It also emphasizes the need, on the part of the criminal justice system, to re-think the strategies that they currently employ and to develop more efficacious ways of combating crime.

My argument, so far, applies to all forms of criminality, but it is particularly relevant to those forms of crime which are officially conceptualized, in the literature, as white-collar crime and organized crime. The view taken in this paper is that those theories attempting to explain the nature of economic and organized crime, have failed to pay sufficient attention to the recent identifiable developments in a variety of criminal behaviours. There has been a tendency on the part of researchers and law enforcement agencies to address only those facts which have been consistent with the accepted wisdom about the causes and origins of white-collar crime. Consequently the theories developed are built upon the ideological positions held by those concerned[8]. One of the effects of this has been the inefficaciousness of laws passed against the types of crime because the legal paradigms were already obsolete.[9]

From organized crime to the organization of crime

Taking Sutherland's definition and theory of differential association, researchers into sectors of white-collar crime have operated "on the pragmatic view that everybody pretty much knows what is meant by white-collar crime".[10] This view has placed more emphasis on descriptive rather than theoretical aspects[11] and has, as a result, failed to produce well developed explicatory theories. The same may be said of organized crime although the wealth of analysis is considerably greater. The debate around this form of crime has been developed by three competing schools: the adherents to enterprise as the key to understanding organized crime, the adherents to conspiracy, and the adherents to ethnicity[12]. The "enterprise school" begins with Landesco's description of organized crime in Chicago in the late 20's.[13] After World War II and the development of the narcotics problem in American society, the enterprise paradigm was substituted by the alien conspiracy paradigm posed by the Federal Narcotics Bureau. It was a time when Mafia was considered to be a sinister criminal organization within which the major criminal syndicates of the country were active. This view was criticized by the supporters of the "ethnic school". For example, Daniel Bell explained through the ethnic paradigm, why many Italian-Americans were involved in organized crime, and why it was considered to be "one of the queer ladders of social mobility in the American life".[14] Between the late 50's and 70's, "the conspiracy theory" re-emerged in relation to some particular events: the testimony of Valachi and the reports of the President's Commission on Law Enforcement and Administration of Justice (1967). That theory, according to Smith "was institutionalized in federal legislations of 1968 and 1970 (i.e. Omnibus Crime Control and Safe Streets Act of 1968 and Organized Crime Control Act of 1970)".[15] Each of these three paradigms contain some elements of truth but they offer inadequate explanations of organized crime. They provide a distorted view of the dynamics of crime and it is precisely in the interpretation of the dynamic of criminal behaviours that these two forms of organized and economic crime tend to become confused.

Close attention to and a deeper exploration of the behaviours associated with organized and economic crime, primarily through the judicial material in a variety of countries, provide the means for a number of important observations.

> "... (It) is becoming obvious that criminal phenomena constitute an uninterrupted continuum ... (which) ranges from the simplest crimes of every-day experience, ... to crimes of state and serious violations of fundamental human rights ... Between these extremes one could find a variety of criminal activities such as organized crime, the activities of terrorist groups, the criminal activities of a variety of economic operators, and the illicit activities of certain national and transnational corporations whose operations had a deleterious impact upon the economies of entire countries and upon the environment".[16]

> As Leslie Wilkins has put it, "There is a range of economic activity that is continuous from the very saintly to the most sinful... (and) of behaviour along which any type of business can be conducted; legality — the litmus test that traditionally has separated business from crime — is an arbitrary point on that range. Its placement varies by industry (and in some cases, by establishment type) and it can be relocated if new laws are passed. It is one variable factor in the business environment, not an intrinsic characteristic of a process by which legal goods and services are produced differently from illegal ones." [17]

And Smith[18] "... Behind these assertions lies a fundamental philosophical issue that cannot be ignored: the relationship between Good and Evil. The traditional alien conspiracy perspective is premised, knowingly or not, on assumptions about good and evil, and the reality of 'criminality' as a master trait that distinguishes between them in some absolute and irrevocable way. These beliefs have enabled some theorists to view organized criminals as a class apart. That is probably why theories of white-collar crime are so popular — they provide a rationalization for not applying the master trait distinction in all cases (i.e. the white-collar criminal remains a businessman). In contrast, I am contending that good and evil are not absolute determinants according to which behavioural theories can be constructed. Existing theories of enterprise and crime have perceived bankers, retailers, importers, and other businessmen as conforming to a set of behavioural rules having nothing to do with loansharking, fencing, smuggling, and other forms of criminal behavior that conform to their own set of rules. A spectrum of enterprise enables the analyst to perceive instead that the businessman of impeccable standards, the sharp or questionable operator, and the underworld supplier are the entrepreneurs who must be distinguished on grounds other than a master trait of 'criminal'. The loanshark is a credit establishment; the fence is a retailer".

If one considers that criminality produces a continuum within which there are various forms of organized crime, then the functional interdependence between them becomes evident, and so do the inadequacies of the definitions and theories that separate them. There are, within this continuum, a variety of economic activity components subject to market forces, which are called business if legal, and crime if illegal. This means that the old enterprise paradigm can be used to understand and explain the behaviour contents of crime. It has been observed that "common to both the Lockheed and Valachi cases is the concept of organization"[19]. However, criminal organization does not exist in a vacuum. It tends to maximize its profits through illegal acts. This means that in the future a new theory of rationalized crime in the changing world must confront three main concepts: behaviour (which defines the type of crime), organization, and its interaction with the forces of the market which orient criminal/non-criminal choices. From this perspective the distinctions between different forms of criminality carry a meaning if used exclusively for descriptive purposes. It is for this reason that I prefer to talk about the organization of crime rather than organized crime. The former is a process which facilitates the understanding and explanation of trends in recent criminality, the latter is a concept which has, at different times, had different meanings.

These conclusions are very important for the development of criminal policies. There is an obvious interrelationship between present day conceptual paradigms, explicatory theories and the resultant efficacy of the criminal justice system. Examples are found in the USA where the conspiracy paradigm has misled those attempting to understand crime and, as a result, have caused the failure of those concerned with the task of controlling it. Similar failures apply in Italy, where organized crime was for a long time explained exclusively within the classic typologies of the Mafia, Camorra and N'drangheta. The restricted level of conceptualization and analysis with regard to the understanding of crime has had deleterious consequences for the efficacy of counterstrategies, as evidenced in the USA and Italy. To elaborate on this, until the end of the 70's in Italy little or no judicial weight was attached to the organization of crime, whereas, in fact, criminal organizations were already conducting illegal traffic on a business level and at

111

war with each other. In Sicily, institutional heads were being eliminated one by one, whilst the judiciary simply regarded Mafia in the light of a conspiracy to offend.

The view of the judiciary reflected society's interpretation of the Mafia at that time as an organization that was not very dangerous. It was not until the beginning of the 80's, when there was an unprecedented increase in public concern and greater awareness on the part of the mass media, that it was possible to pass the Rognoni-La Torre Law: a law that was built on a paradigm of mafia as a business organization. This new law gave criminal investigators adequate tools to examine criminal organizations, and it also raised the judiciary's consciousness leading to the achievement of considerable successes in the struggle against organized crime. Although only a short time has elapsed since the law was passed and its subsequent changes adopted, crime has already developed a response to it, showing an inexhaustible capacity for innovation and development. Those involved in combatting the mafia at an operative level know only too well the capacity organized crime has to spread into new markets, to expand frontiers and to make new alliances, all of which increases the difficulty in "keeping up" with them. Given the speed with which criminal organizations manage to evade attempts to repress them, it is necessary for the criminal justice system to be equally capable of updating their structures. This means that in spite of the difficulties resulting from economic, political and cultural differences among modern states, it is essential that they reconsider the problems of modern criminality. These differences, above all, make it difficult, albeit necessary, to develop a greater rationalization of international means for controlling criminality.

Rational strategies and the organization of crime

It is not within the scope of this paper to concretely identify the best strategies for combatting organized crime.[20]

What must precede the identification of such strategies is a new approach, to be adopted internationally and to be applied to problems created by the organization of new forms of crime which, as we have already shown, include organized crime. This new approach should be to recognize the pressing need for an increasingly rational response on the part of modern society and it's criminal justice system to the problems of developing criminality. In other words, one can only respond with greater rationalization to the growing rationalization of criminal forms which reflect the complexity of modern social systems. A new approach must include the identification of practical objectives and an evaluation of the costs and benefits of possible alternatives chosen to achieve these objectives. In order to do this we may take the aforementioned concepts that describe new forms of "crime as business", those that "operate according to market laws", and "in illegal and legal activities", "with different organizational typologies", and apply them analogously. We might use these models for an economic analysis of criminality in our endeavour to interpret and combat crime. In other words, use criteria of efficiency and effectiveness as well as those of justice.

Within this framework rationality is the starting point from which to interpret criminal behaviour. It must be understood that criminal behaviour has a rational basis and so, too, must the criteria for the allocation of resources to counteract it.

My concern is with developing a possible approach to the problems presented by new organizational forms of crime, which include organized crime. This involves the rationalization of a criminal justice system which has to respond to the challenges posed by recent changes in criminality.

At a micro-level, the paradigm of rational criminal man demonstrates that criminal action is born out of an evaluation of the various possibilities that exist to maximize benefits (the value of the products of illegal activity), and to

113

minimize costs (punishment, time and expense). At a macro-level this paradigm of the rational criminal man might be applied usefully to the wider organization of rational forms of criminality. It can be used to develop policies that counter act problems created by the organization of crime. "It is a strategic analysis which could help in identifying the incentives and disincentives to organized crime, in evaluating the costs and the losses due to criminal enterprises, and in restructuring laws and programmes to minimize the costs, wastes, and injustices that crime entails."[21] Such a strategy entails choices directly related to the specific problems of organized crime and to the relationships between organized and other forms of criminality.

The problem we face may be summarized in our response to the question "do we want to reduce the amount of organization or the amount of crime?".[22] Schelling argues that organization can lead to the internalization of the costs of violence which may lead to less violence.[23] If we choose to reduce the amount of organization, we have to consider the assumption that "crime becomes organized or monopolized when there is some service which all criminal firms in a particular activity need and which can be monopolized. In most operations, entry at the retail end is too easy for efficient monopolization to occur; attempts to reduce the amount of organization in criminal activities should, therefore, focus on monopolized services. Apparently the most important service required by criminal firms is capital. Anything which reduces the use of capital in the production of a particular illegal good will tend to reduce the market power of providers of that good, and hence reduce the amount of organization."[24] This means that the need to create and use economic capital constitutes the most fundamental drive for organization. Therefore, it is necessary to develop strategies to prevent the accumulation and use of capital in criminality.

114

It is now evident that there is an urgent need to confront the increasing organization of criminality with an equally rational counter-strategy. I am aware that the problems we face in the control of present day crime require more than exhortations about the need for rationality. Within a framework of rationality we must make a detailed cost-benefit evaluation and costs of the possible alternative strategies. Only in this way shall we be able to attack the phenomenon of widespread criminal organization. The absence of adequate strategies to defeat it now, will guarantee a flourishing future for the organization of criminality.

References and Notes

[1] The only available sources are the international Interpol statistics. For a comparative analysis on trends of criminality, 1970-1980 in a number of developed and developing countries, see United Nations, "Second United Nations Survey of Crime Trends, Operations of Criminal Justice Systems and Crime Prevention Strategies", Report prepared by the Secretariat, A/CONF.121/18 and Corr. 1, Seventh United Nations Congress on the Prevention of Crime and the Treatment of Offenders, 1985.

[2] But, see for example, Asuni, T. (1970) "Focus of Social Defense Research in the Developmental Context", *International Review of Criminal Policy*, No. 29; Clifford, W. (1975) "New Dimensions in Criminality - National and Transnational", *Australian and New Zealand Journal of Criminology*, 8.; Clinard, M. B. and D. J. Abbott (1973) *Crime in Developing Countries: A Comparative Perspective*, N. Y., John Wiley & Sons.; Leone, U. and U. Zvekic (1987) "Sviluppo e Criminalità" in Ferracuti F. (a cura di) *Trattato di Criminologia, Medicina Criminologica e Psichiatria Forense*, vol. II, Milano, Giuffré; Lopez-Rey, M. (1964) "Economic Conditions and Crime with Special Reference to Less Developed Countries", *Annales Internationales de Criminologie*, 1.; Rizkalla, S. (1974) "Crime and Criminal Justice in the Developing Countries", *Acta Criminologica*, 7.; Scandinavian Research Council of Criminology (1974) *Crime and Industrialization*, Stockholm, University of Stockholm; Shelley, L. I. (1981) *Crime and Modernization*, Carbondale, Southern Illinois University Press; UNSDRI, *Economic Crises and Crime*, 1976; United Nations, "Social Change and Criminality", *International Journal of Comparative and Applied Criminal Justice*, 3, Spring 1979.

³ United Nations, "Second Survey...", *op. cit.*

⁴ United Nations, General Assembly, "Crime Prevention and Control", Report of the Secretary General, (A/32/199), 22 September 1977; H. J. Kerner, *Professionelles und Organisiertes Verbrechen*, Weisbaden, Bundeskriminalamt, 1973.

⁵ P. Arlacchi and N. Dalla Chiesa, *La Palude e la Città*, Milano, Mondadori, 1987.

⁶ S. Bisi, S., "La Criminalità Violenta in Italia" (1981-1982), *Quaderni del GIRS*, N. 1, Università di Roma "La Sapienza", 1986, p. 13.

⁷ G. Chinnici and U. Santino, *L'Omicidio a Palermo e Provincia negli anni 1960-66 e 1978-1984*, Palermo, Università di Palermo, Istituto G. Impastato, 1987.

⁸ According to Smith, "it should be possible to extend Miller's (1973) methodology [a research arguing for a wider recognition of an ideological scale undergirding beliefs about the sources of crime and other criminal policies], and to demonstrate that ideological biases affect prevailing assumptions and positions concerning economic crime". See D. C. Smith Jr., "The Ethics of Economic Crime Control" in F. Elliston and N. Bowie, Eds., *Ethics, Public Policy, and Criminal Justice*, Oelgeschlager, Gunn and Hain Publishers Inc., Cambridge, Mass. 1982, p. 138; W. B. Miller, "Ideology and Criminal Justice Policy: Some Current Issues", *Journal of Criminal Law and Criminology*, 64, 1973.

⁹ J. S. Albanese, "What Lockheed and La Cosa Nostra have in Common. The Effect of Ideology on Criminal Justice Policy", *Crime and Delinquency*, April 1982.

¹⁰ G. Geis and R. Meier, Eds., *White-Collar Crime: Offenses in Business, Politics and the Professions*, 2d ed., N. Y., Free Press, 1977, p. 254.

¹¹ D. H. Newman, "White-Collar Crime: An Overview and Analysis", *Law and Contemporary Problems*, Autumn 1958.

¹² D. C. Smith Jr., "Paragons, Pariahs, and Pirates: A Spectrum-Based Theory of Enterprises", *Crime and Delinquency*, July 1980, p. 374.

¹³ J. Landesco, "Organized Crime in Chicago" part III, in Illinois Association for Criminal Justice, *Illinois Crime Survey*, Chicago, IAC, 1929.

¹⁴ D. Bell, "Crime as an American Way of Life", *Antioch Review*, 1953, 13, 2, p. 133.

¹⁵ D. C. Smith, Jr., "The Ethics...", *op. cit.*, p. 375.

¹⁶ Report of the Ad Hoc Group of Experts on International Cooperation for the Prevention and Control of the Various Manifestations of Crime, including Terrorism, Organized by United Nations Crime Prevention and Criminal Justice Branch, Centro Nazionale di Prevenzione e Difesa Sociale and the International Institute of Higher Studies in Criminal Science, Siracusa, Italy, 20-24 January 1988.

[17] L. T. Wilkins, *Social Deviance*, Englewood Cliffs, N. J., Prentice-Hall, 1965, pp. 46-47.

[18] D. C. Smith, Jr., "Paragons, ...", *op. cit.*, p. 371.

[19] J. S. Albanese, "What Lockheed ...", *op. cit.*, p. 230.

[20] On this see D. A. Hellman, *The Economic Crime*, New York, St. Martin's Press, 1980, pp. 174-179; and F. T. Martens, "Organized Crime Control: The Limits of Government Intervention", *Journal of Criminal Justice*, No. 14, 1986, pp. 244-245.

[21] T. C. Schelling, "Economics and Criminal Enterprise", *The Public Interest*, 7, 1967, p. 61.

[22] P. H. Rubin, "The Economic Theory of the Criminal Firm" in Rottemberg, S. (ed.), *The Economics of Crime and Punishment*, Washington D. C., American Enterprise Institute for Public Policy Research, 1973, p. 165.

[23] T. C. Schelling, "Economic Analysis of Organized Crime", Appendix D, *Task Force Report: Organized Crime*, Washington D. C., G. P. O., 1967, p. 122.

[24] P. H. Rubin, "The Economic ...", *op. cit.*, p. 165.

THE INTERNATIONALIZATION OF CRIME: THE CHANGING RELATIONSHIP BETWEEN CRIME AND DEVELOPMENT

Louise I. Shelley *

Once it was possible to speak of distinct patterns of crime in the developed and developing nations.[1] Research conducted by the United Nations a decade ago sharply differentiated between the crime patterns of countries grouped as developed and developing.[2] Very disparate countries were grouped in these separate categories. The developed nations included such culturally, politically and socially different countries as Western Europe, the United States, Japan and Australia. Whereas the developing nations included the even more disparate countries of Latin America, Africa, Asia and the Middle East. Despite the dissimilarities among the countries grouped together, many common criminological traits were identified.

The first survey of the world crime situation, using data from the periods 1970-75, found significant differences in crime rates and forms of crime commission between the more and less economically developed countries. Crime patterns in the more industrially advanced nations were characterized by lower growth rates in crime commission, a higher percentage of crime commission attributable to property offenses and a higher level of female participation in crime than in the developing countries.[3]

Despite these distinctions certain important similarities were noted in all of the world's countries. Crime levels were

---

* Professor, Department of Justice, Law and Society, The American University, Washington, D.C., USA.

significant in almost all nations of the world and were affecting the quality of life. Drug related offenses were already a noticeable share of crime commission accounting for eight percent of total crime commission in both developed and developing countries.

The economic developments of the past decade have made it much more difficult to divide the countries of the world into two separate groups. Primary among the problems is that the concept of development has become increasingly problematic. There is no uniformity in the developing world. Political, social and religious differences always divided these diverse countries. But economic developments of the past decade made it even harder to group these countries collectively. While certain of the Asian economies have made rapid advances since the 1970s, many countries in Africa and Latin America are not only stagnating but are experiencing negative economic growth. Living standards are now below what they were at the start of the decade. This fact challenges earlier hypotheses on the relationship between crime and development.

The Criminological Relations between the Developing and Developed World

During the past decade the links between the nations of the developing and the developed world have expanded. A decade ago I predicted that the spread of mass transport, communications and international computer networks would have a major impact on future crime developments.[4] This prediction has unfortunately proved true. Coinciding with the contribution of modern technology are other developments linking the developed and developing world. These include large scale population movements between developing and developed countries, terrorist acts that manifest local political agenda on the international arena and the relationships that arise out of the internationaliz-

120

ation of the world's markets. The third world debt and the increasing disparities in income between residents in the developed and developing world has also contributed to the rise of international crime, particularly in the drug arena.

All of these factors create a situation in which crime is more transnational and international. Therefore, it is no longer as clear that development clearly differentiates and divides the criminality of the industrialized and the developing world. Developed countries, however, still share such crime attributes as higher female and youth participation in crime. Yet in certain respects there are now shared characteristics of developed and developing nations — a consequence of their increasing financial and political interdependence. For example, homicide rates in such American cities as Washington, D. C., New York and Detroit are presently higher than in many third world countries noted for their high violent crime rates.[5] This noted similarity in crime patterns, as will be explained later, is a visible consequence of the international drug trade. But the increasing interdependence is manifested in other crime patterns as well.

First, the significant movement of individuals from developing to developed countries has had criminogenic consequences even though many who move are law-abiding individuals. As Thorsten Sellin explained half a century ago in his theory of culture conflict, crime commission is more likely when individuals of different social, political and cultural groups come into contact. The problem is particularly accentuated among the off-spring of migrants who experience the discrimination of outsiders in their country but do not have the expectations for success that motivated their parents to relocate. European, Australian and some American researchers attribute some of their crime growth to the influx of migrants.[6] Their offspring are seen to contribute disproportionately to urban crime problems.

In addition to the voluntary movement of individuals from developing to developed nations, there has been a certain number of expulsions of offenders from developing countries to industrialized nations. Probably the most publicized of these is the case of Cuban inmates emigrating along with the Mariel boat people to Florida. Many of these released offenders have been placed in American penitentiaries where many presently remain.[7]

Second, terrorist crimes are perpetrated by third world nationals in developed countries against their residents. This is done to command greater media attention and to give greater visibility to the terrorists' political agenda. Their objectives can include the advocacy of a local cause or the crime can be committed to affect the policies of an industrialized nation with influence in their region. An example of this is the bombing of a West German nightclub frequented by American soldiers. This offense was committed by citizens of a developing country in a developed country to show Arab disapproval for American policies. Yet the hijacking of an international flight to Malta in which several passengers were killed[8] was done to press more local objectives in the Middle East. These crimes, although limited in number in relation to the total crime picture, highlight the problem of distinguishing between the crimes of the developing and developed world.

Third, sophisticated economic and computer crimes are no longer associated only with the developed countries. With the increasing internationalization of the world's markets, residents of developing countries are increasingly capable of committing such offenses. The insider trading scandal on Wall Street that rocked the financial markets leading to the arrest of many major figures in the financial community did not begin in the United States. Rather an anonymous tip from a branch of an international brokerage house in Caracas, Venezuela triggered the major American investigation. Part of illegal stock trading occurred through a Panamian partnership.[9] Such crime would not have been so possible decades ago when financial communications between developing and developed nations were more restricted and the volume of international financial activity was more limited.

Criminal activity in global financial markets can also have major political as well as economic consequences. Illustrative of this is the recent resignation of a leading member of the Swiss cabinet because her husband was an officer of a bank accused of laundering money for third world drug dealers.[10]

Fourth, the third world debt has a more direct impact on criminality than the Swiss example cited previously. The increasing dependency of many third world countries on industrialized nations as a consequence of the debt and the decline of raw material prices makes criminal activity one of the few feasible ways of acquiring sorely needed capital presently concentrated in the industrialized nations. Drug trafficking is one of the primary vehicles of transferring wealth, albeit illicitly, from the industrialized to the third world. In some societies such as Colombia the wealth of the kingpins of the drug industry is sufficient to pay off the country's national debt. In Bolivia, the illicit export of drugs exceeds the legitimate national exports. With the transfer of such significant capital to financially strapped nations, many leaders willingly or begrudgingly turn their backs on the illicit drug trade.

Terrorist acts and insider trading are limited in number but the illicit drug trade involves hundred of thousands of individuals in both developing and industrialized countries. It is this criminality more than any other that epitomizes the increasingly complex relationship between developing and developed nations. It is a crime with almost unequaled impact on political, economic and social life in industrialized and third world nations. The international nature of drug crime forces us to reconsider the relationship between crime and development on both a practical and theoretical level.

International Drug Crime: The Nexus of the Developed and Developing Worlds

Drug crime is different from most criminality in that it is a complex offense or series of criminal acts. This makes it difficult to differentiate between criminal acts that belong solely to the developed or developing world. Drug crime is different from many other transnational crimes that are a single or even a series of related offenses committed across borders often within a defined period of time. Narcotics trafficking knows no time and few geographical limits; it is not one crime but rather a series of activities ranging from drug cultivation, processing, shipment, sale and then the investment of the profits. The narcotics business, operating from the mountains of the Golden Triangle and the remote regions of South America to the streets of the world's metropoli, closely links the developing and developed worlds in an on-going illicit economic and political relationship.

International drug crime links the developed and developing world in three different respects. The volume of trade is so significant that it is an important element of international commerce. The attempts to combat drug cultivation and trafficking have an important impact on bi-lateral and multilateral political relations. The social effects of this problem are felt not only domestically but have international consequences as well.

Drug trafficking is very different from the international crimes of the world's financial markets or the visible terrorist acts in industrialized nations. These acts represent new relationships between the developing and the developed world. Yet in certain ways the drug trade resembles the traditional relationship that has existed between third world and industrialized nations.

The illicit international narcotics business in several important ways mirrors the international and political relations of the licit multi-national corporations. In the international drug trade as in legitimate multinational business, the raw materials are generally produced in the third world to meet the consumer needs of the industrialized nations. The processing of the drugs as in the manufacturing stage of legitimate international business may occur in either the developed or the more developed countries of the developing world such as Colombia using materials from the developed world. Drug production, like the operations of multinational corporations, also exists with the tolerance or even encouragement of some local political leaders in the developing countries.

Part of the explanation for the rapid growth in this illicit international activity is the general economic relationship between the nations of the developed and the developing world. The foreign debt of many third world nations has widened the gap between industrialized and developing countries. The cost of raw materials, the source of revenue for many third world residents, has dropped on world markets while the cost of industrialized goods has risen. Services to residents have been cut as government's have used their limited resources to pay their foreign debts. No visible legitimate means of obtaining large amounts of capital is available to the residents or the countries of the financially pressed third world. Rural farmers turn to drug cultivation that yields more profit than raising agricultural products. Poor peasants and urban dwellers may support the drug dealers who distribute social and medical services to the indigents that the hard pressed governments can not provide.

Governments of economically depressed countries choose or are forced to turn a blind eye to the drug crops that bring so much foreign currency into their countries. Drugs is a multinational business that returns significant foreign capital to Latin America and to a lesser extent to other financially depressed regions.

Yet the analogy between the multi-national corporation and the illicit drug trade can not be drawn too closely.

Important differences exist. While multi-national corporations are often staffed by individuals from developed nations, many drugs are marketed by entrepreneurs from third world nations as epitomized by the Medellin cartel. Whereas the legitimate multi-national enterprises generally operate with the encouragement of the governments of developed nations, illicit drug activity flourishes despite the expressed hostility and suppressive activity of the governments of many industrialized nations. The proceeds of multi-national corporations can be legitimately invested either in the developed or the developing world. Drug traffickers have greater difficulty investing outside of their region.[11] The billionaires of the Medellin cartel have deposited much of their money in foreign banks. Faced with increased difficulty in laundering money they are increasingly purchasing farm land and real estate in Colombia.

Drug trafficking is perceived by many countries, in particular the United States, as a political problem. Yet it is a quite different problem from the overtly political crime of terrorism. Terrorism and drugs are the only offenses that permanently command the attention of established offices at the State Department and the analytical branch of the CIA (Central Intelligence Analysis). Yet important differences exist between the political handling of such criminality. Terrorism does not permanently affect relations among many countries. Rather concerns about terrorism are generally triggered by a particular incident. Then for a defined period high level diplomatic contacts may be initiated between an industrialized and a developing country.

In contrast, drug production and trafficking remain continuous and key political concerns affecting relations between the industrialized and industrializing world. This statement is particularly characteristic of the United States but applies to a lesser extent to certain European countries. American relations with many of the nations of Latin America and the Golden Triangle are affected by their drug policies and their readiness to comply with American efforts to combat drug cultivation and production.

Terrorism has forced countries and private corporations to spend large amounts of money for enhanced security. Much of it in response to third world rather than domestic terrorism. These expenditures are matched or surpassed by the efforts mounted by many industrialized countries to combat drug production and trafficking. The affluent countries of the industrialized world are able if not eager to allocate the funds for these activities. Certain industrialized nations are also pressuring third world countries to combat drug production domestically. These efforts to control drug crime are often diverting resources badly needed by the social sector into the drug enforcement arena. The social consequences of this policy are all too evident in Mexico and other Latin American countries.

The drug trade's impact is more visible on the individual rather than the economic or political levels. The growth of this major illicit commerce in recent decades has had catastrophic effects on the citizens of the industrialized societies. The social consequences of the drug problem are clear and not easily irradicable. Domestic drug dealers sometimes working in conjunction with dealers from developing countries have become a seemingly permanent feature of urban life in the United States and many Western Europe countries.

Drug abusers are an ever more visible part of the third world urban environment as well. Producer countries, many which felt themselves exempt from the drug abuse problem, are now being confronted with a problem they are less equipped to combat. For example in Pakistan, "there are now between 670,000 and one million addicts, who consume more opium than the country produces." [12] Pakistan's situation may be anomalous but the impact of drug crime is all too universal. Drug addiction and crime related criminal activity have risen worldwide.

Drug cultivation and production also exists as an integral and vital part of many societies. Drugs are now a major element of the economy of such nations as Afghanistan, Bolivia, Burma, Colombia, Ecuador. The very survival of many of the inhabitants of these countries is linked to the perpetuation of drug cultivation. Without alternative legitimate means of survival, peasants pursue their own financial interests without any understanding of the criminogenic consequences for their or other societies of their agricultural activity.

The increasing political, economic and social inter-dependence of the world is clearly illustrated by contemporary drug crime. There is not one cause and consequently neither is there one way of tackling the problem. No where have its political, social or economic consequences been more pronounced than in the United States.

Drugs in the United States and the Developing World

Examining the drug situation in the United States illustrates the increasing complexity of the relationship between the developing and the developed nations. The United States as the largest user of drugs with a policy of intercepting drugs and halting their cultivation provides a concrete illustration of many of concepts previously presented.

The drug issue is no longer merely a criminal problem in the United States. Former President Reagan in a 1986 directive made drug trafficking a national security issue. Yet its policy in this area has still not recognized that "cocaine is not simply a law enforcement issue but is also a complex foreign policy matter".[13] Its dealings with the developing nations that supply drugs are coercive rather than reflective of larger bi-lateral concerns. The extent and the immediacy of the domestic drug problem may partially explain the reason that the United States has taken a one-sided perspective on the drug problem.

128

There are approximately twenty million users of drugs in the United States at the present time. Approximately 18 million use marijuana, approximately one-third of which is produced in the United States. Estimates indicate that five-to six million people in the United States regularly use cocaine while approximately half a million are addicted to heroin.[14] None of these drugs can be acquired legally and most of the drugs consumed are imported.

The United States has paid comparatively little attention to the reduction of demand and the treatment of the offender, placing more emphasis on the destruction of crops and interdiction. This policy perspective has treated the drug problem not as an American problem but has transferred much of the onus to the developing world.

Since 1986 the President of the United States needs to certify whether countries where major trafficking occurs are fully cooperating with the United States in combatting the drug trade.[15] This "cooperation" includes the acceptance of American drug enforcement agents to work with local law enforcement personnel in joint raids to eradicate crops and halt production. It may include the use of airplanes by the narcotics division of the State Department in aerial eradication programs of poppy fields. Treaties of cooperation as well as willingness to extradite drug dealers are other indications of compliance with American drug policy. Without such certification of cooperation, countries may lose their foreign assistance.

The major effort to control drug trade by attacking it at its roots has proved to be an ineffective policy. Furthermore it has exacerbated relations between the United States and many developing countries whose governments, even when willing, do not have the resources or the influence in the cultivation regions to limit drug production. The traditional relationship between an industrialized and developing country continues in this most important area of criminality. Developing countries are being forced to assume

129

particular domestic policies as a result of external pressure. Moreover, American law enforcement personnel have been militarized assuming a visible and coercive presence beyond their borders. The American response to the drug trade is confirming many stereotypes of the meddling big neighbour to the North.

Drug crime has, however, altered the previously established relationship between industrialized and developing countries in one important way. Urban crime patterns were clearly different in developed and developing countries. Presently urban crime in many major American cities can no longer be differentiated from those found in the metropoli of developing countries. Violent crime rates, particularly for homicide, have risen dramatically and presently equal or surpass those of many third world cities. A majority of the individuals killed are victims of the drug wars presently waged in many American ghettos. Like their counterparts in the third world, the offenders are poorly educated, unemployed and marginalized. The sophisticated drug rings that have penetrated the urban ghettos have caused a major transformation in urban crime.

A hallmark of the transition to development was an increase in property crime relative to crimes of violence.[16] High levels of violence were more closely associated with pre-industrial society. But in the United States with a drug problem that is outside the reach and the capacities of the law enforcement apparatus, violence has recently again become a major problem of city life. This violence is unlike the collective violence of the 1960s associated with the political consciousness of a developed society.[17] Rather it is violence that bears striking similarities to that of cities in developing countries whose residents have been left behind in the developmental process.

Conclusion

A significant change has occurred in the past decade in crime patterns internationally. The impact of development can not be as clearly charted now as in the past because of the increasing interrelationships among the peoples and economies of the world's nations. Yet certain consequences of development still remain.

Development in almost all societies has led to higher crime rates. Crime rates worldwide were much lower before industrialization when much of the world's population resided in rural areas. Furthermore, a very different offender has emerged with development. Increasingly women and juveniles are involved in crime. The participation of these population groups becomes more pronounced with increasing industrialization. These differences in crime commission between the industrialized and developing world endure even as there is lessening differentiation in other aspects of crime commission.

Increasing international communications, movement of populations and the internationalization of the world's markets have caused significant changes in criminality. The prime example of this change is the international growth of drug crime that has established many and to a certain extent new relationships between developing and developed nations. Yet drug crime is only the most evident but not the only example of this changing relationship.

The increasing mobility of the world's population and the growing communications and financial links among different countries of the developing and developed world have profoundly influenced the nature of contemporary criminality. These global changes are likely to continue, fundamentally altering the development of crime. Drug crime, the most visible evidence of the increasing inter-connections among the world's nations, is unlikely to recede even in the face of growing pressure from developed nations. Even a profound worldwide economic crisis would only stem but not halt the development of drug trade. Drug usage is now an integral part of many societies and the residents of many countries are financially dependent on its perpetuation.

This paper has not tried to examine the entirety of the international ramifications of the drug problem. By focusing briefly on the relationship between the United States and the drug producing countries of the developing world, a better understanding of the complex and changing relationship between crime and development is possible.

Focusing on the problem from an american perspective, however, underestimates the impact that this criminality has on the development process. Although an American president has declared the drug problem a national security problem issue, it is no way clear that the integrity of the American governmental or political structure is threatened by the drug trade. Yet many analysts would suggest that the drug trade has undermined the political integrity of Colombia and to a lesser extent other countries heavily dependent on the drug trade. Crime is not just then a symptom of the developmental process but may prove an obstacle to its future development. The relationship between crime and development becomes ever more complicated.

References and Notes

[1] For a discussion of this see L. I. Shelley, *Crime and Modernization*, Carbondale, S. Illinois University Press, 1981.

[2] United Nations, *Crime Prevention and Control*, Report of the Secretary General, A/32/199, 1977.

[3] *Ibid.*

[4] L. I. Shelley, *op. cit.*, pp. 99-100.

[5] L. Duke, "Death Cast Long Shadow Over '88", *The Washington Post*, 1 January 1989, p. 1.

[6] M. Killias, "Criminality among Second Generation Immigrants in Western Europe: A Review of Evidence", Presented at the American Society of Criminology meetings, 9-12 November 1988; R. D. Francis, *Migrant Crime in Australia*, St. Lucia University of Queensland Press, 1981; G. Volsky, "Clamor Ruses over Detention of Cuban Refugees by U. S.", *New York Times*, 4 April 1987, p. 23.

[7] A. L. Goldman, "From Tiny Cuban Port to Rampage in Louisiana", *New York Times*, 23 November 1987, p. 14.

[8] Associated Press, "Egyptian Jet Hijacked to Malta; 3 or 4 Aboard are Reported Slain", *New York Times*, 24 November 1985, p. 1.

[9] K. Eichenwald and S. Lohr, "Boesky Misled Drexel, Inquiry is Said to Find", *Washington Post*, 16 November 1988, D1.

[10] "Billion-Dollar Drug Scandal Rocks Political, Money World", *C. J. International*, March-April 1989, p. 3.

[11] A. Dodds Frank, "See no Evil", *Forbes*, 6 October, 1986, pp. 38-41.

[12] E. Sciolino, "Drug Production Rising Worldwide, State Department Says", *New York Times*, 2 March 1989, p. A12.

[13] State Department report quoted in E. Sciolino, p. A1.

[14] L. K. Altman, "U. S. to Ease Methadone Rules in Bid to Curb AIDS in Addicts", *The New York Times*, 3 March 1989, p. A1; E. Marshall, "Flying Blind in the War on Drugs", *Science*, 1988, p. 1606.

[15] E. Sciolino, *op. cit.*, p. A12.

[16] L. I. Shelley, *op. cit.*

[17] For a discussion of this violence, H. D. Graham, "The Paradox of American Violence: A Historical Commentary", *Annals of the American Academy of Political and Social Science*, 1970, Vol. 391, pp. 74-82. The article contained in a special issue on collective violence has other articles that illustrate this point.

CRIME AND DEVELOPMENT IN AFRICA: A CASE STUDY ON NIGERIA

Adedokun A. Adeyemi *

Criminogenic factors in development

"Development is not criminogenic *per se*, especially where its fruits are equally distributed among all the peoples, thus contributing to the improvement of overall social conditions; however, unbalanced or inadequately planned development contributes to increases in criminality".[1]

African societies have undergone and are still rapidly undergoing considerable cultural changes in a process which is producing a blending of the traditional systems and outlook with modern European/American systems and approaches in the various facets of life. Modern technology, aided by modern rapid and large-scale transportation systems, has reduced the spatial gaps between countries and peoples of the region, and between these and peoples of Europe, America, Latin America and Asia. Technological advancement in the fields of transportation and the print and electronic media have made peoples spatially removed from one another, feel as if they are close neighbours and, sometimes, compatriots.

Socio-economic Conditions of Contemporary African Societies

The United Nations Economic Commission for Africa Conference of Ministers expressed its concern in 1984 for

* Professor of Criminology and Public Law, Department of Public Law, University of Lagos, Nigeria.

135

"the very alarming and significant deterioration in the economic and social conditions of the African countries, and in particular, by the effects of the drought which now affects thirty-four of our member states; and the devastating impact of the global economic recession which is still gripping the African countries with its attendant collapse in commodity prices, the unprecedented high level of interest rates, sharp exchange rate fluctuations, increased protectionism, balance of payments difficulties, mounting external debt and the decline in real terms of official development assistance."[2] The Ministers observed that these factors, along with wide-spread, severe and persistent drought, have created "economic and social problems of unprecedent proportions the solution to which is beyond the ability of African countries for many of which the issue is sheer survival."[3] In fact, the Executive Secretary of the Economic Commission for Africa (ECA) warned that should the trend continue, the future of the African society would become horrendous since, among other things, "all services would deteriorate in terms of quantity. A smaller portion of the population would be able to have access to education, health and water. Cities would become over-populated shanty towns as housing would become less available. As a result of such socio-economic difficulties, the political situation would worsen. Then riots, crime and misery would be the order of (the day)."[4]

The situation revealed here is quite grim. It will, in fact, be better appreciated when examined in more specific terms. For instance, in 1980, the average *per capita* income of the African region was only $US741, as compared with a *per capita* GNP of $US9,684 in the industrialised countries. For the Sub-Saharan African countries, the *per capita* income was, in fact, only $US239. Even then, about 70% of Africans were found to be either destitute (i.e. with a *per capita* income below $US59) or on the verge of poverty (i.e. with a *per capita* income of $US115). The deteriorating

136

economic condition of the African countries continues to increase mass poverty, coupled with high unemployment and underemployment. Yet, again, 20% of the African population have an income which is four times the income of the poorest strata (40%), whilst there is a dependency rate of three persons per each employed African.[5] On the food situation, the African region still remains calorie deficient, with over 20% of the population having an energy intake below the critical minimum limit of 1.2 BMR (Basal Metabolical Rate), and an average of 2,197 calories *per capita* in food consumption.[6] Yet the performance of the African countries in the field of agriculture continues to remain disappointing, with the drought only aggravating the various problems.

To these one must add other factors such as massive urban migration and rapid urbanization (resulting in a continental average annual urban growth rate of 5% for the 1980-90 period),[7] rapid population growth (with rates of 2.9% for 1980 and projected 3.02% for 1990),[8] and improperly planned and executed educational policies and programmes. These have not been related to the economic needs of the respective countries; in 1980, 70% of primary school age children, 14% of secondary school age children and 1.8% of university age group were enrolled in educational institutions.[9] The considerable decrease between primary and secondary school attendance, and between the latter and university, has thereby increased the mass of literate and somewhat qualified unemployed.

On the political scene, African societies have had to endure considerable amount of political instability. This is not surprising since human beings cannot be expected to endure with continued passive docility the harsh economic conditions indicated above. However, instability is also fuelled by the nature of the political arrangements in contemporary African societies, namely, the adoption of alien European or American styles of government in socio-culturally different African societies. The result has been that Africans have been fixing imported political square pegs into their traditional political round holes. There can be little wonder, therefore, that the imported systems, be these Western democratic types or the socialist/communist types, have no roots in Africa, since the required underlying conventions which have cushioned and oiled the efficient operation of these political systems in Europe and America are not present in Africa. Our own conventions are culturally geared to cushioning and oiling totally different types of political arrangements. The cultural anomie in this field is self-destabilising on its own. Consensus, even where achieved in consequence of compromises, is the very heart of the African political systems, as opposed to the imposition of the majority's will on the minority. This is the philosophy adopted by the proponents and practitioners of one-party states in Africa. But its operation has led to the emergence of a totally "unafrican" totalitarianism, which is neither European nor African in form and character. Also current African democracies are neither European, American nor African in character. Hence, the political instability in the continent.

This cultural anomie is not restricted to the political field. It pervades through the whole of African life, ranging from the form and content of our education programmes which, with the exception of Ethiopia and the Arab countries, are conducted in either English, French, Portuguese or Spanish in the rest of the African countries. It is clear that the European cultural undertones of the various text books often dominate our educational scene. The same is now true of American and European cultures which have been massively transmitted in the area through entertainment for the African youth. In business and industrial sectors, the adoption of Western dominated management styles and structures, coupled with the transplantation of European and

American technology, have widened the cultural conflict in the African continent. This has been accentuated by the backlash of the colonial heritage which established the European educational, political and economic systems upon which most African countries are now developing their systems.

As a result of this, African youths today are experiencing the conflict between traditional African cultures and European and American cultures.

When one considers this socio-economic, socio-cultural and socio-political framework, one must realise that crises are largely the result of unbalanced and inadequately planned and executed development programmes, which have been recognised as contributing to increase criminality.[10] This increase in criminality has not only been a prominent phenomenon of the African societies in the 1970s and 1980s, but it has been predicted that it might reach "riots" and "misery" dimensions by the turn of the century if something is not done to arrest the situation.[11] It is already apparent that a solution to these crises can only be achieved by a combination of individual and collective African efforts, coupled with "massive assistance from the international community"[12]. These factors have become particularly significant inasmuch as it is now generally accepted that.

> "Socio-economic transitions occurring in consequence of rapid development taking place in developing countries have generally been observed as resulting in the decrease in the role of the family in socialisation and value transmission, mainly because increased urbanization, migration and industrialization create conditions conducive to a weakening of family ties, whilst poverty weakens family authority and autonomy."[13]

Within these parametres, we can now examine the various factors which may be considered to be specific criminogenic factors in development in Africa and, particularly, in Nigeria.

Socio-economic Conditions in Nigeria: 1975-84

Massive Industrialization in Urban Areas

The most prominent issue that comes to mind here is the biased focus of our developmental efforts in terms of the urban/rural dichotomy. Although rural areas have always contributed immensely to the wealth of the country, in the development process, one government after another has concentrated most development efforts in urban centres of

Table 1

Structure of Production in Nigeria, 1975 (Percent) *

Sector of the Economy	Valued added	Employment
Agriculture, livestock, fishing and forestry	26.3	64.0
Mining and quarrying	13.3	1.0
Manufacturing and crafts	13.8	10.7
Electricity, gas and water	0.8	0.2
Building and construction	10.6	0.9
Distribution	11.5	12.2
Transportation, ports and communications	4.9	0.6
Public administration	14.0	1.5
Other services	4.8	8.9
Total	100.0	100.0

* Constructed from Wilbur Smith & Associates, "Master Plan for Metropolitan Lagos", Lagos State Government, Lagos, Vol. 1, Table 3.18.

the country and neglected the rural areas. The structure of the Nigerian economy revealed that for 1975, for example, agriculture, livestock and forestry, as a group, constituted the largest contributor to our economy in terms of their overall contribution to our gross domestic product, namely, 26.3% (see Table 1).

This group, the biggest contributor to our gross domestic product, largely consists of rural activities. This fact has been definitely confirmed by evidence over a much longer period spanning the following financial years: 1975/76, 1979/80, 1980, 1981 and 1982. The pertinent contributory sectors were all definitely rural, namely "Agriculture (crops and other) and livestock."

Again, as shown in Table 2 that follows, the prominence of these combined sectors is rivaled only by that of "Mining, quarrying and petroleum."

Table 2

Percentage for Selected Contributory Sectors to the Cross Domestic Product by Industrial Origin at Current Prices*

Contributory sectors	1975/ 1976	1976/ 1977	1977/ 1978	1978/ 1979	1979/ 1980	1980/ 1981	1981	1982
Agriculture (crops and others) and livestock	51.10	45.94	46.70	48.24	45.16	38.44	41.28	44.38
Manufacturing	5.58	5.40	4.97	5.35	5.10	5.12	5.72	5.64
Mining, quarrying and petroleum	42.70	48.41	47.86	47.90	54.57	63.69	51.69	47.80
Construction	8.66	9.78	9.56	9.22	7.98	7.99	8.65	8.53
Housing	4.16	3.79	3.46	3.40	3.04	2.85	3.02	3.18

* Constructed from the data provided in "Economic and Social Statistics Bulletin" (Special Number), p. 4, Table 4, January 1984, Federal Office of Statistics, Lagos, Nigeria.

Table 2 reveals the declining contribution made by these "largely" rural sectors to the Gross Domestic Product as compared to the contribution by its rival group of sectors, namely, "Mining, quarrying and petroleum". It is interesting to note that the relative contribution of the two groups of sectors are inversely related, namely, that the latter group increased its contribution in the financial years in which the former decreased, and conversely decreased in the years in which the latter increased its contribution. Also, the growth rates of the relative contributions of the two groups have exhibited significantly different patterns. The group of "rural" sectors have, except for 1981 and 1982, noticeably maintained a relatively consistent decrease in contribution, while the mining, quarrying and petroleum group exhibited a more erratic pattern (see Table 3).

Table 3

**Growth Rates of Selected Contribution Sectors
to the Gross Domestic Product by Industrial Origin at Current Prices ***

Contributory sectors	1976/ 1977	1977/ 1978	1978/ 1979	1979/ 1980	1980	1981	1982
Agriculture (crops and others) and livestock	18.24	17.67	12.06	10.22	1.33	8.45	8.73
Manufacturing	25.11	6.19	14.80	14.12	15.58	12.45	—
Mining, quarrying and petroleum	44.16	16.66	6.74	36.60	34.18	−18.28	−6.25
Construction	43.60	14.78	2.89	3.74	15.00	9.00	—
Housing	16.00	7.00	5.00	7.13	7.65	6.76	6.71

* Constructed from Table 6, p. 6, "Economic and Social Statistics Bulletin" (Special Number).

Demographic Structural Changes and Rapid Urbanization

Structurally, the decade has shown relative changes in the demographic pattern of Nigeria in relation to age, sex and rural/urban dichotomy (see Table 4).

The steady decline in the contribution of the "rural" group of sectors' can be said to be the result of the relative neglect of those sectors, particularly in the financial years 1976/77 to 1980. Although complete definitive figures are not as yet available, the indications, however, are that the trend continued in 1982 and 1983 financial years.

Furthermore, the structural change in the rural/urban population appears somewhat significant. Urban population increased from 21.00% in 1975 to 30.2% in 1984 (see Table 4).

Table 5 reveals significant structural changes in the rural/urban population; the latter increasing from 21.00% in 1975 to 30.02% in 1984.

Table 4
Population Distribution by Sex and by Age Group *

YEAR	1 0-5			2 6-11 YEARS		
	Total	Male	Female	Total	Male	Female
1975	15,269,100	7,543,500	7,721,600	12,312,700	6,525,000	5,787,700
1976	10,022,919	4,878,689	5,144,230	13,794,852	7,310,418	6,484,434
1977	10,241,200	4,988,100	5,257,100	14,072,300	7,468,000	6,624,300
1978	10,572,100	5,145,900	5,426,200	14,550,600	7,710,900	6,839,700
1979	10,915,600	5,313,200	5,552,400	15,023,700	7,961,600	7,062,100
1980	11,270,900	5,485,900	5,785,000	15,512,200	8,220,500	7,291,700
1981	11,637,200	5,664,500	5,972,700	16,016,700	8,487,800	7,523,800
1982	12,015,800	5,848,700	6,167,100	16,537,400	8,763,800	7,773,600
1983	12,406,300	6,038,800	6,367,500	17,075,200	9,048,800	8,026,400
1984	12,809,900	6,235,500	6,574,400	17,630,500	9,343,100	8,287,400

YEAR	5 18-24 YEARS			6 25-30 YEARS		
	Total	Male	Female	Total	Male	Female
1975	11,667,600	5,330,100	6,337,500	11,291,100	5,310,800	5,980,300
1976	13,072,081	5,971,711	7,100,370	12,650,333	5,950,140	6,700,193
1977	13,353,900	6,100,500	7,253,500	12,923,100	6,078,400	6,844,700
1978	13,788,200	6,298,800	7,489,300	13,343,300	6,276,100	7,067,200
1979	14,236,600	6,503,700	7,732,900	13,777,200	6,480,200	7,297,000
1980	14,699,500	6,715,200	7,984,300	14,225,200	6,690,900	7,534,300
1981	15,177,500	6,933,500	8,244,000	14,687,800	6,908,500	7,779,300
1982	15,671,000	7,159,000	8,512,000	15,165,400	7,133,100	8,032,300
1983	16,180,600	7,391,800	8,788,800	15,658,600	7,365,100	8,293,500
1984	16,706,700	7,632,100	9,074,600	16,167,800	7,604,600	8,563,200

* The figures for this Table were supplied by the then Ministry of National Planning, now Ministry of Finance and Economic Development.

144

| | 3 | | | 4 | | |
| | 12-14 YEARS | | | 15-17 YEARS | | YEAR |
Total	Male	Female	Total	Male	Female	
4,446,200	2,427,000	2,019,200	4,629,800	2,444,400	2,389,400	1975
4,981,450	2,719,205	2,262,245	5,187,071	2,510,077	2,676,994	1976
5,088,900	2,777,000	2,311,000	5,298,900	2,560,200	2,734,700	1977
5,254,300	2,868,200	2,386,200	5,471,200	2,647,600	2,823,600	1978
5,425,200	2,961,400	2,463,800	5,649,200	2,733,700	2,915,500	1979
5,601,600	3,957,700	2,543,900	5,832,900	2,822,600	3,020,300	1980
5,783,800	3,157,200	2,626,600	6,022,500	2,912,400	3,100,200	1981
5,971,800	3,259,800	2,712,000	6,218,300	3,009,100	3,209,200	1982
6,166,000	3,365,800	2,800,200	6,420,500	3,107,000	3,313,600	1983
6,366,300	3,475,000	2,891,300	6,629,300	3,208,000	3,421,300	1984

| | 7 | | | 8 | | |
| | 31-60 YEARS | | | ABOVE 60 YEARS | | YEAR |
Total	Male	Female	Total	Male	Female	
13,097,600	7,185,300	5,912,300	1,809,000	1,066,000	7,743,000	1975
14,674,230	8,050,260	6,623,970	2,026,718	1,194,281	832,437	1976
14,990,600	8,223,800	6,766,800	2,070,400	1,220,000	850,400	1977
15,478,100	8,491,300	6,986,800	2,137,700	1,259,700	878,000	1978
15,981,400	8,767,400	7,214,000	2,207,300	1,300,700	906,600	1979
16,501,100	9,052,500	7,448,600	2,279,100	1,343,000	936,100	1980
17,037,600	9,346,800	7,690,800	2,353,100	1,386,600	966,500	1981
17,591,700	9,650,800	7,940,900	2,429,600	1,431,700	997,900	1982
18,163,700	9,964,600	8,199,100	2,508,700	1,478,300	1,030,400	1983
18,754,400	10,288,600	8,465,800	2,590,200	1,526,300	1,063,900	1984

Table 5

Rural and Urban Population Distribution by Sex 1975-1984 *

YEAR		Total Population			Rural Population			Urban Population		
		Total	Male	Female	Total	Male	Female	Total	Male	Female
1975	No	74,523,100	37,632,100	36,891,000	58,873,300	29,929,400	29,143,900	15,649,800	7,902,700	7,747,100
	%	100.0			79.0			21.0		
1976	No	76,409,654	38,584,781	37,824,873	59,446,710	30,018,959	29,427,751	16,962,943	8,565,821	8,397,122
	%	100.0			77.8			22.2		
1977	No	78,059,300	39,416,800	38,642,500	59,793,500	30,193,200	29,600,200	18,265,800	9,223,500	9,042,300
	%	100.0			76.6			23.4		
1978	No	80,595,500	40,698,500	39,897,000	60,769,000	30,686,700	30,082,300	19,826,500	10,011,800	9,814,700
	%	100.0			75.4			24.6		
1979	No	83,216,200	42,021,900	41,144,300	61,746,400	31,180,200	30,566,200	21,469,800	10,841,700	10,628,100
	%	100.0			74.2			25.8		
1980	No	85,922,500	43,388,300	42,534,200	62,723,500	31,673,500	31,050,000	23,199,000	11,714,800	11,484,200
	%	100.0			73.0			27.0		
1981	No	88,716,200	44,799,300	43,916,900	64,053,100	32,345,100	31,708,000	24,663,100	12,454,200	12,208,900
	%	100.0			72.2			27.8		
1982	No	91,601,000	46,256,000	45,345,000	65,403,100	33,026,800	32,376,300	26,197,900	13,229,200	12,968,700
	%	100.0			71.4			28.6		
1983	No	94,579,700	47,760,200	46,819,500	66,773,300	33,718,700	33,054,600	27,806,400	14,041,500	13,764,900
	%	100.0			70.6			29.4		
1984	No	97,655,100	49,313,200	48,341,900	68,163,200	34,420,600	33,742,600	29,491,900	14,892,600	14,599,300
	%	100.0			69.8			30.2		

* SOURCE: Compiled from data from the National Planning Office and the National Population Bureau.

146

Table 6

Percentage of Rural/Urban Population in Nigeria *

Population type	Percentage by years						
	1950	1960	1970	1975	1980	1985	1990
Rural	89.5	86.9	83.6	81.8	79.6	77.0	73.9
Urban	10.5	13.1	16.4	18.2	20.4	23.0	26.1

* From United Nations, DIESA, "Demographic Indicators of Countries: Estimates and Projections as Assessed in 1980", ST/ESA/SER.A/82, (Sales No. E.82.XIII.5), 1982.

Table 6 shows that increase of urban population equals the decrease undergone by the rural population. It is therefore evident that the rural population's losses have become the gain of the urban population. This then clearly establishes the fact that the phenomenon of rural/urban migration is the result of Nigeria's neglect of the rural areas in the course of its development process.

In numerical terms Table 7 shows the projection, in percentages, of the growth of some thirteen Nigerian urban population centres, namely: Abeokuta, Ado Ekiti, Benin City, Enugu, Ibadan, Ilorin, Jos, Kaduna, Kano, Lagos, Mushin, Maiduguri and Port Harcourt.

Table 8 shows the comparative growth rates for Nigerian urban and rural centres. Whilst the figures show a consistent increase in the urban population from the 1950-55 to 1985-90 period; for the rural areas a modest increase was recorded up to 1975-80; stabilized at the same level for the period 1980-85, and the beginning of a decline in 1985-90. Even then, the growth rates for the urban centres maintained levels that were throughout more than double the growth rates of the rural population.

147

Table 7
Percentage Urban Population Growth in Nigeria *

Urban Centres	Specific Years					Overall Period Growth up to	Annual Mean Overall Growth by
	1950	1960	1970	1980	1990	1990	1990
Nigeria	—	56.94	59.68	64.40	73.28	613.91	15.35
Abeokuta	—	—	54.41	46.67	50.00	239.71	7.99
Ado Ekiti	—	—	—	189.60	95.11	465.03	23.25
Benin City	—	—	—	27.73	40.31	79.21	3.96
Enugu	—	—	52.48	46.75	50.00	235.64	7.86
Ibadan	—	33.80	25.43	33.79	33.61	200.00	5.00
Ilorin	—	—	232.77	194.95	117.64	2,036.13	67.87
Jos	—	—	—	—	—	43.63	43.63
Kaduna	—	—	—	135.15	92.80	353.56	17.68
Kano	—	71.15	56.54	50.15	50.70	441.42	11.04
Lagos	—	90.64	94.81	81.21	65.12	1,011.23	25.28
Mushin	—	—	—	168.73	107.90	458.69	22.93
Maiduguri	—	—	—	65.70	60.70	166.28	8.31
Port Harcourt	—	—	72.22	63.13	58.76	346.03	11.53

* This table was constructed with data supplied in: United Nations, DIESA, *Patterns of Urban and Rural Population Growth*, ST/ESA/SER.A/68, (Sales No. E.79.XIII.9), Table 48, pp. 127-128 (corrigendum).

Table 8
Nigerian Annual Urban/Rural Growth Rate *

Population type	Growth rates						
	1950-55	1960-65	1965-70	1970-75	1975-80	1980-85	1985-90
Urban	4.6	5.0	5.1	5.2	5.5	5.8	5.9
Rural	2.0	2.4	2.5	2.6	2.7	2.7	2.6

* From "Democratic Indicators of Countries: Estimates and Projections as Assessed in 1980".

148

Urban growth rate in Nigeria is extremely high: it has not only maintained a higher level than world and African rates as from the 1950-60 period, but also the highest West African rate as from the 1960-70 period. It would appear, therefore, that Nigerian urban centres have been exposed to higher pressures than those at world, African and even West African levels (see Table 9).

Table 9

Average Annual Growth Rates of Urban Centres *
in Africa, West Africa and World Total

	1950-60	*1960-70*	*1970-75*	*1975-80*	*1980-90*
World total	3.35	2.91	2.84	2.93	2.93
Africa	4.42	4.85	4.97	5.10	5.00
West Africa	4.97	4.87	5.10	5.34	5.43

* From "Patterns of Urban and Rural Population Growth", Table 5, p. 13.

Table 7 shows that Ilorin, Lagos, Ado Ekiti, Mushin and Kaduna are at the very top of the list of urban centres in which rapid urbanization is likely to become a prominent criminogenic factor. The next category includes Port Harcourt and Kano, followed by Abeokuta and Enugu. The same applies, in descending order, to Ila, Zaria and Ede (not included in the table). It therefore becomes imperative to do something about halting this rural/urban drift. When in fact, Table 7 is read within the context of Table 9, the need to act becomes more compelling.

In terms of aetiology of crime, the phenomenon of massive rural/urban migration becomes significant when the migrant group consists mainly of young able bodied citizens, usually with only the first level (primary) edu-

149

cation, and mostly in the juvenile age group. Emigration atomizes the family thereby neutralizing the youth's most fundamental traditional social control bonds. With the neutralization of the family's ability to guide and control its jurisdiction, the migrant youth in the host community tries to exist without the influence of the strongest medium capable of enhancing his continued socialization. The young migrant is also often disappointed in his dream of finding suitable employment in the urban centre that will sustain him adequately. Moreover, he joins the labour force, when he is able to secure employment, at an age when he is not emotionally ready for such a level of burden and responsibility. Furthermore, he does not usually have access to urban facilities and utilities, and is consequently, forced to join what can be described as "the marginal population", who reside in the shanties of the urban centres. In such a situation, a youth without his family's love and control, without adequate housing, without suitable employment and without adequate financial resources for his maintenance will, of necessity, become an alienated member of the community in which he now resides and bound to be in conflict, attitudinally, with his host community — which he invariably perceives as hostile towards him.

Anyone familiar with Fregier's description of the "dangerous classes"[14] is bound to shudder at the prospects of nurturing such groups in urban centres. When a youth is viewed in the contexts of the ecological theories of crime causation[15] and the delinquent subculture theories,[16] operating within the framework of the theories of broken homes,[17] differential association,[18] economic conditions,[19] culture conflict[20] and anomie,[21] it is clear that he is a potential recruit for the rank and file of the criminal population. Invariably, it is such youths who have so far constituted the "labourers" for armed robbery gangs, the peak-age for which is 17 to 23 years. They also abound in other areas of property offences, such as stealing, burglary and housebreaking, as well as in those of personal offences like assault, indecent assaults, and rape.[22] The migrant youth, whose profile is given above, also finds himself absorbed by a very highly concentrated and heterogeneous population. These factors are strongly responsible for the culture conflict and for the anomic situations referred to above. The relative economic welfare of the main host population tends to cause conflict and antisocial reaction in the socially marginated migrant youth.[23]

It is clear, therefore, that the dangers arising from over-concentration of development efforts in urban centres continues to pose enormous social pathological dangers to our society and its health. Consequently, for the sake of economic wisdom Nigeria needs to review urgently the imbalance resulting from the biased developmental focus in order to remove or, at least, to reduce the criminogenic factors analysed above.

Rapid Population Growth

The World Bank has recently noted that "(r)apid population growth is a development problem ... (particularly) in

Table 10

Nigeria – Selected Population Indicators *

Population indicators	1950/ 1955	1960/ 1965	1965/ 1970	1970/ 1975	1975/ 1980	1980/ 1985	1985/ 1990
Net reproduction rate	1.87	2.09	2.20	2.30	2.40	2.51	2.53
Crude birth rate/1,000	51.80	51.80	51.00	50.30	49.80	49.50	47.80
Crude death rate/1,000	29.00	24.10	21.80	19.70	17.80	16.00	14.10
Natural population increase/1,000		22.80	27.70	29.20	30.60	32.00	33.50	33.70

* From "Demographic Indicators of Countries: Estimates and Projections as Assessed in 1980", p. 166, Sales No. E.82.XIII.5, ibid.

151

countries where the population is still largely dependent on agriculture, and the amount of new land or other resources is limited ... progress in the face of rapid population growth will be extraordinarily difficult." [24]

It is clear from Tables 10 to 12 below, that Nigeria's rates of populations growth (Table 10) are not only higher than those for the African Region as a whole (Table 11), but also higher than those for the World as a whole (Table 12).

It is estimated that the decline in net reproduction rates will begin over the 1990-95 period (2.49), and reach their lowest level in 2020-25 (1.38). The same is true as regards natural population increase rates, 33.3 in 1990-95 decreasing to 19.9 in 2020-25.

Table 11

Africa – Selected Population Indicators *

Population indicators	1950/ 1955	1960/ 1965	1965/ 1970	1970/ 1975	1975/ 1980	1980/ 1985	1985/ 1990
Net production rate	1.82	2.02	2.10	2.16	2.24	2.30	2.30
Crude birth rate/1,000	47.90	47.90	46.90	46.20	46.00	45.60	44.10
Crude death rate/1,000	27.40	22.80	20.60	18.90	17.20	15.60	13.90
Natural population increase/1,000	20.50	25.10	26.30	27.30	28.80	30.00	30.20

* From "Demographic Indicators Estimates and Projections as Assessed in 1980", p. 166, Sales No. E.82.XIII, 5, ibid.

Crude birth rates started to decline in 1965-70 (51.00), and should reach 25.80 in 2020-25; whilst crude death rates started to decline over the 1960-65 period (24.00) and should reach 6.0 in 2020-25.

The decline of net reproduction rates commences in 1990-95 (2.25) and reaches 1.36 in 2020-25. Natural increase rates decline from 29.8 in 1990-95 to 19.00 in 2020-25; whilst crude birth rates decline from 46.90 in 1965-70 to 25.50 in 2020-25, and crude death rates from 22.80 in 1965-70 to 6.50 in 2020-25.

Table 12

World Total – Selected Population Indicators*

Population indicators	1950/ 1955	1960/ 1965	1965/ 1970	1970/ 1975	1975/ 1980	1980/ 1985	1985/ 1990
Net reproduction rates	1.67	1.80	1.79	1.72	1.55	1.47	1.40
Crude birth rate/1,000	36.30	34.80	33.10	31.50	28.50	27.50	26.50
Crude death rate/1,000	18.90	15.10	13.60	12.50	11.40	10.60	10.10
Natural population increase/1,000	17.40	19.70	19.50	19.00	17.10	16.90	16.40

* From "Demographic Indicators Estimates and Projections as Assessed in 1980", p. 64, Sales No. E.82.XIII, 5, ibid.

Net reproduction rates decrease from 1.79 in 1965-70 to 1.09 in 2020-25. The same is true for net increase rates which are 19.50 in 1965-70 and 9.50 in 2020-25. Crude birth rates and crude death rates respectively decline by 34.80 and

Table 13

Population Density per Square Kilometres*

$ (£) 1950	1960	1970	1975	1980	1985
31.86 (+20.14% over)	52.21 (+63.87%)	71.32 (+36.60%)	80.81 (+13.35%)	95.50 (+18.18%)	112.87 (+18.19%)
1940			(33.90)		

* Calculated from figures supplied by the then Ministry of National Planning. These figures show an increase of 354.27% in 1985 over the figure for 1950.

153

15.10 in 1960-65, and 17.9 and 8.4 in 2020-25. In terms of population density, the pressure, in fact, becomes more evident when one considers the population growth in relation to the available land area (see Table 13).

Table 13 shows that available land is becoming rapidly crowded, and when read in conjunction with Table 9 above, the urgent need to do something about population control is evident.

In the aetiological sense, such density tends to result in acute shortage of housing which, in turn, encourages the emergence of squatter settlements. By their very nature, squatter settlements are illegal and one needs not look far to discover that the milieu underlying the formation and persistence of such settlements no doubt symptomises a pattern of behaviour favourable to the violation of the law.[25] In such a neighbourhood, the emergence and perpetuation can be expected of: delinquent subculture,[26] neighbourhood criminality,[27] and dangerous categories — fuelled by the theories of differential association, with a possible interplay of Gabriel Tarde's theory of imitation.[28]

Besides housing and residential issues as resultant criminogenic factors due to rapid population growth, this factor is also closely linked with economic conditions with strong potentials for criminogenic consequences.

Economic Conditions

The data presented in Tables 1 to 7 all have the direct economic implications referred to earlier. Economic factors that can have criminogenic effects, such as unemployment, inflation, gross domestic product, *per capita* income, factors relating to balance of payments and credit worthiness of the country, as well as composite consumer price index, can now be examined (see Tables 14 to 18).

Table 14

Unemployment and Inflation Rates in Percentages *

Year	Unemployment Rate	Inflation Rate
1975	4.50	14.30
1976	4.30	23.90
1977	4.46	15.90
1978	4.44	16.60
1979	4.42	11.80
1980	4.40	9.90
1981	4.57	22.30
1982	4.74	6.40
1983	4.90	23.20
1984	6.30	40.00

Unemployment Rates Broken into Rural/Urban Rates

Year	Rural	Urban
1983	2.4	7.3
1984	4.4	7.9
1985	3.0	9.7

* Source: Ministry of National Planning, March 1986.

Table 15

Gross Domestic Products at Current Prices *

	1975	1976	1977	1978	1979
Gross Domestic Products (Nm)	21,778.73	27,571.45	32,510.37	35,454.70	43,105.81

	1980	1981	1982	1983	1984
Gross Domestic Products (Nm)	49,754.87	52,255.34	55,679.34	55,226.21	56,716.27

* Supplied by the National Planning Office of the Ministry of National Planning in March, 1986.

When one examines the data on foreign reserves, the relationship between the magnitude of our imports and the meagreness of our exports, the levels of our net domestic credit, our unemployment rates, inflation rates coupled with the pattern of composite consumer price index, and the pattern of our *per capita* income, the seriousness of the Nigerian economy becomes clear. In 1975, 1977, 1978, 1981 and 1982 importations exceeded exportations. The level of international reserves dropped in 1976, 1977, 1978, rose through 1979-1980, and started to drop again in 1981-1982. As of 1974 the lowest ebb was reached in 1983, when it was reportedly down to N781,6 million; it rose to N1,1 billion and N1,2 billion in 1984 and 1985 respectively.[29] Prices steadily rose from 1976 onwards; whilst unemployment steadily rose as of 1979. Our erratic inflation rate pattern settled to a steady rise, standing at 40.00 in 1984. Yet, *per capita* income faced a downward trend since the 1982-83 twist. Table 2 shows that as from 1980 the contribution of the mining, quarrying and petroleum group of sectors has been declining; although the agriculture (crops and other) and livestock group of sectors appear to have picked up again as from 1981. However, the increase of this group's contribution could most probably be more particularly attributed to the decline in oil revenue,[30] from the latter half of 1981 onwards, rather than to the actual increase of contribution on the part of the group of sectors. The present slump in oil price is bound to add to the relatively serious economic problems Nigeria is facing.

Table 16

Gross Domestic Products Per Capita at Current Prices *

Year	GDP Per Capita (N)
1975	291.90
1976	357.40
1977	407.58
1978	431.00
1979	505.49
1980	564.29
1981	573.17
1982	590.65
1983	566.58
1984	562.74

* Calculated from the new GDP and population figures supplied in March 1986 by the Ministry of National Planning.

Again, on examining the pattern of the Fourth Plan disbursements in the various sectors revealed that, with one exception, the previous governments did not actually evaluate the seriousness of the situation (see Table 19).

Table 17

Other Economic Factors, Value in N¹m*

Economic Factors	1975	1976	1977	1978	1979	1980	1981	1982
Level of International Reserves	3,582.4	3,282.4	2,738.7	1,192.4	3,043.0	5,445.0	2,424.8	1,026.5
Exports, Goods & NFS	5,322.7	6,593.2	8,519.7	7,189.4	10,726.1	14,806.0	11,449.1	9,268.2
Imports, Goods & NFS	5,030.9	6,573.4	8,702.6	9,260.7	9,213.3	11,472.6	14,408.5	13,405.5
Net Domestic Credit **	—	2,610.5	5,529.4	8,059.9	8,855.2	10,780.1	16,261.4	19,768.2

* The first three factors were extracted from Table 18, whilst the last factor. (**) was extracted from Table 24 of "Economic and Social Statistics Bulletin".

158

Table 18

Composite Consumer Price Index *

Component	All Items	Accomoda-tion Fuel & light	Food	Drinks	Tobacco and Kola	Clothing	H. H. Goods and other Pur-chases	Trans-port	Other Services
Yearly Averages									
1976	123	109	122	132	143	135	145	139	148
1977	143	127	146	140	183	141	137	141	146
1978	167	131	172	154	186	176	147	158	156
1979	186	167	186	176	203	219	156	196	178
1980	205	170	200	188	229	270	182	197	235
1981	248	173	250	193	264	314	195	202	253
1982	267	180	272	208	278	335	213	224	296
1983	328	240	336	236	318	398	328	271	357

* This table was extracted from Table 41, page 40 of "Economic and Social Statistics Bulletin".

159

Table 19

Fourth Plan Disbursements by Functions. Federal Government *
(Percent)

Sector	1981	1982	1983
Economic sector	21.36	17.80	14.89
Social services	20.89	18.13	16.70
Environmental development	23.64	17.43	22.20
Administration	20.39	19.55	30.31

* From "Economic and Social Statistics Bulletin", p. 34, Table 35.

Table 19 shows that while disbursements to the economic sector and social services group decreased from 1982 onwards, those assigned to the administrative sector exceeded each of the other three sectors in 1982 and leaped up, in 1983, to a level which more than doubled the disbursement of the economic sector.

This situation led to a serious and structural deterioration of our economy. As a result, money was no longer available for the provision of adequate food, health services, education, and housing. The consequent shortage of goods and services brought about an increase in prices; and, coupled with a drop in external reserves, an increase in external and domestic debts.[31] All this ultimately resulted in the inability to pay for goods and services abroad and in the devaluation of the Naira,[32] thus causing the vicious spiral of inflation.[33] In turn, factories found it difficult to purchase raw materials to manufacture their products, which consequently led to large scale retrenchment of workers. This of course worsened the unemployment situation.[34] Many citizens who had been able to assist their unemployed dependents and relatives were themselves forced to join the unemployment scene. This situation widened the poverty striken class and, consequently, the number of the discontented and alienated groups of society. The spread of unemployment and consequential poverty was further aggravated by the government's various resorts to large-scale retrenchment of workers.

Poverty may force dependent family members, such as wives and children, to have to work. This results in a break in the traditional intra-family dependence pattern and even family unity. In extreme cases it can lead to separation of the spouses and/or children leaving home to look for work. Economic independence of the children at a very early age seems to make them less amenable to parental control and discipline, which may lead to behavioural difficulties, including involvement in crime.[35] Female employment, on the other hand, particularly when the woman has to bring up her children on her own, often results in the inability to maintain a satisfactory relationship with the children as the impossibility to provide the necessary amount and quality of parental discipline and supervision.[36]

In general or in specifically individual terms, unemployment may, on the one hand, result in poverty and, on the other, it may also be the result of poverty; and, as explained above, the consequent poverty may be criminogenic. Furthermore, unemployment may also lead to idleness. In Merton's typology the situational adjustment to this may be either retreatism (as in drug addiction or alcoholism) or rebellion, which may lead to malicious damage.[37] In this sense, unemployment leading to idleness can be said to be criminogenic. Unemployment may also be the result of affluent progress, as in the case of unplanned automation, which may lead to the retrenching of former manual operators. This, however, is not the case in Nigeria where retrenchments are the consequence of economic recession.

Employment, on the other hand, may also provide an opportunity to commit certain offences, such as corruption of/by public officials, stealing by bank employees, servants embezzlement of master's money, etc.

161

Furthermore, society's attitude towards certain crimes may conduct to its encouragement, e.g. swindling insurance companies which are themselves regarded as swindlers. An interesting example is the development of the banking industry, in particular, in relation to its lending functions. This practice grew out of public tolerance of the criminal practice which consisted in the conversion of customer's money by its early custodians. The tolerance of this criminal behaviour eventually became so widespread that it was legalised and regulated, giving birth to the banking industry as it as known today. In a certain sense, therefore, the crime, in retrospect, was "necessary".[38] On the other hand, public intolerance tends to discourage such crimes as the swindling of a poor individual's meagre salary, the defiling of a seven year old child, or the killing of a respectable citizen in his home; an extreme example of intolerance is the lynching of armed robbers through "tyre burning". Public intolerance is very high, and public feeling of insecurity increases whenever it is felt that police protection is inadequate; at such times lynching increases.[39]

Again, unbearably high inflationary pressures in a widespread poverty stricken context generates considerable amount of tension and frustration in the individual citizen.[40] Whenever the individual's inhibitional mechanism reaches its breaking point he may, in protest, commit economic crimes or inflict personal violence.

It is a favourite aetiological theory, particularly among theorists who accept the Marxist ideology, that poverty can be a cause of crime.[41]

Affluence and prosperity have also been identified as criminogenic factors.[42] Thus, poverty has been suggested as a possible aetiological explanation for such crimes as stealing, burglary, housebreaking, and robbery;[43] whilst affluence has been suggested as the explanation for an incidence in fraudulent offences, such as forgery, cheating, and achieving a goal through false pretences.[44] These are, by

162

and large, offences that are committed as a consequence of the availing of an opportunity for their perpetration.[45] Such opportunities tend to dwindle at times of economic recession.[46]

Housing

It is obvious from the above described socio-economic profile of the country, namely: massive rural/urban migration, rapid urbanization leading to high population density and its overconcentration in marginal areas, depressed economic conditions, and the spread of poverty arising out of high rates of inflation and unemployment, that housing is in very short supply. In fact, the United Nations has estimated that, on the average, for every urban housing unit in Africa, ten new families migrate from rural areas to urban centres.[47] Furthermore, the World Bank has observed that more than half the urban population of developing countries live in slums and squatter settlements, and half of these have no access to water supply or facilities for the disposal of human waste.[48]

Aetiologically speaking, slums have been known to feature prominently in ecological theories;[49] whilst squatter settlements actually involve unilateral land invasion by migrants, or illegal land deals (such as sale of land by non-owners or against legal prohibitions), and illegal developments (such as those that infringe various town planning regulations). These illegal practices are in themselves crimes, in addition to other criminogenic factors associated with the existence of slums and settlements such as subculture factors, culture conflicts, family factors, economic factors, etc. It is within this context that one can understand the reasons for the high incidence of criminality in areas like Ajegunle, Mushin and Maroko in Lagos State. Numerous researchers have variously confirmed high criminality rates for these areas.[50]

163

It is pertinent at this stage to advert briefly to the intervention of the Land Use Act [51] in this area. This Act aimed, *inter alia*, at limiting the size of land to be allocated in urban areas, to half an hectre per person, with a view to preventing the activities of land speculators and making land readily available to Nigerians irrespective of their place of origin. It is doubtful whether one can say that land is now more readily available to the common man than it was before the Act. In fact, it would appear that, in practice, the Southern common man is worse off now than he was before the Land Use Act. Before he could gain access to the use of land through his family connections; whilst at present he must go through the Governor of his State. It cannot be seriously argued that drivers, mechanics, factory workers, clerks, messengers and cleaners (— the Nigerian common man —) have, on their own, the necessary leverage to obtain government allocation of land for housing purposes. Consequently, it seems that the Act has, in actual fact, reduced the chances of the common man becoming owner/occupier of his own residence, thereby facing the prospects of never leaving the ranks of tenant/occupier.

The housing loan situation further confirms this sad situation, as it is doubtful any bank will operate a policy which will make it possible for the common man to borrow enough money to build a house for his six to eight-member family. Everything in the rules governing loans appear to be loaded against his chances. Also the limitation of urban land holding to no more than half an hectre has become a hindrance to private companies wishing to participate in housing development. Such companies, with their enormous resources, could have gone into house building and have operated convenient mortgage systems — like those operative in other parts of the world; this would have notably supplemented government efforts in providing houses for needy Nigerian citizens. Such a feat is definitely beyond the ability of any single government of a developing country, including that of Nigeria. I believe that the existing gap between expectations placed on the Land Use Act and its practical application could be "an eye opener" to the possibilities of a socialist system being totally imposed in Nigeria. Furthermore, it is not certain that private land speculators and shylocks have not now been replaced by governmental equivalents.

The criminogenic implications of the acute housing shortage are deducible from the approach to an ecological explanation of crime causation which considers tenant-occupation the resultant high mobility rate and lack of commitment and integration to the immediate community, and ultimately to the larger community, as very significant.[52]

Education

The Nigerian Constitution directs the government to ensure the provision of "Equal and adequate educational opportunities at all levels".[53] It would appear from Table 20 below, that there is some evidence that all governments have taken steps consistent with this directive, since enrolments in the educational institutions continued to increase from 1975 to 1984 at all levels. In fact, the percentage of primary school children in relation to the portion of primary school age population increased as follows: 1975 - 48.33%; 1979 - 71.88%; 1980 - 78.12%; and 1984 - 84.38%.

Enrolments in secondary level institutions have also increased, *intra se*, as well as in their proportional relationship to the primary school enrolments for those same four years, as follows: 1975 - 11.86%; 1979 - 11.06%; 1980 - 12.82%; 1984 - 20.56%. It is clear that as the institutional level increases, the proportional relationship reduces. In fact, there is a considerable number of overall dropouts between the primary school and admissions to the secondary and tertiary institutions. This is clearly reflected in Table 21 which shows that dropouts increased by 124.08% between 1975 and 1984. See also Table 20.

166

Table 20

Total Enrolments in Educational Institutions 1975 to 1984 *

No	Levels of education	1975	1976	1977	1978	1979	1980	1981	1982	1983	1984
1.	Primary Schools	5,950,297	6,165,547	8,100,324	9,867,961	10,798,550	12,117,483	13,760,030	14,397,946	14,533,676	14,876,220
2.	Secondary Grammar/ Commercial Schools	705,516	601,652	730,899	913,648	1,194,640	1,553,345	1,993,417	2,503,952	2,899,015	3,059,088
3.	Secondary Technical/ Vocational Colleges	25,943	27,843	20,858	40,538	46,712	61,856	67,943	83,899	75,392	76,242
4.	Grade II Teacher's Training Colleges	112,995	116,222	144,174	176,926	210,051	249,512	282,244	292,429	260,037	267,335
5.	Polytechnics	—	11,993	17,454	14,882	16,709	35,777	42,381	52,226	61,223	70,455
6.	Universities	26,448	31,511	38,877	41,811	46,384	57,772	70,395	85,210	96,233	104,380
7.	GRAND TOTAL	6,821,203	6,954,768	9,052,586	11,055,837	12,313,046	14,075,745	16,216,410	17,278,226	17,925,576	18,453,720

* Compiled from the figures supplied by the Federal Ministry of Education, Lagos, 1985.

Table 21

Estimates of School Dropouts and their Percentage Proportions to Youth Population of 12-30 Years *

Year	Estimates of school dropouts	% estimates of dropouts	Youth population 12-30 years	% school dropouts 12-30 population
1975	827,816	83.47	32,034,700	2.58
1976	879,298	85.57	35,890,935	2.45
1977	1,173,226	86.90	36,664,800	3.20
1978	1,419,898	86.33	37,857,000	3.75
1979	1,515,063	84.18	39,088,200	3.88
1980	1,656,900	82.04	40,359,200	4.11
1981	1,844,373	80.42	41,671,600	4.43
1982	1,853,891	77.35	43,026,500	4.31
1983	1,827,300	75.44	44,425,700	4.11
1984	1,854,991	74.82	45,361,100	4.09
Cumulative no. of dropouts by 1984	14,852,756		45,361,100	32.74

* Compiled from figures supplied by the Federal Ministry of Education, Lagos, 1985.

It is, therefore, to be expected that such a large cumulative school dropout population, coupled with an increase in unemployment and urban population, and combined with a decrease in *per capita* increase will augment community hardship — particularly the vulnerable 12 to 30 years age group — thereby propelling an increase in criminality.

In 1984, this age group totalled 45,361,100. Cumulatively school dropout population reached 14,852,756, thereby constituting 32.71% of the 12 to 30 years age group, (— a sort of marginated population —) as against 20.69% of the same age group in 1975. This, therefore, means that from 1975 to 1984 there was an increase of 58.24% of the marginated population within the vulnerable age group. Thus, it would appear that these grim socio-economic factors could be adduced to explain the record crime figure of 372,558 and a crime rate of 381,50 for Nigeria in 1984.

It is important to observe that at the conclusion of whatever educational programme a youth has been exposed to — whether total or partial — his expectations of gainful employment tend to raise. The thwarting of such expectations due to the lack of job vacancies might well cause discontent in the educated youth and alienate him from society. He may respond, according to Merton's anomie theory, by chosing a situational adjustment of innovation (e.g. robbery or stealing), rebellion (e.g. malicious damage) or retreatism (e.g. drug abuse and addiction).[54] The criminogenic situation would be still more serious if the educational ladder was blocked by lack if vacancies in post primary institutions. The resultant acute frustration typifies the youths' adjustment to innovation, rebellion or retreatism. Statistics on robbery and drugs tend to support an association between these respective response patterns and school dropout. By and large, the increase in the number of school dropouts from 1975 to 1982 appears to match the increase in the number of crimes: up to 1980 for robbery — with the exception of 1978 when narcotics/drug offences prevailed.

Furthermore, we have fashioned our educational pattern and programmes after certain British and/or American models. This practice has imposed on our children and youths the value systems underlying those policies and programmes. Such models subject Nigerian children to mental culture conflict, which can lead to behavioural difficulties, including criminal behaviour.[55] The problem is further accentuated by the fact that these educational models have been imported from relatively stable societies which no longer seek to emphasize their social differences. We are applying these models in a developing society, with rapid social change and with very heterogeneous communities which, almost above the concept of nationhood (still in its infancy), tend to emphasize that of ethnicity. These models are by now quite glaringly unsuitable, and the factors stated above seek to give a clear indication of the mental culture conflict element that involves children and youths under such educational systems. In fact, on a massive scale, it can escalate to anomie in a Durkheimean sense. Therefore, a revitalization of education as a force for development and social cohesion is urgently needed.

It has become imperative that formal school education promotes basic values common to all sectors of our nation, and that the school be used to transmit and build a socialization process oriented towards social justice, co-operation, national solidarity and respect for others and the environment. The military regime that preceded the present civilian government, in its last days in power, appeared to make an attempt to commence action towards the development of these objectives. Thus, the National Pledge and a new National Anthem were introduced and are now regular features of opening and closing school sessions. These, in part, can be regarded as fulfilling some of these objectives, similar to the American school system of "flag salute". All State ministries of education should co-ordinate their efforts in this regard and direct their capabilities to the fulfillment of the objectives suggested above. In addition, educational materials (books, etc.) should be adopted to meet these objectives. The present practice of Nigerian/African authors aiming at securing foreign applause for a locally presented drama to a Nigerian/African audience should be clearly recognised as self-imposed mental apartheid, which we must all reject without any reservation whatsoever. The World Community has accepted that "(e)ducation is a machinery which must commence from the home. The formal edu-

169

cational system must of necessity build on the home foundation, if education is viewed from its eventual perspective of socialization. In this regard, book knowledge needs to be complemented with normative/legal, moral/religious, and civic education ... There was ... the need for such wide supportive educational outlook in the socialization programmes of youths ...".[56] Thus, the dichotomy between the home, as the socialization medium, and the school, as the skill and book knowledge training medium, should be eliminated. Both media should complement each other in the socialization processes. Accordingly, schools must be involved in and, just as much as they emphasize book knowledge, they should also emphasize the development in and acquisition by youths of acceptable standards of behaviour and socially acceptable value orientations. Consequently, schools should re-emphasize in their curricula subjects like civics and religious instruction.

It is pertinent at this stage to advert our attention to the need to integrate our educational policies and programmes with our political, economic and social policies and programmes. Education has hitherto been seen as a mere tool for producing "an enlightened man", with qualifications which will enable him to earn his living. This is not necessarily a bad idea. However, such should not be our main purpose in education. Our main educational objective should be human resource development. In practice this means that, to begin with, stock should be taken and human resources assessed. In other words, how many lawyers, doctors, para-medical personnel, physicists, technicians, etc. — and of what type and level — are needed in Nigeria? Our educational system should be then geared specifically towards the production of the estimated quantity and quality of ascertained manpower needs. An educational system, planned with a view to human resource development is not only bound to support and accelerate the pace of development, but would also constitute a good control mechanism for unemployment rate. There is no gainsaying the fact that a system of education capable of preventing a rise in unemployment rate and capable of adequately supplying specific manpower needs is to be preferred to one which bears higher and higher rates of unemployment, including among graduate youths. In other words, not efficient enough to supply specific manpower needs.

In order to find a remedy to this situation it is necessary that the Nigerian government(s) carries out a manpower survey in the immediate future to determine the specific needs of the country. Subsequently, an educational policy and programme(s) should be devised to ensure the production of such manpower.

At this point it is, therefore, pertinent that attention be given here to the new educational policy, popularly referred to as the "6-3-3-4" system. This system envisages a shift of emphasis to science- and technology-based disciplines. Firstly, as stated above, the policy has not yet answered the question: what type of scientists and technologists do we need, and in what number? Secondly, the curriculum operating under the system does not appear to have the potential to inculcate a "science culture" in the Nigerian child that is being subjected to its programmes. On the other hand, unless the education system clearly orientates the child from its earliest grades, future state expectations for the educational system will not be achieved. The difficulties of our Universities in filling their science admission quotas have proved to be a clear testimony to the present state of affairs.

Crime trends in Nigeria

The nature, extent and trends of criminality over a ten-year period spanning 1975-1984 will now be examined.[57]

It is clear from Table 22 that, except for 1979, when a 7.59% decrease was recorded, criminality steadily increased

171

Table 22

General Crime Figures *

Years	Figures	% of total criminality	Rates per 100,000 of population	Annual % increase/ decrease
1975	193,633	100	259.83	+ 0.60
1976	214,286	100	280.44	+10.66
1977	219,112	100	280.70	+ 2.25
1978	220,475	100	273.56	+ 0.62
1979	203,733	100	244.82	− 7.59
1980	210,908	100	245.46	+ 3.52
1981	253,952	100	286.25	+20.40
1982	271,240	100	296.11	+ 6.80
1983	311,961	100	329.84	+15.01
1984	372,558	100	381.50	+19.42

* This table, as well as tables 23 to 26, have been compiled from the Nigerian Police statistics for 1977 to 1984.

throughout the decade. As against a population increase of 31.04% in 1984 over the figure for 1975, criminality rose from 1975 to 1984 by 92.40%. It is clear, therefore, that inasmuch as the rate of increase in criminality was 2.98 times that of population increase for that period, the increase in criminality was not necessarily attributable to mere increase in population. In fact, the recorded 43.83% increase in the rate of criminality between 1975 and 1984 (by 100,000 population) belies any attempt to attribute the increase to mere population growth. Structurally speaking, the increase of the 12-30 age group amounted to 41.60%; whilst in terms of its proportion to the total population, its increase amounted to 58.53%.[58]

The group of offences against persons now includes murder, manslaughter, attempted murder, attempted suicide

Table 23

Offences against Persons

Years	Figures	% of total criminality	Rates per 100,000 of population	Annual % increase/ decrease
1975	56,197	29.24	75.41	+ 0.59
1976	58,555	27.33	76.63	+ 4.19
1977	72,424	33.05	92.78	+ 23.68
1978	68,521	31.07	85.02	− 5.38
1979	64,726	29.35	77.78	− 5.53
1980	55,875	26.49	65.03	− 13.67
1981	64,346	25.33	72.53	+ 15.16
1982	88,433	32.60	96.54	+ 37.43
1983	93,752	30.05	99.13	+ 6.01
1984	112,116	30.09	114.81	+ 19.58

grievious harm and wounding, assaults, rape and indecent assaults, and unnatural offences. The participation of this group of offences in the structure of total criminality was 29.24 in 1975, 33.05 in 1977, 31.05 in 1978, 25.33 (its lowest) in 1981, rising again to 32.60 in 1982, and 30.09 in 1984. Except for 1981, where unlike the percentage share, the crime rate rose, both measures followed a similar pattern. The number of crimes covered by this group increased from 56,197 in 1975 to 112,116 in 1984: a 99.51% increase; on the other hand the population increase of the 18-30 age group — the age most involved in the commission of these offences — amounted to only 43.19%, out of which the male population increased by 56.75%. Hence, as mentioned with reference to Table 23, the explanation must go beyond the mere increase in population, even if this includes the age group at risk. It seems that additional explanation must be sought for in some other factors, like the growing culture

173

conflict caused by the increasing importation of foreign culture through the mass media, educational materials and foreign technology. Also, the increasing economic hardship put greater burden on earning money, consequently imposing long working hours away from the home for both parents, thus, leaving their children alone. At the same time the children are exposed to the stark reality of their economic situation. Further, the frustation of the ever increasing number of school dropouts, is conducive to the effects of the combination of Merton's anomie: lack of family supervision, differential association and delinquent sub-culture.[59] Also, the deprivation experienced by parents as a consequence of the 1967-1970 Civil War has manifested its impact through the resulting so-called "Delinquent Generations", in particular from 1980 onwards.[60]

Table 24

Offences against Property

Years	Figures	% of total criminality	Rates per 100,000 of population	Annual % increase/ decrease
1975	108,282	52.82	145.30	− 5.35
1976	115,688	53.98	151.41	+ 6.84
1977	100,416	45.82	128.64	−13.20
1978	107,879	48.93	133.85	+ 7.43
1979	109,308	53.65	131.35	+ 1.32
1980	104,780	49.68	121.95	− 4.14
1981	91,856	36.17	103.54	−12.33
1982	131,408	48.44	143.46	+43.05
1983	145,607	46.67	15.95	+10.80
1984	187,610	50.35	192.12	+28.84

174

This group increased from 108, 282 in 1975 to 187,610 in 1984, having a percentage increase of 73.26%, and a rate increase of 32.22%. However, its percentage share of total criminality of 52.82 in 1975, which rose to 53.98 in 1976 and 53.65 in 1979 fell to 50.35 in 1984 with its lowest ebb of 45.82 reached in 1977, followed by 46.67 in 1983. The increases were quite steady in the last three years, coinciding with the steady decrease in the national *per capita* income over the last five years of the decade, as well as with steady increase in the unemployment rate for the last four years of the decade and a worsening of the inflation rate, the worst peak being reached in 1984. When one adds to these a cumulative school wastage of 14,852,756, most of which emigrated to the urban centres, without being able to get the opportunities which they hoped to get in the cities, and constituting a marginal population, without access to the various urban facilities, it is not difficult to see the

Table 25

Other Offences – Social Disorganisation Crimes

Years	Figures	% of total criminality	Rates per 100,000 of population	Annual % increase/ decrease
1975	16,502	8.52	22.14	+ 29.65
1976	19,820	9.24	25.94	+ 20.11
1977	20,848	9.51	26.71	+ 5.18
1978	19,541	8.86	24.25	– 6.26
1979	15,323	7.52	18.41	– 21.58
1980	18,177	8.61	21.16	+ 18.63
1981	16,917	6.66	19.07	– 6.93
1982	29,058	10.71	31.72	+ 71.77
1983	23,402	7.50	24.74	– 19.40
1984	26,009	6.98	26.63	+ 11.14

emergence of innovation and rebellion in Merton's typology of anomie response, and the eventual crystallisation of criminal sub-culture and criminal areas. These combinations can possibly explain the trend of property offences during this period. The offences in this group include theft and other stealing, robbery and extortion, burglary, house breaking, store breaking, false pretences and cheating, forgery, receiving stolen property, unlawful possession and arson.

Social disorganisation crimes include gambling, offences against public order, perjury, and bribery and corruption. In the first three years under examination, crimes within this group rose throughout (even though the percentage of increase consistently dropped). In 1978 the figure, when expressed as a percentage of total criminality, dropped below the 1977 figure and remained there until 1982 when it rose above 1977 levels. However, from 1980 onwards it rose and dropped alternately until 1984. Nonetheless, the overall increase from 1975 to 1982 was 76.09%. The pattern from 1979 onward can possibly be explained by, among other things, the imitation theory with respect to bribery and corruption and anomie with respect to offences against public order, keeping in mind the political climate in 1979 — transition from thirteen years of military rule to a democratic presidential system as yet unknown in Nigeria which, before the military take-over of 1966 practised the Westminster system of democracy. 1980 was the period when those involved in the implementation of the new system were as yet unsure of themselves and the system. The emergence of new confidence in running the political system characterized 1981; eventually overconfidence took over which resulted in a reckless mismanagement of the economy. These circumstances yielded the first economic crisis in 1982, when the Federal Government was forced to introduce some austerity measures which sought to set out some guidelines regarding economic policies, particularly with respect to transactions involving the spending of foreign exchange. At that time social disorganization crimes recorded a slight drop. However, uncertainties, socio-political antagonisms (1983 was election year), and consequent social discontent over the conduction and results of the election — coupled with deteriorating economic situation and political tension — led, on 31 December 1983, to still another military take-over.

The new military government did not leave the citizens in any doubt as to the difficult times ahead of them. The various economic measures and the accompanying tightening of the national economy established more firmly the socio-cultural revolution conceived of as "the war against indiscipline" campaign (WAI), launched that same year. With so many things happening at once, and within such a short space of time, skepticism mingled with the earlier hope causing an increase of social disorganization crimes to 26,009 in 1984. It is hoped that when the various socio-economic and socio-cultural measures begin to show results, and social, political and economic stability is achieved again, the incidence of this group of offences will once again decrease. It is significant, however, that 1982 was the year in which this group of offences reached its peak in figures: 29,058; with a 10.71 percentage share of criminality, a rate of 31.72 and an annual increase of 71.77%. 1982 was a year of shock and dismay; a year in which citizens were really apprehensive about the social, political and economic conditions of the country. Figures for that year are given in the table that follows.

This group consists of miscellaneous crimes such as traffic offences, offences against liquor acts, and drug/narcotics offences. These offences increased by 246.09% from 1975 to 1984, with a rate increase of 164.08%. The increase can be understood, in part, by the social disorganisation explanation given above for Table 25. Another partial explanation could be the increased number of automobiles, the

Table 26

Offences against Local Acts

Years	Figures	% of total criminality	Rates per 100,000 of population	Annual % increase/ decrease
1975	12,652	6.53	16.98	+ 8.23
1976	19,820	9.24	25.94	+ 56.66
1977	25,425	11.60	32.57	+ 28.28
1978	24,534	11.12	30.44	− 3.50
1979	14,376	7.05	17.28	− 41.40
1980	32,076	15.20	37.33	+123.12
1981	37,598	14.80	42.38	+ 17.22
1982	44,018	16.22	48.05	+ 17.07
1983	48,965	15.69	51.77	+ 11.23
1984	43,787	11.75	44.84	− 10.57

improvement of road conditions, technological advancement, and education; in addition to socio-economic frustration theories — including the economic theory in both Durkheimean and Mertonian senses: culture conflict and delinquent sub-culture as well as imitation and differential association theories.

Crime control strategies

Within the context of development, consideration of crime control strategies must, of necessity, be viewed from the perspectives of formal and informal control measures. It is, therefore, proposed that the issue be considered within these perspectives in this section.

a) Traditional forms of social control

Factors like the extent of the community, strong kingship bonds — and consequent strong primary ties —, the reduced scale of social interaction, the localization and immediacy of the criminal justice system, and the importance of religious and mystical beliefs and sanctions, tended to contribute in no small way to ensuring conformity in traditional Nigerian societies. Also present were strong punitive measures such as expulsion and exile from one's community. These were quite effective because there were no alternative competing normative political or religious systems, and because the traditional Nigerian communities were essentially homogeneous with definitive authority systems.

However, external contacts through trade, foreign, missionary-influenced education and the embracing of an alien political system, created changes at various levels. These also brought about massive social changes related to modernization, modern urbanization and industrialization, all of which had a weakeningeffect on the homogeneity of the Nigerian urban communities, it eroded traditional authority, values, social control and sanctions, and created alternative and competing sources of possible orientation, motivation and legitimacy.

In addition, changes in demographic structure in relation to such variables as age, rural/urban and urban/urban migration — both of which lead to the development of metropolitan communities — also contribute to changes in the social structure and to the weakening of traditional trends of social control and synomy.[61] The situation has been further aggravated by the emergence of religious diversities, fuelled mainly by the spread of Christianity and Islam, changes in occupational structure,[62] and levels of literacy and education, as well as involvement in technology and with foreign culture.[63]

179

These factors could generate culture conflicts and, in extreme cases, anomie in the Durkheimean sense. In addition, migration, changes in occupational structure and, in particular, educational levels also have a tendency of weakening family ties, family authority and family autonomy.[64] It has, in fact, been suggested that such developmental factors have lead to an increase in crime, especially property offences such as stealing, corruption and forgery.[65] On the basis of Merton's anomie approach,[66] it has also been sustained that inequality in opportunities and material wealth might also have fuelled offences such as stealing, robbery, burglary and house/storebreaking.

However, citizens have also developed adaptive or adjustive mechanisms which have a tendency to reduce the adverse effects of rapid social change, urbanization and unplanned development, such as have been taking place in Nigeria. Examples of such mechanisms are voluntary, religious and ethnic associations, and friendship networks.

Voluntary associations have received extensive attention in the literature. They have been cited as constituting one of the major organizations used by migrants to cope with urban life in the early days of colonization and change. Kenneth Little's seminal work on their significance as modes of adjustment, remains unassailable. Other authors, such as Wallerstein, have identified their significance in the political sphere, whilst Okediji has pointed out further adjustments these associations are constrained to make, particularly in connection with the recruitment of domestic servants in Lagos.[67] Recent works on the importance of synoretic religion as source of strong social bonds and control, are almost non-existent, but contributions by J. D. Y. Peel on certain religious sects are relevant in the light of recent proliferation of such sects.[68] The importance of ethnic and religious bonds as strong elements of social control among migrant communities is seen in Cohen's work on Housa trading communities in Ibadan. Here Cohen shows the strong factors of endogamy, homogeneity and the uses to which these were put in politics and economics. He showed further how control is strengthened through the ritualization of political authority and the use of ritual moral sanctions.[69] Other sources of adjustment were stressed by Peace, whose emphasis here was on the use of friendship networks and the development of the concept of 'brother', which were used as instruments for managing social instability and creating bonds for assisting new migrants to Agege in getting jobs and settling in.[70] All these served as instruments of adjustment to change, but did not necessarily prevent the emergence of structural problems caused by 'change'.

b) Informal strategies for crime prevention and control

The informal method of crime prevention and control is essentially a survival of the traditional synomy bonds of social control. This is a result of the traditional social arrangement whereby a family, in the extended sense, lives in the 'compound', under a *pater familias* — the household head who may or may not be a chief. All family disputes are ultimately settled by him. If, however, he is unable to resolve these, he then refers the matter to the ward or communal authorities whose decision is usually final. This system is still predominantly in force in most Nigerian communities; it is mainly operative among the indigenous population, but it also operates among those migrants who reside in new areas and are under the protection of the local *pater familias*. This system is equivalent to the "King's Peace" under the old English Common Law.

Apart from the indigenous population, the system operates also among the immigrant population, on the analogy of the system described above, where the community is composed of those who have built up para-synomy mechanisms of voluntary associations, religious or ethnic associations, friendship ties, etc. This is because the immigrant himself is used to such a tradition in his home town or village.

To a much lesser extent, the system also operates among strangers since a Nigerian's (and indeed African's) first reaction to a violation of a person's rights is to seek redress by conciliatory means. Consequently, even when cases have entered the formal criminal process ambit, the parties concerned can always settle the matter out of the police station or the criminal court, usually with no objection on the part of officialdom, irrespective of whatever redress is agreed upon between the parties. Reconciliation is the central pivot of our traditional criminal justice system.[71] To Europeans and Americans, this may come under "diversion", however, for Africans, it is the normal and accepted method of settling disputes, civil or criminal.

From the statistical point of view, this system of dispute settlement contributes to a very high 'dark figure' rate.[72] It is only very serious cases like murder and armed robbery that are ordinarily no longer settled this way. Settlement outside police and judicial jurisdictions are rare in such cases. However, most other offences, including rape and defilement, are still not unusually dealt with by formal criminal justice unless the offender is a total stranger who does not have someone to intercede on his behalf. Burglary and housebreaking, on the other hand, are more readily reported to the police because they usually involve strangers. However, sometimes the offender is exposed to public ridicule and disgrace; this occurs particularly when an unsuccessful attempt has been committed, or when the offence was completed but the appropriated property was restored. In the more serious cases of burglary, involving threat of violence, or in the cases of robbery, such an offender risks being lynched; although ordinarily, he would be handed over to the police. It is clear, therefore, that the informal procedure of crime control is applied in most cases, except in the serious cases or in the case of strangers who are in no relationship with their victim or with someone known to their victim.

In the area of crime prevention, citizens' in the higher social strata employ a range of preventive measures. Apart from installing burglar-proof devices in their homes, and employing security guards to supplement police protection, citizens also form 'vigilante' groups for night-patrol in their areas of residence, in order to protect themselves against the various crimes mentioned, particularly property crimes.[73] These, of course, are only supplementary to ordinary police patrols.

Formal Crime Prevention and Control Strategies

Nigeria, like most developing countries, has its share of colonial heritage; and the English system of laws — including those governing administration of criminal justice — are still operating. Individualistic culture is inherent in this criminal justice system, while Nigerian and African culture in general is essentially communal as evidentiated in the preceeding subsection on traditional mechanisms of control which operate also in today's urban context. Yet, criminal justice systems of European origin, are based on strict sustainance of individual rights and obligations, breaches of which normally result in sanctions. Developments in European criminal justice systems can be regarded as attempts to lessen the problems created by this main thrust of the criminal justice systems.

Obviously, in the Nigerian environment, such an approach engenders problems of conflict and crisis in the operation of the criminal justice system. First, increase in criminality necessarily requires an increase in the quality and quantity of human and material resources allocated to the criminal justice system. However, like virtually all developing African countries, Nigeria cannot allocate resources sufficient to meet the increasing demands for the operation of its criminal justice system. Consequently, the informal strategies of crime prevention and control should be encouraged to reduce the need to rely too heavily on the very costly formal strategies of prevention and control.[74] Failure to encourage the sustenance and further development of the informal strategies is bound to worsen the present apparent overburdening of the criminal justice system, which in turn generates inefficiency. Secondly, the 'alien' systems have never generated sufficient confidence in the population, and Nigerians still very much believe in settling their criminal disputes outside the ambit of the formal criminal justice systems, thereby producing a 'dark figure' rate of 87.5%[75]. Hence, there is need for us to resort to the more culturally acceptable methods of dispute settlement, even at the formal level. This has led to the proposal that conciliation should be entrenched in our criminal process and that only those cases which the parties and courts have failed to achieve conciliation should proceed to criminal trial.[76] Further simplification of both the criminal procedure laws and the law of evidence have also been advocated, with a view to making the system more comprehensible to the generality of Nigerians and enhance a greater degree of public participation and confidence in the criminal justice system.[77] Complementarily, there is need for serious judicial reforms through which the Nigerian judiciary should be made to serve Nigerians in a Nigerian (not English) manner, thereby balancing the universal need for justice and fairness with those of relevance. Our traditional criminal justice systems had largely achieved these standards in the past.[78] Thirdly, within the context of formal judicial intervention, the disposition methods employed by Nigerian criminal courts have shifted over the years from those of personal reparations to those of imprisonment in the main, followed by fines, discharges and binding over.[79] Even the terms of imprisonment have become noticeably more severe.[80] This sentencing trend of the courts can be said to reflect the frustrations of the society; these are also reflected in the judicial practices where continued increase in criminal incidents seemes to have baffled an officialdom that is not

184

well prepared to cope with the resulting increased pressures. Consequently, the courts have relied heavily on imprisonment which is not only contra Nigerian culture, but which has also had a very high failure rate in the Nigerian penal scene.[81] In addition, where resort has been made to fines, the weakness of the courts' conviction in this form of sanction is betrayed not only by their refusal to allow for payment in instalments or the granting of a certain amount of time in which to make the payment, but also by their refusal to take the offenders' means into consideration when deciding on the amount of fine, thus disregarding the existing legal provisions to the contrary.[82] As a result, courts have been committing to prison roughly above 15% of those in default of payment.[83] Similarly, except for customary courts, and despite ample cultural and popular support[84], personal reparations are not constructively practised by the criminal courts[85].

An addition to these problems, is that concerning the processing of criminal laws which are largely alien in substance. This has added to the crisis of confidence which is plaguing our criminal justice system today. The police, for instance, usually have problems enforcing as offences those acts that are traditionally acceptable, such as bigamy, and small scale offences such as simple assaults between parties who belong to the same primary contact group. Similar difficulties are encountered in the area of property offences, particularly where the parties have agreed upon and effected restitution and/or compensation.[86] These problems have led to many proposals for reform.[87] In June 1987, the Attorney-General of the Federation and Minister of Justice addressed a meeting of resource persons at his Ministry on the need for unification and reform of the Nigerian criminal laws and procedures, thus setting the machinery in motion. In the course of a National Conference on the Unification and Reform of the Criminal Laws and Procedures (October 1987) these laws and procedures were reviewed and further

185

developed by a task force or commission set up by the Minister for this purpose; the new legislations will be based on the recommendations presented by this body.

Parallel to this, the realisation has developed of a need for modernization of the police force and prison service, with a view to making them more efficient and relevant within the social, economic and cultural conditions of the context in which they function. These modernisation processes are now in progress and it is hoped that, together with the modernisation exercises, societal relevance is constantly kept in mind. As in the case of Japan, where this has been successfully achieved, with conscious efforts on our part this need can be fulfilled.

Rapid changes and increases in the magnitude and complexity of the crime problem have augmented the workload of the criminal justice agencies to the point that they now need to adopt modern record-keeping and information retrieval methods on a fast and efficient — but still relatively cheap — basis. None of our criminal justice agencies has as yet reached this point. It is for this purpose that Nigeria, with the help of the United Nations, is now seeking to establish its own Crime Information Network (CIN). This is planned to aid the compilation and storage of crime prevention and criminal justice data with easy retrieval, which will provide quick access to the information thereby stored in data form. It is also planned to expand further the Decision Support Information System to aid the personnel of the criminal systems and other agencies and decision-making bodies that have bearing on crime prevention, in taking informed decisions and having the necessary information when needed. This Crime Information Network Project is being implemented at present.

Conclusion

We have looked into the problems which unplanned development is capable of causing. Development *per se* is not criminogenic. It is development without the necessary capacity to develop which is problematic. This has now been appreciated in Nigeria; the necessary capacities to appreciate problems of backwardness, collecting and digesting the needed information about same, developing a holistic, systemic and systematic policy of development and for development, whereby the inter-sectoral components are well alligned, must be fully and urgently addressed if we are to depart from the generally convenient but ineffective haphazard, piece- meal approach to solving the various problems.

It is for this purpose that we have nationally embarked on a Structural Adjustment Programme on the economic front, a population containment policy and 'health for all by the year 2000 policy' on the social front, and the preparation of a new constitution for the return of the country to civil rule on the political front. For the development of consistent and thorough economic, political and socio-cultural policies, the President created the Directorate of Mass Mobilisation for Social and Economic Self-Reliance (MAMSER), and the Directorate for Food, Roads and Rural Infrastructure (DIFRRI). This Directorate ensures not only the end of the erstwhile neglect of the rural areas, but also their sustained and comprehensive development, with a view to improving the standard of living and the quality of life of the Nigerian rural dweller who still constitutes approximately 68% of this population. This policy seeks to promote agriculture, and agro-allied and other industries in the rural areas, coupled with the provision of good roads, potable water, and electricity, as well as good but cheap housing, with the necessary — Nigerian designed and oriented — sanitation systems. It is clear that such a policy would stem the massive influx to urban areas by rural people in search of improving their living conditions. Additionally, the Directorate of MAMSER aims at changing Nigerians from a nation of job-seekers, not only to a nation of self-employed but also to a nation of job-generating people. Thus, young school leavers and University graduates are provided with government assistance to enable them start small-scale farming and small-scale industries which will enable them to live independent, self-reliant and self-employed lives. They are not only assisted financially, but they are also assisted with technical and professional advice and support. These aim not only at stemming rural/urban migration, but also at promoting urban/rural migration. When these economic, social and political programmes start yielding their dividends tangibly in the next year or two, Nigeria will be on the way to alleviating many of its development-originated criminogenic factors. In addition, citizens' morale should also improve once health policies, complemented by the MASS TRANSIT Programme, are enacted.

Contemporaneously, the educational policy now being implemented ("6-3-3-4" System), with a more relevant syllabi, is seeking to switch the educational system from mere book-knowledge and qualification acquisition, to purposeful manpower training. However, if we are eventually to achieve turning our educational programmes into human resources development programmes, we need to make more fundamental changes even in the content of our "6-3-3-4" curricular. Thus, in the same way as we had hitherto built the liberal acts into our old programmes, if we now build a science and technology culture into our primary education, we can only accomplish a science and technology culture.

In addition, the necessary substantive reform of the legal and procedural system, of the judiciary, the police force and our prison system, must be effected in order to make them more relevant to our needs along the lines suggested in the preceding section. For this purpose, staff training on a continuative basis, is absolutely essential.

It is only in this way that our "Criminal Justice System can become fully responsive to the diversity of political, economic and social systems and to the constantly evolving conditions of society"[88] in Nigeria.

188

References and Notes

[1] United Nations, *Report of the Seventh United Nations Congress on the Prevention of Crime and the Treatment of Offenders, para. 2, "Milan Plan of Action"*, A/CONF. 121/22/Rev. 1, (Sales No. E.86.IV.1), endorsed by the General Assembly Resolution, 1985, (GA/RES/40/32).

[2] United Nations, *ECA Conference of Ministers on Africa's Economic and Social Crises, Para. 2 of the Preamble to the Special Memorandum*, adopted at the Nineteenth Session of the Commission held in Addis Ababa, Ethiopia, from 24 to 28 May 1984 and presented to the 1984 Second Regular Session of the United Nations ECOSOC and the 20th Ordinary Session of the Assembly of Heads of State and Government of the Organization of African Unity, United Nations ECA Document (E/ECA/CN. 10/37/Rev. 1), p. 1. (hereinafter referred to as *ECA Conference of Ministers on Africa's Economic and Social Crises*).

[3] *Ibidem*, para. 12, p. 5.

[4] Adebayo Adedeji, *ECA and Africa's Development, 1983-2008: A Preliminary Perspective Study*, (Addis Ababa, 1983), p. 2.

[5] *Ibidem*, pp. 7-8.

[6] *Ibidem*, p. 9.

[7] United Nations, DIESA, *Patterns of Urban and Rural Population Growth*, ST/ESA/SER.A/68, (Sales No. E.79.XIII.9), Table 5, p. 13.

[8] United Nations, DIESA, *Demographic Indicators of Countries*, ST/ESA/SER.A/82, 1982, (Sales No. E.82.XIII.5), Table 8, p. 25.

[9] Adebayo Adedeji, *"ECA and Africa's..."*, *op. cit.*, p. 8.

[10] United Nations, *Report of the Seventh United Nations Congress...*, para. 2, "Milan Plan of Action", *op. cit.*, pp. 2-3.

[11] Adebayo Adedeji, *ECA and Africa's...*, *op. cit.*, p. 2.

[12] *ECA Conference of Ministers on Africa's Economic and Social Crises*, *op. cit.*, pp. 1-2.

[13] United Nations, *Report of the Sixth United Nations Congress on the Prevention of Crime and the Treatment of Offenders*, A/CONF.87/13/Rev. 1, (Sales No. E. 81. IV.4), Agenda Item 4, *Juvenile Justice: Before and After the Onset of Delinquency*, para. 143, p. 163.

[14] Freigier, *The Dangerous Classes in Paris*, 1839. Compare with Mayhew, H., *London's Labour and the London Poor*.

[15] C. R. Shaw and H. McKay, *Juvenile Delinquency and Urban Areas*, 1942; Bernard Lander, *Towards an Understanding of Juvenile Delinquency*, 1954.

[16] A. Cohen, *Delinquent Boys*, 1955; R. A. Cloward and L. E. Ohlin, *Delinquency and Opportunity*, Ill., Free Press of Glencoe, 1961.

[17] Sir Cyril Burt, *The Young Delinquent*; O. Oloruntimehin, "A Study of Juvenile Delinquency in a Nigerian City", *British Journal of Criminology*, 1973, Vol. 13, No. 2, p. 157.

[18] Edwin H. Sutherland, "A Sociological Theory of Crime Causation", in E. H. Sutherland and D. R. Cressey, *Principles of Criminology*, Chapter 4, 1960.

[19] For the marxist viewpoint, W. Bonger, *Criminality and Economic Conditions*, 1916; for the point of view that affluence causes criminality, H. Mannheim, *Comparative Criminology*, Vol. 1, London, Routledge and Kegan Paul, 1965. Both view points are admirably well summarized in G. B. Vold, *Theoretical Criminology*, 1958, London, Oxford University Press.

[20] T. Sellin, *Culture Conflict and Crime*, N. Y., Social Science Research Council, 1938.

[21] E. Durkheim, *Division of Labour*; also R. K. Merton, "Social Structure and Anomie", *American Sociological Review*, October 1938, No. 3, pp. 672-682.

[22] A. A. Adeyemi, "Treatment of Young Offenders in Nigeria", paper presented at the National Workshop on Child Welfare Policy, January 1986.

[23] This is deducible from a combination of B. Lander's socio-cultural factor of minority populations' social marginality, in his ecological analysis of Baltimore, and Merton's reaction typologies of innovation and rebellion as the offender's response to society's socio-economic anomie.

[24] *World Bank Development Report*, 1984, pp. 7-8.

[25] Recall here the importance attached to this phenomenon by E. H. Sutherland in his enunciation of the theory of differential association in relation to crime causation.

[26] A. Cohen, *Delinquent Boys*, 1955. Also R. A. Cloward and L. E. Ohlin, *Delinquency and Opportunity*, 1961; and D. Downes, *The Delinquent Solution*, New York, The Free Press, 1966. See further, M. Wolfgang and F. Ferracuti, *The Subculture of Violence*, London, Tavistock, 1967.

[27] C. R. Shaw and H. McKay, *Juvenile Delinquency and Urban Areas*, *op. cit.*; B. Lander, *Towards an Understanding of Juvenile Delinquency*, *op. cit.*; H. F. Morris, *Criminal Area*.

[28] G. Tarde, *Penal Philosophy*, Translated by R. Howell, 1912.

[29] *The Daily Times*, March 3, 1986, p. 16.

[30] *Economic and Social Statistics Bulletin*, "Oil Sector Basic Data and Indicators", Table 29, p. 28.

[31] *Economic and Social Statistics Bulletin*, "Balance of Payments", Table 18, p. 18.

[32] *The Daily Times*, *op. cit.*, "How Naira has fared since '84", March 3, 1986, front page.

[33] Table 12, ante.

[34] Situation illustrated in Table 12, *op. cit.*

[35] J. B. Mays, "Crime and Social Structure", London, Faber, 1963.

[36] O. Oloruntimehin, "A Study of Juvenile Delinquency ...", *op. cit.*

[37] R. K. Merton, "Social Structure and Anomie", *op. cit.*

[38] E. Durkheim, *Division of Labour, op. cit.*

[39] Otegbade, *Lynching in Lagos State*, 1977.

[40] E. Faris, "Some Results of Frustration", *Sociology of Social Research*, 31, pp. 87-92, November 1946; Healy and Bromer, *New Light on Delinquency and its Treatment*, 1936.

[41] Karl Marx, *Critique of Political Economy, op. cit.*; W. Bonger, *Criminality and Economic Conditions, op. cit.*

[42] Aristotle, *Politics*, ii, pp. 7, 11, 13; H. Mannheim, *Comparative Criminology*, Vol. II, 1965.

[43] W. Bonger, *Criminality and Economic Conditions, op. cit.*

[44] H. Mannheim, *Comparative Criminology, op. cit.*

[45] Leslie Wilkins, *Crime and Crime Control: The Next Ten Years*, Preliminary Paper prepared for the Fifth United Nations Congress on the Prevention of Crime and the Treatment of Offenders, 1975.

[46] Sir Leon Radzinowicz. "The Influence of Economic Conditions on Crime", *American Sociological Review*, I and II, 1941, pp. 1-36 and 139-153 respectively. His findings tend to suggest that prosperity is more effective in reducing criminality rates than poverty is effective in increasing it.

[47] United Nations, *Report on the World Social Situation*, 1978, p. 35.

[48] World Bank, *World Bank Development Report*, 1979, p. 81.

[49] C. R. Shaw and H. McKay, *Juvenile Delinquency and Urban Areas, op. cit.*

[50] O. O. and F. O. Okediji, "The Sociological Aspects of Prison Reorganization in Nigeria", in T. O. Elias, Ed., *The Prison System in Nigeria*, Table VIII, p. 121. The latest figures on the breakdown of the Lagos State Criminal Statistics also confirms this fact for the years 1977 to 1985.

[51] No. 6 of 1978, so designated by virtue of the Adaptation of Laws (Redesignation of Decrees, etc.) Order. 1980.

[52] B. Lander, *Towards an Understanding of Juvenile Delinquency*, op. cit. The same deduction can be drawn from the description of the "interstitial areas" of Chicago given by C. R. Shaw and H. McKay in *Juvenile Delinquency and Urban Areas, op. cit.*

[53] Section 18 (1) of the Constitution, as amended by Decree No. 1 of 1984.

[54] H. K. Merton, "Social ...", *op. cit.*

[55] T. Sellin, *Culture ..., op. cit.*

[56] United Nations, *Report of the Sixth United Nations Congress on the Prevention of Crime and the Treatment of Offenders, op. cit.*, para. 144, pp. 63-64.

[57] Because of the lack of space in this Section, offences will be considered in groups rather than individually.

[58] This has been calculated from Table 4, ante.

[59] See references 14-23, 27-28 and 35-49, ante.

[60] Leslie Wilkins, *Delinquent Generations*, London, HMSO, 1960.

[61] P. O. Ohadike, "Urbanization: Growth, Transitions and Problems of a Premier West African City (Lagos, Nigeria)", *Metropolitan Lagos*, Vol. 3, No. 4, June 1968, pp. 69-90. See also A. L. Mabogunje, *Urbanization in Nigeria*, 1968.

[62] From the broad categories of farmers, artisans and traders on the one hand, to employers of the public and private sectors, on the other, and now to the additional categories of self-employed job generators such as small scale industrialists, etc., which the difficulties of the employment market have brought about.

[63] P. O. Ohadike, "Urbanization: ...", *op. cit.*; A. Izzett, "Family Life among the Yoruba in Lagos, Nigeria", in A. Southall, Ed. *Social Change in Modern Africa*, 1964; P. C. Lloyd, *Power and Independence: Urban Africans' Perception of Social Inequality*, London, Routledge and Kegan Paul, 1974; and M. Pail, "Migration and Labour Force Participation: A Study of Four Towns", in A. Adepoju, Ed. *Internal Migration in Nigeria*, 1976.

[64] A. A. Adeyemi, "Crime Prevention and Control in the Context of Development: A Casa Study of Nigeria", Inaugural Lecture, 1986.

[65] O. Oloruntimehin, "Crime and Development", paper presented at the NISER Seminar on Innovative Approaches to Development Theory, 1984.

[66] A. A. Adeyemi, "Crime Prevention...", *op. cit.* Odekunle's interpretation, however, was based on the socialist theory similar to that of Bonger's approach in *Crime and Economic Conditions*, 1916; "Capitalist Economy and the Crime Problem in Nigeria", 1977. (Mimeograph)

[67] F. O. Okediji, "The Role of Voluntary Associations in West African Urbanization", *American Anthropologist*, Vol. 59, No. 4, 1957. I. Wallerstein, "Voluntary Associations", in J. S. Coleman and G. G. Resberg, Jr., Eds. *Political Parties and National Integration in Tropical Africa*, 1966; and F. O. Okediji's "On Voluntary Associations as an Adaptive Mechanism in West African Urbanization: Another Perspective", 1967. (Mimeograph)

[68] J. D. U. Peel, *Aladura: A Religious Movement among the Yoruba*, 1968.

[69] A. Cohen, *Customs and Politics in Urban Africa*, 1969.

[70] A. Peace, *Choice, Class and Conflict: A Study of Southern Nigerian Factory Workers*, 1979.

[71] A. A. Adeyemi, "Criminology in Contemporary Africa, *Nigerian Journal of Criminology*, Vol. II, No. 1, pp. 1-30, at pp. 16-17.

[72] A. A. Adeyemi, "Criminology ...", *op. cit.*, p. 17; see also O. O. Oloruntimehin, "Differences between Real and Apparent Criminality", in

A. A. Adeyemi, Ed. *Nigerian Criminal Process*, University of Lagos, 1977, chap. 1, p. 4, where the 'dark figure' rate given is 87.5%.

[73] Nigeria's contribution to the United Nations University Research, A. A. Adeyemi, et al., "Ordinary Crime and its Prevention Strategies in Metropolitan Lagos, Nigeria", 1987.

[74] There should not be too much problem with this as it is in accordance with our cultural orientation.

[75] O. O. Oloruntimehin, "Differences...", *op. cit.*, p. 4.

[76] Chap. 3 of the Report of the Ogun State of Nigeria Commission on the Reform of Administration of Criminal Justice (hereinafter referred to as Oyemade Commission), June 1981.

[77] Oyemade Commission, chap. 3, pp. 32-36, *op. cit.* See also A. A. Adeyemi, "The Problems of the Criminal Justice System in Nigeria", in A. A. Adeyemi, Ed. *Nigerian...*, *op. cit.* p. xx.

[78] T. O. Elias, *Nature of African Law*; Bohanan, *Justice and Judgement among the Tiv'*; Meek, *Law and Authority in a Nigerian Tribe*; Gunn, *Pagan Peoples of the Central Area of Northern Nigeria*, etc.

[79] A. A. Adeyemi, "Administration of Justice in Nigeria: Sentencing", in *Proceedings of the National Conference on Law Development and Administration in Nigeria (LAWDEV '87)*, pp. 22-24.

[80] A. A. Adeyemi, "The Prospects of Improvement within the Nigerian Criminal Justice System", *Law Reform - Journal of the Nigerian Law Reform Commission*, No. 3, November 1983, p. 10.

[81] The situation is reviewed in A. A. Adeyemi, "Administration...", *op. cit.*, pp. 13, 27-31.

[82] For a review of the Judicial Practices, A. A. Adeyemi, "Administration...", *op. cit.*, pp. 33-35.

[83] *Proceedings... (LAWDEV '87)*, *op. cit.*, p. 34.

[84] Oyemade Commission, *op. cit.*, chap. 3, para. 3: 11.3.2, p. 43.

[85] Oyemade Commission, *op. cit.*, Tables 1 and 2, pp. 22 and 23 respectively.

[86] These attitudes, coupled with institutional inefficiency have led to considerable back-log in police investigations, which now result in a high proportion of prisoners awaiting trial, ranging from about 30% to almost 80%. When the remand and awaiting trial category and that of those committed to prison in default of payment of fines are added to the population stabilized by longer terms of imprisonment, it is no wonder that our prison congestion rates have exceeded the 50% level.

[87] Oyemade Commission, *op. cit.*, chap. 3; A. A. Adeyemi, "Administration...", in *Proceedings... (LAWDEV '87)*, *op. cit.*, pp. 21-69.

[88] United Nations, *Report of the Seventh United Nations Congress...*, *op. cit.*, para. 4, "Milan Plan of Action", p. 3.

193

LA MEDIATION:
UNE FORME DE REACTION SOCIALE

*Nsimba Masamba S. **

Le terrain

La perspective théorique développée ici est induite d'un matériel collecté sur le terrain: Kivunda une collectivité (secteur) de la zone (territoire) de Luozi, dans le Bas-Zaïre au Zaïre, du 1er avril au 15 juillet 1985, par observation participante chez les Manianga ou Nsundi.

Les Manianga sont un des groupes principaux que compose l'ethnie Kongo du Zaïre; les autres étant: les Ndibu, les Mtandu ou Mpangu, les Besi-Ngombe, les Yombe et les Bomboma. Tous les groupes parlent une même langue: le kikongo. Mais chez chacun d'eux on rencontre des variantes: le kindibu, le kintandu, le kisi-ngombe, le kimanianga, le kiyombe, le kimboma. Au-delà des différences propres à chaque groupe, subsiste toujours en dépit de la colonisation, un fond culturel commun indiscutable, qui par ailleurs se retrouve audelà des frontières: au Congo Brazzaville et en Angola, pouvant fonctioner à l'occasion, comme facteur de cohésion;[1] parce qu'ayant constitué l'ancien royaume du Kongo.

Nous sommes à une cinquantaine de kilomètres du fleuve, sur la rive droite, c'est-à-dire sur sa rive "congolaise", par référence à la majeure partie du fleuve, et à une quinzaine de kilomètres de la République du Congo, ainsi qu'à plus ou moins quatre-vingt-dix kilomètres de la route Kinshasa-Matadi (Zaïre).

---

* Unité de Criminologie, Séminaire de Doctorat, Université Catholique de Louvain, Belgique.

Notre terrain intéresse près de 5000 habitants, dans un territoire de plus ou moins 42 km². Il est limité au sud-est par une mission catholique, Mangembo; au nord-ouest par une mission protestante, Sundi-lutete. Une route relie les deux missions. Autour et entre ces deux missions s'agglutinent des villages dont la distribution spatiale reste plutôt classique, bien que certains d'eux ressemblent à un quartier urbain de Kinshasa (capitale du Zaïre). Les matériaux de construction sont résolument modernes: briques, tôles, boiseries.

Pour justifier la qualification de "rurbain", on se servira pour abréger, d'indicateurs qui intéressent le palier de surface;² la présence de certains service publics: l'administration, la santé publique (deux hôpitaux), l'enseignement (sept écoles), le commerce, un petit hôtel, le marché hebdomadaire et le petit marché quotidien de Mangembo. Certains métiers tels que le boulanger (quatre boulangers), le cordonnier, le tailleur, le photographe, le réparateur de montres, de vélos, de télévisions et radios. La télévision est présente chez huit particuliers, et dans trois écoles secondaires. Elle est alimentée par deux faisceaux hertziens, celui de Kinshasa et de Brazzaville. Notons toutefois l'importance du salariat dans notre population. Il s'agit évidemment d'un statut et non pas forcément d'un revenu assuré.

A ce palier de surface, correspondent des niveaux de profondeur de la vie sociale, constitués de structures sociales, mieux de réseaux sociaux à partir desquels nos catégories tirent leur sens, en explicitant leurs différents liens.

La médiation: une forme de réaction sociale

De qui émane cette réaction sociale? La réponse à cette question révèle le caractère éclaté de la réaction sociale. Selon que les acteurs ont ou non un statut précis dans la gestion de la situation problématique, nous distinguons trois formes de réactions sociales: diffuse, organisée et spécialisée.

196

a) *La réaction sociale diffuse (R.S.D.)*

C'est celle qui émane des proches: amis, voisins, collègues de travail, parents, etc., et difficile à structurer, dans l'ignorance de "qui a dit quoi". Ces acteurs peuvent déjà amener les antagonistes à un compromis[3] parce qu'ils inciteront l'auteur de la situation définie par eux comme problématique à réparer la faute; soit pour empêcher ainsi que se déchire le tissu social tendu du réseau social menacé d'éclatement; soit pour le raccomoder s'il s'est déjà rompu.[4] Il apparaît clairement qu'il s'agit d'une réaction sociale à la réconciliation.

b) *La réaction sociale organisée*

Lorsqu'une "solution" émerge difficilement à ce niveau, se met en place à l'initiative d'acteurs de la réaction sociale diffuse, une réaction sociale organisée (R.S.O.): le "kinzonzi", prenant le plus souvent la forme de la négociation ou de la médiation.

Notre matériel se constitue essentiellement de "binzonzi"[5] ayant eu lieu avant et pendant notre séjour sur le terrain. Certains nous ont été rapportés par les concernés et par des intervenants tels que les "nzonzi" et le "duki".[6] D'autres, auxquels nous avons eu l'occasion d'assister, seront décrits dans le cahier de terrain, l'enregistrement ayant été difficile pour plusieurs raisons. Ce cahier comprend aussi différentes observations du quotidien des relations sociales des acteurs du terrain.

A l'examen, un kinzonzi apparaît être tout un réseau organisé de prise en charge des situations conflictuelles. Il se distingue des réseaux de sociabilité tels que: la famille, l'école, le travail, etc. par son caractère plutôt circonstanciel, et se constitue en quelque sorte de la même façon que le sociogramme de Moreno: les partenaires se choisissent en fonction de la tâche à accomplir.

Un proverbe souvent utilisé lors de "binzonzi": "nous ne sommes pas le "kibaku" (couteau),[7] mais le "ntumbu" (aiguille); indique la première préoccupation des acteurs de la réaction sociale diffuse (R.S.D.): la sauvegarde des bonnes relations d'échange des biens et services dans les réseaux de bon voisinage, d'amitié, etc. menacés de rupture.

Il rend compte de l'aspect échange des biens et services du quotidien des relations sociales [8] et d'au moins deux logiques de prise en charge des situations problématiques: celle de "ntumbu" qui raccomode le tissu social et celle de "kibaku" qui coupe les liens sociaux.

L'analyse des réseaux organisés amène à la découverte de processus, dont celui d'échange d'information que décrit bien Gulliver dans son modèle cyclique; [9] et d'acteurs impliqués dans ces processus facilitant la négociation, mieux la réconciliation, ou la bloquant.

Par rapport à ce modèle, notre contribution peut se résumer à la mise en évidence de ces "tierces parties", et de leur importance dans la réussite d'une réconciliation laquelle empêche le renvoi vers les agences officielles.

Le processus d'échange d'information s'amorce bien avant le "kinzonzi". Pour un choix justifié du type de contrôle social, les antagonistes consultent des acteurs de la réaction sociale diffuse (R.S.D.).[10] Lorsqu'ils ne le font pas ou ne prennent pas en considération leurs avis, ils s'exposent à des sanctions redoutables de leur part.[11]

Lors d'un "kinzonzi", ces acteurs se mobilisent. Certains d'eux ont des rôles précis. Il s'agit entre autres d'intermédiaires formels et informels; d'espions et de nzonzi. L'action combinée de ces acteurs garantit la réconciliation.

— L'intermédiaire formel

Est défini comme tel, tout intervenant ayant un statut précis dans la gestion d'une situation problématique: un "duki", un chef de famille, un notable du lieu (un pasteur, un directeur d'école, un enseignant, etc.) centralisant l'information ou chez qui transite l'information destinée à la partie adverse.

Lorsqu'on les suit au mfundu,[12] se défait l'image de simple arbitre qu'ils affichent pendant les débats publics, se limitant au respect de la règle du jeu de la part des parties en cause. L'on découvre leur rôle voilé de négociateur. Ce qui justifie par ailleurs leur participation aux "mfundu" organisés par les deux parties.

Tout n'étant pas dit pendant les débats publics, ils indiquent aux parties les possibilités de réconciliaton offertes par chachune d'elles.

Etant "nzonzi" dans beaucoup d'affaires, ils utilisent leur savoir-faire, même quand ils sont "médiateur formel", pour faciliter la réconciliation. A partir de ce qui est dit d'une part pendant les débats publics – lieu où les acteurs de la réaction sociale diffuse manifestent leur désapprobation ou accord quant à l'orientation donnée à la gestion du problème – et d'autre part aux "mfundu", il conseillent aux parties ce qu'il convient de faire pour la sauvegarde des bonnes relations d'échange entre les antagonistes.

— L'intermédiaire informel

Pour augmenter les chances de réussir la réconciliation, ou simplement pour suppléer à l'absence de médiateurs formels, les réseaux organisés de prise en charge des situations problématiques se dotent d'un deuxième canal de circulation de l'information. Ils sont constitués par le(s) médiateur(s) informel(s).

Il s'agit d'acteurs qui, compte tenu de la très bonne qualité de relations d'échange des biens et services les liant aux antagonistes, et compte tenu également de leur habileté à la réconciliation, se voient confiés par les acteurs de la réaction sociale diffuse la délicate mission de négociateur lorsque les parties se retirent au "mfundu". Il s'agit là d'une mission difficile, vu la très courte marge de manoeuvre dont ils disposent. En effet, dans leurs initiatives, ils peuvent irriter une des parties et rendre ainsi difficile la poursuite de la négociation. Cette mission est le plus souvent confiée aux aînés réputés sages.

— Les espions

Ces acteurs que nous découvrons par hasard lors d'un kinzonzi et qu'un de nos informateurs nous montre en les nommant "espions", nous sont décrits comme étant des "baleke" (cadets) chargés de suivre la partie adverse aux mfundu pour informer les aînés de tout ce qui est dit.

Les deux types de médiateur (formel et informel) ne couvrant pas tout le champ de la négociation, une bonne partie de l'information leur échappe. C'est ici qu'intervient ce troisième type d'acteurs: les espions. L'information apportée par les médiateurs — réputés sages — est digérée. Il ne serait pas digne de leur part de transmettre l'information dans sa forme brute: des injures, etc. ce qui ne facilite pas la négociation. Ce troisième canal: les espions, par contre la livrera brute.

L'information importante ne vient pas seulement du "mfundu". Elle émane aussi d'acteurs de la réaction sociale diffuse, constituant l'assemblée et d'autres tels que: le curé, le pasteur, etc. opérant dans la pénombre. La vraie mission des espions consiste dès lors à faire parvenir aux parties et aux différents intervenants les avis, mieux la demande à laquelle adhère le plus grand nombre d'acteurs de la réaction sociale diffuse. La situation conflictuelle ne concerne pas exclusivement les deux antagonistes, mais tout un réseau ou des réseaux d'échange des biens et services, qui suite à cette situation, risquent d'éclater. Ainsi, tous les acteurs de ces réseaux se mobiliseront-ils pour la sauvergarde des bonnes relations d'échange, de solidarité entre voisins, amis, collègues de travail, etc.; choisissant ainsi le type conciliateur de contrôle social.

— Le nzonzi

Quand on suit cet expert au mfundu, on saisit mieux sa mission de négociateur. Il se distingue d'un avocat par son souci de réconciliaton. Dans ses conseils qu'il fonde sur toute information apportée au "mfundu", il cherche avec beaucoup d'adresse et de façon progressive à amener l'antagoniste à la réconciliation.

Face à la partie adverse, dans le but de recevoir le plus d'information possible pourrait-on dire, le nzonzi de la partie demanderesse s'attache à démontrer la totale responsabilité de celle-ci. Lorsque l'information sera suffisemment échangée et que les nzonzi auront bien préparé les antagonistes, les deux parties convergeront vers la réconciliation ou l'issue la plus juste, la plus satisfaisante pour les deux parties.

Dans cette tâche, les "nzonzi" — une partie peut en avoir plusieurs — sont efficacement aidés par tous ces intermédiaires décrits ci-dessus. Ainsi, malgré la présence de "nzonzi", une réconciliation peut avorter si l'information circule mal.

Une première implication du processus d'échange d'information lorsqu'il fonctionne harmonieusement, est la redéfinition de la situation problématique et de la personne de l'auteur. Les premières sont réductrices (processus de reconstruction d'objet) puisqu'elles sont élaborées à partir d'une situation mal perçue

c) *La réaction sociale spécialisée*

Quand le processus d'échange d'information fonctionne mal, il y a fixation ou confirmation des définitions réductrices; moment ultime du processus de reconstruction d'objet, processus qui aboutit à la construction du fait-prétexte.

Les acteurs de la réaction sociale diffuse se tournent vers un autre type de contrôle social: le type punitif-compensatoire. C'est le renvoi criminologique, un processus indiquant le passage d'une logique de prise en charge (celle de l'aiguille) à une autre (celle de kibaku).[13]

Le caractère punitif tient à ce que les acteurs de la réaction sociale diffuse sollicitent cette prise en charge[14] pour punir le voisin difficile. Généralement il s'agira ici d'affaires à qualification pénale. Tandis que pour d'autres, ils demanderont au réseau de la réaction sociale spécialisée, tel que le tribunal de la collectivité, de poursuivre simplement la gestion du problème, la réconciliation n'ayant pas été possible.

Le fait-prétexte qui justifie la prise en charge spécialisée, trace le cadre au sein duquel le réseau spécialisé doit circonscrire son intervention.

Toutefois, cette prise en charge n'est pas automatique. Elle ne devient effective que lorsque toutes les possibilités de réconciliation sont épuisées. Dans le cas contraire, se déclenche un autre processus dit de substitution de logique de prise en charge et contradictoire à celui de renvoi. Les intervenants renoncent à leurs statut d'acteur de la réaction sociale spécialisée (R.S.S.) au profit de celui d'acteur de la réaction sociale organisée (R.S.O.) pour une nouvelle tentative de réconciliation.

La mise en évidence du rôle essentiel des acteurs de la réaction sociale diffuse (R.S.D.), restitue la dimension diachronique des relations sociales des acteurs du terrain. S'agissant souvent de mêmes acteurs: voisins, connaissances, etc. se mobilisant dans des rôles différents pour la sauvegarde des structures (réseaux) de bon voisinage, d'amitié, etc.; l'issue d'une situation problématique est à chercher dans la logique des précédentes; les antagonistes d'aujourd'hui, ayant été des intervenants d'hier. L'on se rend compte ainsi du caractère lié des incidents constituant notre matériel.

La perspective diachronique

Elle introduit ici le concept de changement social. Les structures sociales de prise en charge (réseaux) examinées ci-dessus, gagnent en compréhension en les articulant à ce concept.

La présence d'institutions (services publics) sur ce terrain indique l'importance — au quotidien — d'une part, des relations professionnelles entre acterus de villages et même d'ethnies différentes et d'autre part des diverses législations qui définissent certains comportements: détournement de fonds, vol de médicaments, etc., comme problématiques et prévoient des sanctions à infliger aux contrevenants.

L'on peut s'attendre à ce que ces institutions prennent totalement en charge la gestion de ces illégalismes ou la confient à des agences spécialisées. Ceci est en partie vrai dans les établissements scolaires par exemple, lorsqu'il s'agit de situations problématiques qui perturbent directement leur bon fonctionnement. Mais ces relations ne sont pas simplement professionnelles. Elles se complexifient avec le temps et les conflits interpersonnels se diversifient.

Le champ d'intervention de ces législations est très limité et en l'absence de relations de parenté et/ou d'alliance entre les antagonistes, d'autres structures de prise en charge se mettent en place.

En se mobilisant, ces réseaux comblent cette lacune. Ils empruntent à la coutume certaines pratiques, telles que le "kinzonzi" et des principes (des proverbes). Ils exploitent d'autres ressources: les relations de bon voisinage, d'amitié, de travail, de connaissance, etc. pour des solutions informelles à leurs problèmes. Ces différentes institutions y ont recours aussi.

Le caractère non-prévu de l'issue — chaque fois qu'il est fait recours à la logique de "ntumbu" — suppose la créativité de la solution de la part des acteurs de la réaction sociale diffuse. Et la définition d'une situation varie selon qu'on adhère à l'une ou l'autre de ces logiques de prise en charge.

L'élément "créativité" rend bien compte de la dimension processuelle du changement: à savoir l'apprentissage, c'est-à-dire la découverte, voire la création et l'acquisition par les acteurs concernés, de nouveaux modèles relationnels, de nouveaux modes de raisonnement, bref, de nouvelles capacités collectives.[15]

Ce changement s'appréhende mieux sur des périodes suffisamment longues. Elles portent à l'observation des modifications importantes des structures, telles que celles de prise en charge des situations problématiques, conséquentes à l'introduction d'éléments culturels nouveaux, dans les espaces sociaux fondés essentiellement sur des relations de parenté et d'alliances, que décrivent bien par exemple Van Wing[16] et G. Balandier[17] cez les Bakongo du Zaïre et du Congo.

La mission de juge, d'arbitre, d'un acteur social comme le nzonzi[18] nous ne la retrouvons plus sur notre terrain, pourtant très proche et très lié à celui de Balandier — au Congo Brazzaville — et composant la même ethnie Bakongo. Dans la mesure où cette étude peut servir de comparaison, nous constatons là après une période de 34 ans (de 1955 à 1989) un aspect important du changement social intervenu sur notre terrain: l'instauration des nouvelles pratiques ayant intégré des éléments traditionnels et ceux empruntés à d'autres univers culturels. Nous avons mis en évidence ainsi sur notre terrain, des nouvelles capacités collectives conciliant une agence officielle telle que le tribunal de collectivité (un réseau spécialisé) à celles diffuses et organisées que montrent les acteurs de la réaction sociale diffuse, des nouveaux modèles relationnels entre des acteurs sociaux (individuels et collectifs), des nouveaux modes de raisonnement, des logiques qui rendent compte plutôt de synergie que de parallélisme[19] entre les différents réseaux de prise en charge.

Pour nous résumer

La négociation ou la médiation est une forme de réaction sociale à la réconciliation. Les acteurs de la réaction sociale diffuse (R.S.D.) ne sollicitent la réaction sociale spécialisée (R.S.S.) que lorsque la première échoue.

Malgré la construction d'un fait-prétexte justifiant la prise en charge spécialisée, celle-ci n'est pas automatique surtout si la demande est l'initiative exclusive du plaignant. Elle ne devient effective que quand toutes les possibilité de réconciliation sont épuisées.

Nous saisissons là un aspect important du changement social opéré par les acteurs de notre terrain: la mise en place de nouvelles structures de prise en charge, se fondant sur d'autres relations que celles de parenté, d'alliance.

Ils se sont dotés de nouvelles capacités collectives de gestion des situations problématiques, qui nous portent à définir la médiation se déroulant dans les espaces microsociologiques, comme étant une forme de réaction sociale, une pression sociale à la réconciliation.

Références et notes

[1] T. K.M. Buakasa, "L'impensé..." du discours: "Indoki" et "Nkisi" en pays Kongo du Zaïre, Aunaza-Cedaf, 1973, p. 11.

[2] G. Gurvitch, *Traité de sociologie,* 1967, Paris, P.U.F., tome 1, p. 158 et svt.

[3] T. K. M. Buskasa, *op. cit,* p. 133.

[4] Y. Brillon, *Ethnocriminologie de l'Afrique Noire,* 1980, Paris, Vrin, Montréal, Presses Universitaires de Montréal, p. 160.

[5] Binzonzi est le pluriel de kinzonzi.

[6] Un nzonzi est un spécialiste de la prise en charge des affaires (nsamu). Tandis qu'un duki ou duc, mot d'origine portugaise, est un chef de village.

[7] Kibaku: outil très tranchant utilisé par le tireur de vin pour tailler les palmiers et préparer le conduit collecteur de la sève, recueillie dans une calebasse.

[8] R. Firth, *Primitive Polynesian Economy,* 2nd ed., Routledge-Kegan, 1964, p. XI.

[9] P. H. Gulliver, *Disputes and Negotiations: A Cross-Cultural Perspective,* 1979, New York Academic Press, p. 81 et svt.

[10] J. L. Comaroff et S. Robert, *Rules and Processes: The Cultural Logic of Dispute in an African Context,* Chicago and London, The Univesity of Chicago Press, 1981, p. 110 et svt.

[11] Y. Brillon, *op. cit,* p. 160.

[12] Le mfundu (ou nenga) c'est la mise à l'écart de chacune des parties, pur examiner les propositions de la partie adverse ou de l'assemblée et prendre une décision.

[13] M. Turmaine et R. Zauberman, *Du renvoi: mécanismes éclatés ou modèle intergré? Le controle social de la deviance*, Vaucresson, D.G.R.S.T., 1978, pp. 249-274.

[14] J. C. Chamboredon, "La délinquance juvénile: essai de reconstruction d'objet", *Revue française de sociologie*, Vol. XII, 1971, pp. 335-377.

[15] M. Crozier et E. Friedberg, *L'acteur et le système*, Paris, éd. du Seuil, 1977, rééd. Coll. "Points", 1981, p. 339.

[16] J. Van Wing, *Etudes Bakongo: sociologie, religion et magie*, 1956, 2e éd., Desclée de Brouwer, Louvain.

[17] G. Balandier, *Sociologie actuelle de l'Afrique noire*, Paris, P.U.F., 1955.

[18] G. Balandier, *Sociologie actuelle de l'Afrique noire: dynamique sociale en Afrique centrale*, 4e éd., Quadrige/P.U.F., 1982, p. 330.

[19] A. Mignot, "La justice traditionnelle, une justice parallèle. L'exemple du Sud-Togo", *Penant*, No. 775, janvier-février-mars, 1982, pp. 5-30.

DEVELOPMENT, CRIME AND PREVENTION:

Reflections on Latin America

Elias Carranza *

Development and Crime

The United Nations has either implicitly or explicitly included discussion on crime trends in its quinquennial congresses on the prevention of crime and the treatment of offenders.[1] This is logical, since the first task of science is to observe the phenomena it deals with, so as to predict their future course. On the other hand, this is the only way, in the criminal justice area, to formulate, prevention and control strategies in order to maximize the results at the lowest material and social costs.

During the Sixth United Nations Congress on the Prevention of Crime and the Treatment of Offenders held in Caracas in 1980, this topic was specifically included and treated in close relation with development. Another specific topic dealing with "New Perspectives in Crime Prevention and Criminal Justice in the Context of Development" was also included.[2] During the Seventh United Nations Congress on the Prevention of Crime and the Treatment of Offenders (Milan, 1985), it was treated under the name of "New Dimensions of Criminality and Crime Prevention in the Context of Development: Challenges for the Future". The Congress likewise yielded important instruments on the subject, such as "Guiding principles for Crime Prevention and Criminal Justice in the Context of Development and a

* Deputy Director, United Nations Latin American Institute for the Prevention of Crime and the Treatment of Offenders (ILANUD).

New International Economic Order" and a resolution entitled "Crime prevention in the Context of Development".[3]

It was rightly observed that a nation or region's style of development is a conditioning structural framework for the type and volume of prevention forms consequently adopted.

It is not necessary to quote further in order to demonstrate the importance of this subject for Latin America and for the socalled "developing" regions in general.

The discussion that follows tries to point out the way in which particular forms of development, common to our countries, affect particular crime trends (rates, increase in the frequency of conventional criminal offences, and the emergence of new preoccupying forms of crime) and determine the type of prevention applied.

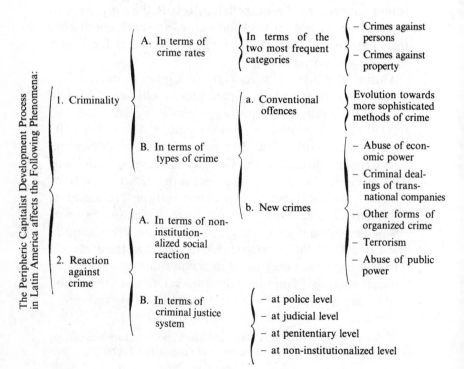

When exploring ways to decrease the cost of crime, which is believed to be much higher in developing countries than in developed countries,[4] the effects of these particular forms of development must be kept in mind.

An overall analysis of the present situation and of the tendencies of development and criminality in the countries of our region — many of which are very different from one another — will logically omit going deeply into the singularities of each state; this would, in fact, be the task of sub-regions or individual country analyses.

The chart shown here presents two major concepts: "development" and "crime". In order to fully understand this chart, existing information concerning the present state of development and future perspectives in Latin American and Caribbean countries must first be analyzed because, as has been pointed out, the evolution of crime rate will be to a large extent conditioned by the way in which the development process evolves.[5]

To accomplish our proposed task we will primarily make use of research carried out by international organisms such as the Economic Commission for Latin America (ECLA), and the World Bank.

Development in Latin America

In this paper the idea of development is not identified with the idea of "growth" — although growth is one of its components. Development demands "that the growth of the different economic sectors be in harmony and bring about an improvement in the levels and in the collective living conditions".[6] The last part of this definition refers to the need of keeping other indicators in mind besides those strictly economic, namely: health, education, and housing indicators which condition the population's welfare.

This is not an arbitrary statement because economic and welfare indicators are necessarily interrelated, "human development depends on the fact that economic growth should offer the necessary resources to broaden the opportunities of productive labour and basic services and, at the same time, those service of primary education and professional training, basic health care, nutrition and family planning programmes, and potable water supply can make outstanding contributions to growth".[7]

Likewise, it is important to point out another characteristic fo contemporary development processes: their inter-dependent character. We can olny speak of the development of this or that nation as an abstraction, since the degree of worldwide interdependency does not allow "autonomous" development processes. However, having described this interdependency, we must also point out that not all the countries in the world depend on each other to the same degree.

There is a marked difference, in the contemporary world, between central capitalist countries and countries with peripheric capitalism.[8] This characterization clearly shows that in terms of economic policy decisions, the economy of countries with peripheric capitalism varies greatly from that of central capitalist countries, and that there is an outstanding lack of equity in the interchange between the two.[9]

This lack of equity is translated into impressive figures; the so-called "developing countries", which account for 70% of the world population, receive only 30% of the wordl income. It is important to point out the ever growing difference in income between the higher and lower social strata within these same countries; difference which places the latter in a critical situation of sub-consumption.[10]

Based on the "Report on Worldwide Development" by the World Bank,[11] we will point out some of the basic indicators that show the huge gap between middle income economies, that is to say, all the nations of our region except Haiti (low income economy), and the countries that the mentioned report classifies as "industrial market economies":

210

- life expectancy at birth: is, on an average, 10 years less;
- education: adult literacy rate, 30% less;
- nutrition: the report states that "both in low and medium income countries, the poorer groups of the rural and urban population are chronically under-nourished;"
- income: average per capita income is 1/7 of the average per capita income in "industrial countries with market economy". In "low income" countries, the amount is decreased to 1/43.

The Need for a New International Economic Order

The situation described inspired the UN to proclaim the need to "urgently work to establish a New International Economic Order based on equity, sovereign equality, interdependency, common interest and cooperation among all the States".[12]

Other international forums reached the same conclusion; here we have only mentioned the most important one. However, in relation to our region of extensive Christian tradition, it is important to mention the outstanding papal encyclicals which came before the aforementioned statement.

"Mater et Magistra" dedicates a chapter to the "Relationship between zones of different development within the same country", and another to the "Relatonship between countries of different economic development"; the topic we are dealing with is extensively discussed in these two chapters.

"Mater et Magistra" and "Populorum Progressio" encyclicals are very clear and direct in stating the situation. For example, the latter says: "While in some regions an oligarchy enjoys a refined civilization, the rest of the population, poor and dispersed, is deprived of almost all possibilities of personal initiative and of responsibility; often tlerating liv-

211

ing and working conditions unworthy of human beings". The document gives great importance to the need for a true development in order to attain peace and to reduce increasing violence; it points out that: "Development is the new name for Peace"; therefore, peace is not an abstraction but, instead, peace is the fruit of justice.

Future Perspectives as Regards Development and Crime in Latin America

Bearing in mind the above quoted authoritative sources, a deterioration of the social development situation in the developing regions can be expected in the near future. The income gap between rich and poor countries will continue to increase and it is very likely that by the end of the decade, the number of persons in our planet living in "absolute poverty" will have increased by one hundred million, reaching 850 million persons.[13] The cited World Bank Report likewise foresaw further deterioration of the situation sustaining that, in combatting the crisis, policies adopted could aim at reducing human or social development programmes. Unfortunately, the World Bank's prediction is becoming true in Latin America: a recent study carried out in seventeen countries of the Economic Commission for Latin Ametica shows that fourteen of them have decreased, some drastically, their budgetary percentages for education and health.[14]

A large number of documents prepared by the Economic Commission for Latin America or by its experts, point out that the development process of the countries in our region is restrained by its inability to accumulate capital. It goes on to explain the two main reasons for this: a) the insertion of transnational corporation in our economy exerts a centripetal rather than centrifugal force, whereby the wealth transferred to the centre is greater than the wealth that remains in the countries, and b) a considerable part of the

212

wealth which remains in the countries is in turn misspent in the "consumer society" that the same transnational corporations introduce to the periphery, instead of injecting the wealth in the productive process, creating thereby a greater purchasing power among the population.[15]

Due to the aforementioned, it is important to emphasize the knowledgeable view taken in the most recent UN congresses on crime prevention and the treatment of offenders, focusing on the study of the crime problem in connection with the development/criminality relationship. It is likewise important to point out that in order to plan a realistic crime prevention policy for our region, one must begin by taking a clear and realistic view of the situation of development and of its future perspectives. It is foreseeable that, to the extent to which development is related to the existing socio-economic structure, unless the basic conditions vary and a more evenly distributed justice is reached within a New International Economic Order, criminality will either continue or get worse if the socio-economic situation deteriorates.

The Criminological Theory in Latin America

The elements gathered to date indicate, on the other hand, that regarding not only the theories that give the reasons for criminality but also possible preventive measures, we must not make the mistake of transferring, without analyzing, said theories and forms of prevention from developed countries to developing countries.

This does not mean to flatly refuse the contribution criminology in developed countries can provide. This would mean denying criminology as a science. We must take from criminology in developed countries that which we can use and try to validate its theories together with others which may emerge from direct knowledge of our reality.

From here on we will try to describe some of the most interesting delictive typologies and problems in our sur-

213

roundings so as to then move towards identifying the most adequate forms of prevention. We will start from the structural framework we have applied so far and from the interpretative elements contemporary criminological theory provides.

Conventional Crime Offences Against Property

The preceding chart suggests that the process of capitalist-peripheric development in the countries of our region leads to an increase in conventional crime rates and also to new forms of criminality.

Regarding conventional crimes, we will specifically refer to the most frequent offences against property throughout the world. They add up to more than 60% of total offences in all Latin American countries and, for the previously mentioned reasons, those with the fastest growth rate.

Based on theories which attempt to explain the phenomenon at least two large categories of offences against property can be identified in Latin America: 1) those which are the result of need, and which therefore can be explained on the basis of the theory of deprival; and 2) those which can be explained on the basis of Merton's theory of differential access to legal means to obtain social objectives.

Concerning the first group, it is important to state that a large sector of the population in our region live on the so-called minimum vital salary or even less; at the same time, studies carried out reveal that a large number of individuals in this category pass through our penitentiary system and fill our prisons. The minimum vital salary can be taken as a good indicator to characterize people in absolute deprival. Regarding this, the Economic Commission for Latin America shows that 40% of the families in the region live in poverty; their income is insufficient to meet the essential needs. Twenty percent live in conditions of indigence, that is, their income does not permit adequate nutrition.[16]

214

Over the last few years there has been a remarkable increase in the rates of specific types of crime against property due to the incidence of variables brought about by "criminogenic development processes". These variables are: unplanned rapid urbanization, unemployment, lack of housing, lack of trained labour, etc.[17]

This category of crimes includes larceny, qualified larceny, simple robbery, forced entry and gang robberies (association of two or more people). With a few exceptions, these crimes are not as sophisticated as one may find in Europe and the United States.

In order to avoid sanctioning and imprisonment, judges sometimes apply the justifiable cause of the "state of need"; nevertheless, it is applied only in those cases where the "state of need" arises due to the existence of a serious and imminent, present and immediate problem. Traditional jurisprudence and doctrine attribute the justifiable cause of the state of need to situations such as fire or immediate danger of death. Nevertheless, it would be important to elaborate in further detail the theory of the "state od need" so as to increment its use. When quantitatively measuring the degree of need of sectors of the population that incur in this type of crime, it can be observed that there are objective situations such as, lesser life expectancy, larger degree of incidence of certain serious diseases, etc., that are easily measurable. This circumstance should, at least within the limits granted by "judicial discretion" (minimum and maximum penalties established by law for each crime) help judges to regulate penalties to the state of deprival which has caused these persons to commit the offence.

In general , every penal code in the region foresees that punishment be dictated taking into account the individual's personal circumastances as well as his social conditions; however, judges' interpretation of this principle is extremely restricted.

Within the category we are analyzing, female deviant conduct is mainly prostitution; chiefly low level prostitution.

It is true that most legislations do not consider female voluntary prostitution a crime. However, prostitutes are pursued for infringement by municipal and police codes and, in most countries, punished by deprivation of freedom which is, in fact, more severe than the punishment inflicted for many crimes which are given conditional execution penalties. Summary proceedings that constantly allow that these women be deprived of their freedom, on an average of approximately thirty days, in many cases makes it possible for authorities unlawfully applying this power, to play the role of "extra-official mafia" exploiting prostitution among sectors of the population. This is a case of "collusion of public power abuse with economic power abuse".[18]

The analysis of this type of female deviant behaviour is, as in the aforementioned cases, based mainly on the theory of deprival. The analysis concerning the behaviour of those who exploit this activity is very different.

The second large group of crimes against property is that which can be explained based on Merton's theory of the differential degree of access to the legal means of reaching social objectives. This theory explains a good part of the criminal offences committed by the medium and lower classes in our society which, obsessed by the so-called "consumer society" usually pursue with determination, and by any means, the so-called "socially valuable" objectives although the social structure itself limits their access to them.[19]

Non-Conventional Crime: Economic Crime and Abuse of Economic Power

Within the so-called "economic criminality" category, the most serious crime in the countries of our region and which affects most our development process, is that usually committed by transnational companies.

216

Contrary to what happens when they operate illegally in their country of origin, when they carry out their activities in developing countries, transnational companies remove from the national and regional economic environment of the host country, the product of their illegal transactions. This is an almost irreparable social damage.

Some authors have well-argumented that crimes "against property", as well as economic crimes, when committed in the transnational corporation's country of origin (in what we have called "centre" countries), hardly produce any social damage, what they cause is a simple transfer of wealth from one sector to another or from one person to another. In this transfer there is logically a victim, but society as a whole is not directly affected (although, as a consequence of the crime, it may be affected by other types of hazards).[20]

However, this reasoning is not valid when the crimes are committed by transnational corporations in developing or peripheric countries, since in these cases, besides the individuals directly affected, important damage is caused to the society in general.[21]

Among these crimes, some of the most serious ones are: fraudulent bankruptcy, tax evasion, illegal flight of foreign currency, dumping, ecological damage to the environment or dangerous activities such as nuclear disposal sites which are being established in our region.

This type of criminality can be economically and structurally explained by means of the reasons previously pointed out. Furthermore, the social psychology contribution made by the differential association theory outlined by Edwin Sutherland is extremely revealing in relation to this type of crime as was practiced in the 40's in the United States.[22]

As the theory points out, the learning process of criminal conduct includes both criminal techniques, and rationalizations and attitudes; these rationalizations allow the individual to justify his behaviour to himself and to others. Within

217

the context we are dealing with, these rationalizations go beyond the world of isolated individuals and become accepted or even valued by wide sectors of society in general.

Specifically regarding criminal law, they contribute to the subtle distinction between the so called "illicit penal" and "illicit civil" ethically reproachable conduct but for which there never seems to be enough evidence to classify them as criminal. In this case, rationalizations have helped to "de-institutionalize" prison sentence (when punished, these conducts are not given a prison sentence but fines which are meaningless to the large companies behind the individual or which are simply transferred into cost to the consumer). In this respect and as regards penology, economic crimes have really been "pioneers". For many years criminologists and humanists have advocated the need to de-institutionalize prison sentence for minor crimes that cause little or no social damage. Nevertheless, large economic interests have, for a long time, successfully avoided that this sentence be applied to their representatives.

Non-conventional crime. Crimes against human rights (terrorism, kidnapping and hi-jacking, missing persons, torture, illegal loss of freedom, etc.); Crimes against public powers and constitutional order: (rebellion mutiny, conspiracy, corruption of security forces, claim on peoples' rights and removal from officee of duly constituted authorities, etc.)

This type of crime in our area cannot be explained on the basis of contemporary theories on criminality in European countries and in the United States. It fits into a structural explanation of our development process which brings about highly criminogenic conditions favouring this type of criminality in a manner and frequency that is unknown to Centre countries and that makes its eradication difficult.

218

The analysis of this matter in some documents published in recent years by the Economic Commission for Latin America is very revealing, particularly in some of the works by Raul Prebish.[23] Mention is made of this specific body and economist because of their authority, one as the specialized regional agency of the United Nations on this matter, the other as its president for many years.

The above mentioned studies reached the following conclusion (verified daily in our region): forms of radical economic liberalism are incompatible with democracy and human rights in our countries. Due to the large socio-economic differences which the former brings about, it leads to a process of structural violence which disrupts the democratic-republican system expressed, with slight differences, in the political constitutions of countries in the Latin American region. On the other hand, there exists a whole range of crimes that are linked to the process described.[24]

Drug Trafficking

A subject of great importance in our region is that of the illicit trafficking and consumption of narcotic drugs.

A problem common to all countries in the region is the lack of reliable statistics to evaluate the exact dimension of the problem. Nevertheless, ordinary Meetings of the Commission on Narcotic Drugs, WHO meetings, and various regional seminars organized by the United Nations on the subject, have revealed that in spite of the efforts to combat the problem, the production and illicit drug trafficking are rising in the majority of the countries of the region, reaching always younger groups of the population.[25] Even without complete and reliable statistics, the worsening of the problem is evident, and all the countries of the region are aware of it.

The problem was analyzed at a worldwide level during the "United Nations International Conference on Drug

Abuse and Illicit Trafficking", where consensus was reached concerning the need to carry out an international joint effort, and a "Comprehensive Multidisciplinary Outline of Future Activities in Drug Abuse Control"[26] as prepared to guide this action.

With regard to the consumption of drugs, the inconvenience has been pointed out of acting exclusively on the basis of so-called "negative strategies" which tend to rebound on the addict; instead, emphasis was placed on the convenience of offering positive alternatives to fill the vacuum which the drug user are seeking to satisfy.

In relation to illegal trafficking, international co-operation is indispensable in order to accomplish success. In as far as our region is concerned, ILANUD is exercising all its efforts to coordinate joint activities.

Possible Prevention and Control Strategies

Penal law and crime prevention strategies in our region still retain, in general, the traits of the 18th Century Classical School: severe punishment, mainly consisting in the privation of liberty — aimed predominantly at combatting "conventional crime" — and the absence of alternatives to imprisonment, with limited use or total unawareness of the existence of conditional sentencing.

In spite of the fact that criminological theory has evolved towards the de-institutionalization, as much as possible, of the use of imprisonment,[27] studies on the matter show that in practice its use has not decreased; furthermore, during the last ten years there has been a significant increase in the number of persons sentenced to imprisonment for offences which could be dealt with by probation.[28] It seems, therefore, that the reaction to the increase of crime rate is a mechanical response: it increases the use of the loss of liberty without carefully selecting or categorizing crimes on the basis of their gravity and social damage.[29]

This type of response introduces new criminal factors to the system (effects of imprisonment, transfer of the sentence, etc.) and notably increases the costs, since the use of prisons, even those of a precarious or inhuman nature, is expensive.

The following are some possible guidelines which, in our region's present state of development, could be taken into consideration by the crime prevention policies.

1. Concerning the types of conventional crimes which originate in absolute deprival, prevention must aim at eliminating this conditions. This leads us to forms of primary pre-delictum prevention which the United Nations long ago identified basically as "social justice".[30] Therefore, we must refer back to the idea of integral non-exclusive development, widely distributing its benefits so as to assure not only economic growth but also profitably influencing areas of health, occupation and income, education, housing, etc.

This, of course, implies adopting policies that go beyond the exclusive scope of the ministries of justice and which penetrate the areas of planning, economy, health, education, social welfare and community development. This, on the one hand, would be logical and convenient since true development planning, which produces well-being and rises the quality of life of our people, should be all-enveloping. On the other hand, as long as our criminal policy programmes are not included in national development programmes, we will continue to face serious difficulties.

2. As to the types of conventional crimes which originate in "relative deprival" or which are a product of our contemporary consumer society, primary prevention could also be important and directed at removing those conditions which lead to the pursuance, at any cost, of false objectives created by the international market. Huge resources which could be used to satisfy the basic needs of the population or which could be injected into the productive process, are lost

221

in our economy. "This deals with another spreading phenomenon in the centres, constantly spurred on by the marvellous expansion of social disseminaton and communication techniques".[31]

Evidently, this means adopting economic and mass media policies. Without these policies we would not stop this type of crime, and what is more, the best of our culture would be in danger.

Concerning the individual and post-delictum prevention strategies for this type of crime, it has been proved that the exacerbation in the use of imprisonment is ineffective as long as the basic conditions which give rise to it are not eliminated. As much de-institutionalization of prison as possible in its various forms is therefore advisable.

3. With regard to new criminal tendencies which cause severe individual and social damage, such as economic crimes, it is worth mentioning harshening of penalties and use of prison sentences for perpetrators. Likewise it is worth studying new patterns of responsibility, not only of an individual or personal type, but also collective or corporative. To date, the classical principle of our criminal law *societas delinquere non potest* has served to evade responsibilities in most severe cases of this type of crimes.

One of the greatest problems regarding the prevention of economic crimes is the need to train officers and judges who, for each case and in each situation, must gather the necessary convicting evidence to prove that the offence constitutes a penal case. Regrettably, this is frequently difficult.

Therefore, a number of questions arise: to what extent is traditional criminal law prepared to face these new criminal patterns? To what extent are police and judges trained or have at their disposal the necessary material elements to carry out their duty? Likewise, the need arises to create investigative and judicial bodies specialized in economic penal affairs.

4. Concerning crimes related to the violation of human rights, we feel that not only should the certainty of sentencing be assured, but also the guarantees introduced two centuries ago in the liberal criminal law. These permit the legitimizing action of justice when facing the structural violence pointed out at the beginning of this document.

For this same reason, we believe that ordinary justice should be responsible for this and all other types of crime. In this respect the Italian justice can be considered a positive example.

Finally, it should be mentioned here that this paper could not possibly have dealt with all dimensions of this vast topic. It is, therefore, only meant to supply references for an exchange of views concerning problems which seriously affect developing countries in the Latin American region.

Reference and Notes

1 See reports on: First United Nations Congress on the Prevention of Crime and the Treatment of Offenders, Geneva, 22 August-3 September 1955; Second United Natons Congress on the Prevention of Crime and the Treatment of Offenders, London, 8-19 August 1960; Third United Nations Congress on the Prevention of Crime and the Treatment of Offenders, Stockholm, 9-18 August 1965; Fourth United Nations Congress on the Prevention of Crime and the Treatment of Offenders, Kyoto, 17-26 August 1970; Fifth United Nations Congress on the Prevention of Crime and the Treatment of Offenders, Geneva, 1-12 September 1975; Sixth United Nations Congress on the Prevention of Crime and the Treatment of Offenders, Caracas, 25 August – 5 September 1980; Seventh United Nations Congress on the Prevention of Crime and the Treatment of Offenders, Milan, 26 August – 6 September 1985.

2 United Nations, Sixth United Nations Congress on the Prevention of Crime and the Treatment of Offenders, "Crime Trends and Crime Prevention Strategies", Agenda Item 3, A/CONF. 87/4 and Corr. 1; "New Perspectives in Crime Prevention and Criminal Justice and Development: The Role of International Co-operation", Agenda Item 8, A/CONF. 87/10, 1980.

[3] United Nations, Seventh United Nations Congress on the Prevention of Crime and the Treatment of Offenders, "New Dimensions of Criminality and Crime Prevention in the Context of Development: Challenges for the Future", Topic 1, A/CONF. 121/IPM/5; "Guiding Principles for Crime Prevention and Criminal Justice in the Context of Development and a New International Economic Order", A/CONF. 121/122, 1985.

[4] United Nations, Fifth United Nations Congress on the Prevention of Crime and the Treatment of Offenders, "Economic and Social Consequences of Crime: New Stimuli for Research and Planning", A/CONF. 56/7, 1975.

[5] United Nations, "New Perspectives...", *op. cit.*

[6] A. Birou, *Léxico de Economía,* Barcelona, Lala, 1973, p. 43; also in UNESCO, *Dictionary of Social Sciences,* Vol. I, Madrid, 1975, p. 687.

[7] World Bank, "Report on Worldwide Development 1981", Washington D. C., 1981, p. 115.

[8] R. Prebish, *Capitalismo periférico: crisis y transformación,* Fondo de Cultural Economica, México, 1981.

[9] *Ibidem*: "La periferia latinoamericana en el sistema global del capitalismo" *Revista de la CEPAL,* April 1981, p. 163; "Crítica al capitalismo periférico" *Revista de la CEPAL,* First Semester 1976.

[10] World Bank, "Report on Worldwide...", *op. cit.,* Tables 24 and 25 on "Income Distribution", Washington, D.C., 1981.

[11] *Ibidem,* pp. 7 and 122.

[12] United Nations, General Assembly, "Statement on the Establishment of a New International Order", 1 May 1974.

[13] World Bank, "Report on Worldwide...", *op. cit.,* 1981, pp. 4 and 115.

[14] United Nations, Economic Commission for Latin America and the Caribbean, "Crísis económica y políticas de ajuste, estabilización y crecimiento", Twenty-First Period of Sessions of ECLAC, Mexico, 17-25 April, 1986.

[15] R. Prebish, "Planificación, desarrollo y democracia", *Regional Conference on Social Conditions in Democracy*, San José, Costa Rica, September 1978.

[16] United Nations, Economic Commission for Latin America and the Caribbean, "The Development of Latin America in the Eighties", E/EC-LAC/G.1150, pp. 21 and 23.

[17] Criminological literature on the incidence of each of the said variables on criminology is abundant. United Nations, "New Perspectives...", *op. cit.,* 1980.

[18] United Nations, Sixth United Nations Congress on the Prevention of Crime and the Treatment of Offenders, "Crime and the Abuse of Power: Offences and Offenders beyond the Reach of the Law", A/CONF. 87/6, 1980.

[19] R. Merton, *Teoría y estructuras sociales,* Fondo de Cultura Económica, Mexico, 1980.

[20] United Nations, "Economic and Social Consequences...", *op. cit.,* 1975.

[21] United Nations, "Crime and the Abuse of Power:...", *op. cit.,* 1980.

[22] E. Sutherland and D. Cressey, *Criminology,* 9th edition, Philadelphia/N.Y., J. B. Lippincott, 1974.

[23] R. Prebish, "Planificación,...", *op. cit.; Capitalismo... op. cit.*

[24] J. A. Montero, "Tendencias de la delincuencia y estrategias para la prevención del delito en los países de América Latina", *International Review of Criminal Policy,* 1979, No. 35; United Nations, "Crime and the Abuse of Power:...", *op. cit.*

[25] United Nations, Commission on Narcotic Drugs, Supl. No. 4, New York, 1981; World Health Organization, Twenty Seventh Regional Meeting, Washington, October 1980.

[26] United Nations, "Report of the International Conference on Drug Abuse and Illicit Trafficking, Vienna, 17-26 June 1987", New York, 1987, pp. 3-88.

[27] United Nations, Seventh United Nations Congress on the Prevention of Crime and the Treatment of Offenders, "Reduction of the Prison Population, Alternatives to Imprisonment and Social Integration of Offenders", resolution 16, A/CONF. 121/22, 1985; United Nations, Sixth United Nations Congress on the Prevention of Crime and the Treatment of Offenders, "Deinstitutionalization of Corrections and its Implications for the Redisual Prisoner", A/CONF. 87/7, 1980.

[28] E. Carranza, et al., *El preso sin condena en América Latina y El Caribe,* San José, ILANUD, 1982.

[29] United Nations, "Crime Trends...", *op. cit.,* 1980.

[30] United Nations, Sixth United Nations Congress on the Prevention of Crime and the Treatment of Offenders, "Juvenile Justice: Before and After the Onset of Delinquency", A/CONF. 87/5, 1980.

[31] R. Prebish, "Planificación,...", *op. cit.*

SOCIAL CHANGE, CRIMINALITY AND SOCIAL CONTROL IN INDIA:

Trends, Achievements and Perspectives.

Upendra Baxi *

Notions of Social Change and Criminality

At the level of everyday life, change is ubiquitous; so is control and its transgressions known as "deviance". It requires considerable feats of theory and ideology to characterize certain tendencies and directions of social change as "development" and of deviance as "criminality". While this double transformation informs and enables contemporary discourses on development and crime, it also signifies a loss and a lack. The plenitude of deviance becomes transformed into the locus of "criminality"; not all major forms of deviance remain on the agenda of the state, society and law to cognize and combat. "Criminality" becomes a notion contingent on the very nature of class and state formative practices through legislation and legal administration (enforcement, adjudication).

Similarly, discourse on development valorizes certain types of social changes (for example: acceleration of changes in the forces and relations of production, growth of scientific temper, spread of secularization and individuation; the latter in the form of the citizen as consumer). Contemporaneously,

* Professor of Law, University of Delhi, New Delhi, India.

Acknowledgments: I must here record my appreciation of the Australian Vice-Cancellor's Committee for their award of a Visiting Fellowship at the Department of Law, the Research School of Social Sciences, the Australian National University, which enabled me to complete this paper. Mrs. Audrey Magee faired an irritating manuscript at short notice.

227

the valorization of certain forms of deviance and criminality as inherently developmental, also occurs. The discourse on "development" contains — almost universally — reference to the growth of crime as a necessary concomitant of development. Progressive criminality (an aspect of development) seems to provide indicators of social, economic and political development. The Bhopal catastrophe of 1984 provides an archetypal illustration of progressive criminality. All standards and rules concerning location, manufacture, storage, handling and safety procedures for hazardous products, processes and substances, were violated. Yet the Bhopal plant was considered a developmental good.[1] The developmental rationality (part of which was the production of toxic pesticides by a wanton multinational at Bhopal) was a part of a process designed to make India self-sufficient in foodgrains through the Green Revolution. this in turn sanctioned the creation of exploitative and semi-slave migrant rural labour market and a regime of disability and death for the helpless workers through pesticide poisoning and faulty agricultural equipment.[2] The harvest of occupational illness and disability, winnowed through outworn tariffs of workmen's compensation, is secured through strategies of *de facto* decriminalization of major forms of industrial and agrarian economic development.

Law and order operations, considered essential for development and "nation building", also shelter a whole variety of legal and extra legal police and paramilitary violence. Progressive criminality of this nature is, to be sure, a notoriously global phenomenon, as studies of comparative strife continue to remind us.[3] Also in the absence of adequate legal accountability, the data remains open to charges of inaccuracy. Yet, it is possible to say with available scientific studies, that the use of fatal force by police and paramilitary forces in India, especially through "encounters" (a term of art describing civilian casualties in dealing with 'dacoits', 'extremists', 'militants' and now 'terrorists') is alarmingly on the rise. Standardless use of force by the very custodians of people's security and well-being seems in India to stand justified as an aspect of development, here conceived, in terms of reasons of state, as reinforcing national unity and integration.

Progressive criminality, in its various forms and domains, is certainly often recognized as implying conduct that is proscribed by law through severe criminal sanctions. However, given the assumed tendency of such behaviour to promote "developmental" goals, legal administration (prosecution, adjudication, implementation/enforcement) immunizes it in a variety of *de facto* decriminalization techniques. At the same time, state and society in India are constrained to cognize and combat (what I have to call) "regressive" criminality in two distinct senses of that notion. First, regressive criminality consists in deviant behaviour which is seen to foil or frustrate the objectives of planned development. Second, it manifests of hegemony of the unwelcome, unvalued, unwanted rights to the past time or contemporary modifications of historic temporalities. These manifestations, indicative of (what Vilfredo Pareto called) the "contemporaneity of the non-contemporaneous", are considered regressive insofar as they put to test the very legitimacy of the state and the law, grounded in the new theologies of secular, scientific "development".

The first type of regressive criminality is, broadly speaking, identified by a whole gamut of 'economic crimes'which tend to retard emergent rationalities of industrial and state capitalism. Bureaucratic corruption and tax evasion, generating secret, black, or parallel economy, are considered today serious forms of regressive criminality, as they interrupt India's effort at capitalist development. This is also the case with networks of organized crime which are also seen, especially through narcotic traffic, to endanger national security and integrity. Concern with environmental

229

degradation as threatening economic and democratic development has, similarly, led to the naming and control of new delinquencies, especially in the wake of Bhopal.[4]

Concern with the second form of regressive criminality, asserting rights to a cultural past at odds with the legitimation needs of the state and the laws, is at long last becoming an articulate feature of Indian legislation and criminal justice administration. The revival of the practice of *sati* (burning widows at the funeral pyre of the deceased husband), dowry (burning of brides for inadequate supply of presentations in cash and kind during the first years of marriage as pledges of security and well-being of daughters in their matrimonial homes), amniocentesis of female foetuses and atrocities against untouchables are now being considered as forms of criminality which the state and law must seriously struggle to outlaw.

In a more general way, therefore, the relation between social change and criminality in contemporary India consists in the articulation of modes of progressive and regressive criminality. *De facto* decriminalization of what is perceived to be progressive criminality, and *de jure* criminalization of regressive forms of criminality reflect the accumulated contradictions in the nature of development, articulated by state power and legal administration.

Progressive Criminality, Social Change and the Dark Figure of Crime

The enactment of progressive criminality accentuates in India the dark figure of crime well beyond the narratives of conventional criminology. Many forms of criminality are tolerated, and even legitimated, by the Indian state, society and law. Often regime sponsored, such tolerance is also at times produced, as it were, under the joint auspices of the civil society and the state. The privileging of criminality is usually animated by the belief that progressive criminality is

230

not just a necessary evil but also, and often, a developmental good. Thus, an understanding of the ways in which certain types of criminality are privileged also decodes certain messages concerning societal transformation in India.

Privileging of criminal conduct occurs through various legal processes and modalities and it traverses a whole range of arenas and actors. The modalities of privileging criminal conduct include: non-cognizance and non-prosecution of criminal conduct, strategies of not pursuing prosecutional action in the "public interest" thereby creating the illusion that the administration of criminal justice exists, provision of regimes of amnesty for economic offenders (as well as "dacoits"), total bypassing of the criminal justice system in arenas of grave currruption involving persons in high positions by delegating to conveniently ineffectual devices such as commissions of inquiry, and an almost deliberate policy of negative personpower planning for judiciary positions resulting in what an incumbent Supreme Court Justice (Justice Krishna Iyer) was constrained to describe as "soft justice" syndrome.[5]

Privileging of certain actors and arenas covers rather a formidable range of criminal conduct. The state/regime sponsored privileging of such conduct occurs principally in three major arenas, extending virtual immunity to state security forces for large-scale criminal violence and other serious breaches of criminal law and the Constitution of India. The arenas include: (a) repressive use of force in dealing with revolutionary, secessionist and regional/ethnic movements directed towards greater autonomy, decentralization and self-determination within the Indian federation; (b) corruption offences, mainly when serious allegations are directed against incumbent politicians, upper echelons of the civil service, police and jail administration; and (c) law and order operations against "dacoits"/"social bandits". Privileging of criminality, under the joint sponsorship of the civil society and state/regime occurs in arenas that include: (d) "communal" riots; (e) "atrocities" (heinous offences)

231

against the untouchables (constitutionally christened the Scheduled Castes, they constitute 15% of India's approximately 800 million population and are exposed both to legislative reservation and a whole array of compensatory or preferential discrimination programmes);[6] (f) patriarchal violence against women and (g) campus violence.

Revolutionary, Secessionist and Autonomy Movements

"Revolutionary" movements have come to be symbolized by the phrase "Naxalite movements" in Indian political and legal discourse. Inspired by truly radical, militant ideologies, Naxalite movements aim to accelerate fundamental transformation of state and civil society in India and are characterized by acute critiques of the bourgeois landlord state formation, and by the deployment of force and terror against the "enemies of the people" (especially landlords, money-lenders, recalcitrant local elites, police and paramilitary forces). In certain enclaves, the movement has been able to experiment with alternative legality and regimes of governance. Despite three decades of militaristic repression, custodial torture, and internal fragmentation within the factions of the movement (marked by theoretical bloodletting as well as death to the "traitors" and "informers"), the Naxalite theory and praxis continue to win young adherents throughout India and has, significantly, constrained the state to move less effectively in the direction of agrarian reform and alleviation of mass impoverishment.[7]

"Secessionist" movements seek new frameworks for self-determination outside the Indian federation, if possible, and within it, if necessary. The two decade-long insurgency in Mizoram and the present Khalistan movement in Punjab provide the most striking illustration of an "irredentist" direction of Indian social transformation.

In contrast, autonomy movements constitute endeavours by regional and ethnic groups to secure self-determination within the Indian Union, regarding their rights to identity and destiny through preservation not only of their language but also of their cultural and religious traditions. In the first decade of Indian independence, such movements generated a redrawing of the federal map of India through linguistic reorganization of Indian states. Nevertheless, autonomy movements continue to persist, insisting, on the one hand, on a proliferation of new states within the Indian federation and on the other, on preferential treatment of the "sons of the soil" in the existing state units.[8]

While autonomy movements, even when involving assertion of sub-national identities and aspirations through criminal violence have led, first to militaristic repression and then to fascinating exercises in constitutional and legal accommodation. On the other hand, secessionist and "Naxalite" movements have invited thoroughgoing repression by the Indian security forces. Although legal processes and institutions have been involved (e.g. preventive detention, criminal prosecution, legislative enhancement of executive power, capital punishment), counter-insurgency measures have been preeminently characterized by militaristic use of force (e.g. annihilation campaigns, reign of terror for those suspected of being "Naxalites", torture in jails and detention camps, hamleting, counter-propaganda, brainwashing and indoctrination). The technique of annihilation has been adopted even by the civilian police: especially when it has been entrusted with law and order operations in crime "infested" arenas. The term of art is "encounter deaths": it describes rebel casualties as being the outcome of armed confrontation between police and rebels. Social action litigation in India (still miscalled public interest litigation)[9] has sought to demonstrate the unconscionable loss of civilians life through these encounters; in actual fact, in one case the Supreme Court of India has already awarded substantial damages to the family of the victims in counter-insurgency operations in Nagaland. Judging by the norms of India's Constitution and the values of the Indian legal order, this privileging of criminality in counter-insurgency operations — and associated forms of it — have been described as "governmental lawlessness"[10] and even as "state terrorism".[11] While this articulate indictment of modes of counter-insurgency operations testifies to the vigour of democracy, it also indicates the failure of political democracy and planned development in enhancing the constitutional ideology of consensus and the thrust towards the redemption of India from mass impoverishment and increasingly unacceptable inequalities of income distribution.

Corruption Offences

The second arena, reinforcing the last observation, is that which privileges corruption in high places. This privileging is achieved and articulated through the normative legal system itself. Under the general penal law of India, as well as the special regime for anti-corruption offences, no prosecution may be initiated without prior sanction of a competent state authority. "Public servants" (itself a term of art, including ministers and civil servants) may not be prosecuted without prior sanction, but should such an eventuality arise, special courts for corruption offences may well not cognize a complaint. The executive discretion in granting or refusing such sanction is virtually untrammeled. Standards of constitutional or administrative justice do not provide for court review over delay or denial in sanction. Although private prosecutions for corruption offences can be initiated upon sanction, the first such prosecution in the four decades of independence went through eight years of labyrinthine litigation, resulting in an unprecedented reversal by the Supreme Court of its own earlier decision in the self-same proceeding! The new Prevention of Corruption Act — 1987, while streamlining procedures, jurisdictions and offences, and enhancing punishments, still

234

retains the sovereign prerogative of prior sanction and does not affect minimally the power in prosecution to seek withdrawal from prosecution on the ground of "public interest" at any stage before conviction and sentencing.[12]

This privileging of corruption has led to a certain degree of "privatisation" of state and is steadily transforming the social perception of a democratic state into a mercantilist state. Moral crusades against corruption in their first nationwide manifestation under Jai Parkash Narain-led Total Revolution movement produced, dialectically, the imposition of a national emergency in 1975-1976;[13] the mid-eighties witnessed yet another massive *exposé* of political corruption that almost lead to a major constitutional crisis when the last President of India was said to have considered dismissal of the Prime Minister Rajiv Gandhi's government. In the absence of authoritative vindication of guilt or political honour, the folklore of corruption grows apace, causing considerable strain on the still fragile system of liberal political democracy and illustrates, in the process, the high social cost of privileging investigation, prosecution and punishment for corruption offences.[14]

"Dacoity/Social Banditry"

The response of the state and the law to this problem has been complex and varied. On the one hand, special legal regimes exist to police and punish "dacoity", on the other hand, there have arisen special regimes of rehabilitation and amnesty. In 1959, the entire criminal justice system of India was suspended *de facto* by Prime Minister Jawaharlal Nehru to enable "Saint" Vinoba Bhave to "convert the hearts" of Chambal Valley dacoits; a similar experiment was performed by Prime Minister Indira Gandhi in 1969 this time to enable Jai Prakash Narain to perform similar spiritual tasks. The result achieved by these expeditions have been subjects of some controversy; but the most striking aspect of them was the wholesale suspension of the Indian legal order by executive fiat.[15]

In recent years, ruthless repression entailing standardless use of force seems to be the norm. For example, in the period 1979-1981 approximately 7,879 Indians were killed in anti-"dacoity" operations through police "encounters". Although all those killed were posthumously described officially as "dacoits" or accomplices, a recent sociological study has shown that the majority of those killed were innocent citizens, mainly lower caste Hindus, who could not be proved to have had any complicity with "dacoit" depredation. Despite this, to date, no attempt has been made to punish the guilty nor to compensate the families of those killed. Privileging use of fatal force in policing operations entails obviously heavy costs for the integrity of police force as well as the constitutional integrity of political orders.

The civil society's state-sponsored tolerance of criminal conduct signifies the prevailing orders of consensus among the elite groups in India. Political discourse is suffused with the incantation of the limits of the state and the law in the face of intransigent community values and patterns of behaviour sustained by these. Critical discourse, however, perceives a complicity between agencies of state and dominant elites in perpetuating certain forms of criminality as serving common ends of class power. Yet, if the jointly privileged criminal conduct contains both messages of dominance, it also carries messages of subaltern resistance to domination. They also convey to us the nature of state-formative practices in the process of transformation of Indian society. These contexts are briefly examined below.

"Communal" riots

In terms of aggregate analysis of Indian criminal statistics, the total incidence of riots over a fifteen year period (1966-1980) has shown an increase of 100.17%. Riots constituted 45% of the reported crimes in 1980. Compared with the base year (1966), the total incidence of riots in 1980 increased by 208.27% and its share of the total crime is estimated as 84.09%. "The increasing incidence of riots (100.71%), the incidence per million of population (68.38%) and the share of total crimes (45%) over these fifteen years is specially alarming".[16]

While not all riots are communal (hindu-muslim violent clashes sometimes lasting for days and weeks), available statistics would suggest a salience of communal riots; evidence that may even justify a greater cause for alarm. Since the independence, communal riots have occurred in almost all parts of India. From an average of 65 riots in the fifties, the number increased to 367 in the seventies. Between 1954 and 1959, there were 336 communal clashes; the number increased to a cruel tally of 2,938 riots in 1958-59. The decade 1971-1980 was marked by 2,574 riots. In this period, 816 muslims and 362 hindus were killed, and 15,404 people were injured.[17]

Bare statistics cannot narrate the magnitude of horror and depredation,[18] nor can they bring to bear on discourse the languages of victimhood.[19] Triggered by some trivial-looking incidents (such as kite-flying, routes of religious processions, use of amplifiers in mosques, claims over disputable and often non-existent *mazars* (tombs of saints and temples), these horrible happenings called "communal riots" entail weeks and months of concerted preparation: hostile propaganda (rumours, pamphleteering, door to door campaigns), collection of all kinds of arms (knives, sharp instruments, country-made revolvers, bomb and grenade materials) and conscription of the riot personnel with training of willing or forced recruits. The theatre of riots are usually small-sized towns with around 30% muslim population.[20] The pattern of fatal and other forms of debilitating injuries, as well as damage and destruction of property, increasingly suggest the presence at riot sites of elements from the world of organized crime.[21] Although there has been difficulty in establishing positive correlation between riots and communal parties and movements (as well as responsible elements within major national and regional party formations), these stand indictes (in some official inquiry reports and at the bar of progressive public opinion) for fomenting riot situations. In recent democratic rights movement investigations on the Meerut riots, overwhelming *prima facie* evidence of communally inspired violence by security forces also came to the surface, thus aggravating the overall situation of violence and intolerance.

The question of "causation" of communal violence has been recurrently addressed by theorists of Indian social transformation. Understanding of it involves recourse to one or more of the following constitutive elements:

(a) History: as providing reservoir of collective memories and images of past violence for both hindus and muslims; whether the history of *longue durée* genre of about four centuries of muslim invasion and rule in India or of the colonial tactics of power ("divide and rule") ultimately leading to the partition of India in 1947 or, again, the history of the immediate past replete with riots.

(b) Religion: as especially furnishing to the Indian muslims — through processes of Islamization —[22] with cohesive cultural identity; and the proselytizing aspect of Islam (some communal riots have recently centred on successful conversion of untouchables to Islam and their forcible reconversion to Hinduism; considerable ingenuity seems now to be exercised in conscripting untouchables to fight muslims in riot situations as a strategy to prevent future conversions).

(c) Minority syndrome: constituted by radical uncertainty, persecution complex, low tolerance and high sensitivity to the patterns of apperceived majority intrusions (in late 1988, for example, Salman Rushdie's *Satanic Verses* was

238

banned by the Government of India at the behest of the community leadership to prevent hurting of religious sentiments and probable large scale communal riots; the issues of validity of the ban are now before the Supreme Court of India).

(d) Politics: while muslim votes are highly coveted and decisive in many constituencies and issues of law reform policy, muslim representation in Indian parliament and state legislatures remains at a low level and constitutes approximately the same low percentage as it did at the first general elections in 1952;[23] this has, in part, encouraged militant communally-based fringe parties/movements among Indian muslims and, by way of response, among the hindus as well.

(e) Legislative policy: which has fundamentally assaulted patriarchal elements in Hindu law traditions (assuring, normatively at least, equal rights of inheritance to women, proscribing bigamy and the practice of *sati,* liberalization of divorce — to a certain extent — and provision for suitable maintenance) has, in the name of "secularism", reinforced patriarchal traditions in the law of *shariat* (allowing unilateral *talak,* polygamy, disallowing reasonable maintenance upon divorce beyond the period of *iddat*). The Directive Principle of State Policy commanding the state to move towards a Uniform Civil Code remains a dead letter, despite support from progressive muslim opinion, of both men and women, and activist judicial interpretation which are quickly set at naught by the legislature.[24]

(f) Ambivalence towards the state: while the state is perceived by Indian muslims to be a prize arena for fostering processes of Islamization, it is also contextually perceived as an unjust "Hindu"-"majority" state which fails to protect fundamental democratic rights of muslim communities, including survival and dignity.

239

(g) Geopolitics: according to articulate (as well as inarticulate) majority perception, the "fundamentalist" Islamic states appear to have developed considerable interst in keeping the "communal" cauldron burning at all times in India (riots are constantly shown to be structured by intruding "foreign hands").

(h) False consciousness: "communalism is largely a false consciousness ... as it only serves to hide the structure of deprivations, mainly social, economic and political".[25]

(i) Class elements: comunal riots furnish means of fragmenting class alliances and solidarities amongst the impoverished.

Even this crude survey of constitutive elements of causal explanations reminds us of the complexity of the phenomenon called "communalism" and with it, of the well worn theme of the limits of the law. Even so, state/societal privileging of criminal conduct and violence (virtual non-enforcement of criminal law) is incorrectly identified within the limits of effective legal action. The idea that vigilant and strict law enforcement directed at prevention and punishment would serve as a further catalyst to riotous behaviour in the future, is simply baseless and self-serving and represents in itself a communally based approach to the law. We know, with blinding clarity, that criminal conduct here provides an effective medium for "uncivic" (to say the least) sub-elites to pursue unabashedly their material interests through carefully orchestrated violent means (few riots are spontaneous social events). Effective criminal justice administration appears, on the contrary, to be necessary and wholly justified. Regardless of the long term deterrence effect of interventions by the criminal justice system on riots, the short term effects would indeed be salutary: these would at least deplete the ensemble of social opportunities and initiatives which opportunistic formations, inclusive of politically adventurist elements and elements of organized crime, now wield with impunity. Legal intervention would also enhance the legitimation of democratic policy which stands totally enfeebled by the cruel privileging of communal violence, suggesting complicity or cowardice and feeding paranoia concerning the predatory permanence of certain "uncivic" formations among both communities and insecurity amongst, especially, minority communities.

Atrocities against the Untouchables

The problem of atrocities against untouchables (and tribal populations) has been in the forefront of elite consciousness and is recognized to be a form of regressive criminality which ought to be curbed by sound legal administration. Yet, the available legal instrumentalities — the normative law enunciations, judicial process and procedure, effective investigative instrumentalities, and innovative prosecutorial strategies — do not match this growing awareness.[26]

Indian law contains no offence known as "atrocities". Yet, operationally, law enforcement agencies consider it a distinct category of criminality highlighting two elements. "Atrocities" involve the commission of heinous offences "with an element of cruelty, brutality or wickedness" and the commission of such offences has, as its main objective, "teaching a lesson" to untouchables.[27] Despite the indeterminacies of this notion, which prove critical to effective law enforcement,[28] it offers working insights into the dual character of atrocities. Heinous collective caste violence is inscribed on each text of atrocity; so is its ultimate pedagogic code — simply aimed at making untouchables realise that their place in Indian society is exactly where it has been for millennia, at the bottom of the social heap.

Since atrocities constitute congeries of distinct offences, statistics are hard to come by. Nevertheless, the annual reports to Parliament by the Commissioner of the Scheduled Castes and Tribes privide some reliable accounts,

241

even when the indeterminacy of the notion tends towards keeping the dark figure dark. Even with this caveat, it is still clear that atrocities are on the increase. The period 1973-1978 witnessed 62,295 visitations upon the untouchable life and property (that is to say, the barest means of cheating their way into survival). In 1977-1978, 12,746 atrocities were registered, leaving in their trail at least 354 killed an 306 registered cases of rape.

The theatre of atrocities is mainly rural, though movements against reservations for untouchables (together with tribals and "backward classes") typified by the 1985 prolonged agitation in the State of Gujarat suggest new forms of urban extension.[29] Undoubtedly, criminal violence against untouchables entails conflicts over ritual norms. Nevertheless, assessments which place their incidence as high as 70% in the period 1947-1977 invite suspicion of overstatement. There appears to be enough persuasive evidence, indeed, that the immediate provocation emanated from the untouchables 'pursuit of' material interests and status equality; demand for higher minimum wages, distribution of surplus land, secure tenancy rights, access to drinking water at the village wells, access to common and public places. It is noteworthy that the highest amount of assertion and repression has been associated with the Green Revolution areas, though by no means only confined to these. The untouchable articulation of social justice, and the fierce repression by dominant classes is neither "local in implication nor sectional in interest, nor short lived and transient".[30]

It has even been suggested that "class wars" would be a more apt description than atrocities. Not only the upper peasantry (landlords and rich peasants) but also "socially backward but economically ascendant castes of lower peasantry" provide seat and source of fierce repression of untouchable articulation.[31]

Atrocities, or to borrow Ralph Milliband's striking phrase, "anticipatory class wars" against the untouchables,

242

constitute a bloody intersection of enactment of strong change expectancies among them and the almost Lacanian desire for domination by the old and the new peasant classes.[32] At the same time violence against untouchables is "often a direct attack on the authority of the state itself".[33]

While it would be overly ambitious to assign a critical role to the criminal justice system, and the legal order as a whole, in the struggle against atrocities, it is well to recall that the groundwork for untouchable articulation for justice has been laid down by the Constitution of India in the four decades it has been operating, and by its normative onslaughts against the caste hierarchy. Even when its full impact may remain subject to a variety of probabilistic assessment, there is a need for a national policy on prevention and punishment of atrocities. The lack of such a policy makes not merely the existent legal administration lethargic and lackadaisical but bestows it, extravagantly, with caste bias, inimical to democratic faith. Equally, it emboldens unconscionable and uncostitutional predatory class/caste formations to practice, with relative impunity, the pedagogy of atrocities.

Violence against Women

As noted in some detail in the ensuing section of this paper, violence against women — especially rape and custodial rape (rape in police and prison custody) — has increased phenomenally in the last decade. But, as with atrocities, violence against women has been increasingly recognized by state and society as regressive. As pointed out earlier, this form of violence is comprehensively affecting women from cradle to coffin and includes: amniocentesis (aborting of female foetuses), deferred female infanticide (through sex based nutritional discrimination), statutory rape, bride burning (dowry), the sudden revival of *sati* in some parts of India, and the battered wife syndrome.

243

While during the International Women's Year national attention was focused on problems of inequalities of status,[34] it is the arena of patriarchal violence which has massively mobilized public opinion and constrained vigorous state action. Starting with a *crie de coeur* by four law academics[35] at the Supreme Court's reversal of conviction of two police constables for custodial rape on the ground of lack of evidence that the victim resisted (and, therefore, consented!), we find a vigorous espousal of law reform by women's groups and social activists. Over the last few years this has led to momentous reversal of norms and processes of the criminal justice system. The gamut of law reform includes measures such as "creation" of a new offence of custodial rape, reversal of onus of proof on the accused that the victim consented in situations of custodial rape, the thoroughgoing reformulation of the Dowry Prohibition Act, provision of a rebuttable presumption of death due to unnatural causes (dowry and cruelty related) in case a wife dies within seven years of marriage, stringent rearticulation of prevention of immoral traffic legislation, a state legislation regulating the technique of amniocentesis (in Maharashtra) with a national legislation now on the anvil. Sentencing attitudes have also undergone a profound change, and greater sensitivity to crimes against women is constantly demanded, and increasingly displayed, by the law enforcement agencies.

Only a decade ago, not even a far-sighted futurist would have been able to forecast such fundamental transformations in the direction of combatting patriarchal violence. Yet, it would be too idealistic to say that all these measures and processes have adequately responded to the manifold problems of patriarchal violence. It is significant that the legal order has moved that far to delegitimate such violence, instead of awaiting cultural transformation. It is also significant that law here features and figures as a dominant democratic instrumentality of social transformation. Also, the continued growth of women's movements ensures the prospects of further constraining state action and societal values in the direction of a just social order.

Campus Criminality

Campus criminality is yet another form of privileging criminal behaviour. University youth represents a significant and volatile section of emergent political communities in India. Virtually, all major national parties patronize student unions on campuses. Faced by an uncertain employment prospect, driven by conflicting perceptions of change and dominant ideologies, influenced by overseas models of students movements, excited by their emergence as centres of political power in Indian society, student power manifests itself in diverse forms ranging from ideological politics to a more organized pursuit of such manipulation of academic standards and schedules as facilitates, with relative ease, passing of examinations and attainment of degrees. In the processes of articulation of student power, serious transgressions of criminal law tend to be the norm, rather than the exception; and effective administration of the criminal justice system is here exceptional, when not conspicuous by its total absence.

In the process, and cumulatively symbolic violence on the campuses and cities (damaging public property on and off campuses, burning and "hijacking" of buses, use of force against university authorities and teachers) has become legitimated. Even normal techniques of law enforcement are perceived as "police excesses" and legal "repression": this includes registration of first information reports by the police, arrest, and criminal prosecution. Large-scale law and order operations, when situations get out of hand, dialectically, emerge as police "atrocities" and become the site of further movements.

Toleration of campus criminality is also widespread in civil society. Increasingly, parental authority and control are becoming problematic given the slow, but sure, victory of technology over culture. As has been observed: "Interestingly, the Green Revolution and the demand for new technology has specially contributed to the obsolescence of age as the measure of accumulated knowledge or experience".[36] The moral authority of politics has also declined, since the exemplarship provided by leading politicians in the first decades of Indian independence, has not significantly contributed towards preserving the high ideals which inspired national struggle and animate the constitutional vision of a resurgent India.

The Dimension of Crime in India

Even within the state of art, it is possible to say that the incidence of cognizable (serious) crime in India, measured over a period of fifteen years (1966-1980) is on the increase. The average incidence of crime in this period increased by 37.76% and the incidence per lakh (one hundred thousand) population has registered an increase of 13.78%. A comparison of crime as related to the growth of other social and economic indicators (for the period 1963-1973) demonstrates that while cognizable crime has registered a 4.6% growth *per annum*, the percentage increase *per annum* for national income stood at 2.9; population at 2.2; factory employment at 2.1; *per capita* income at 1.3; literacy at 0.06 and urbanization at 0.02.[37]

The Indian Penal Code broadly classifies crimes as: against persons, property and state. A vast number of penal statutes (both national and state laws) create offences, including "special" offences, which cut across this neat-looking categorization of the Code. In terms of the Code categories, we find that in 1980, as compared with the base years of 1966, a "tremendous increase of 74.23%" occurred in crimes against persons (murder, kidnapping, abduction) and its incidence, per million of population, stands at 28.64%.[38] In particular, data on the period 1971-1980 suggests a rise of 28.35% and 10.26% respectively, for rape and culpable homicide not amounting to murder. The data of 1970 and 1981 suggest "an alarming rise" of 28.64% in culpable homicide and 76.43% for rape. Indeed, when we look at the incidence per million of population for 1980, in comparison with the base year, we find that while culpable homicide has shown an increase of 6.78%, rape has registered a "phenomenal increase" of 46.62%.[39] The latter may, of course, partly be accounted for by the rising feminist outcry against patriarchal violence as well as by the inclusion of statistics of rape committed during communal riots and atrocities against untouchables.

At first sight, crimes against property (dacoity, robbery, burglary, theft, criiminal breach of trust, cheating) constitute a larger share of the total crime. For the fifteen year period the percentage share of these crimes was 22.17 as compared with crimes against persons (2.57%). Yet, on closer exa-mination, when percentage decreases (relative to their total share in overall crime situation) are noted, we find that while the decrease in crimes against property is 7.66%, that of crime against persons is only 1.55%. This difference in decreasing trends suggests a puzzling feature, especially if we were to regard property offences as the "hallmark of modernization".[40]

The share of "miscellaneous crimes" including riots (and it is hard to tell what constitute "miscellaneous" crimes except that they represent a conflation of various offences under what are called "special" laws and relatively minor offences) in the fifteen year period was 24.58%. Nevertheless, when the category "riots" is isolated it reaches the order, as noted earlier, of 100.71%. The other features of riots have already been noted in detail earlier, but we might pause to acknowledge here the peculiar fact that the percentage of women arrested for riot in 1980 stood at 23.66% (the highest percentage catergory for arrests), and 16% of convicted women had been successfully charged with riotous behaviour in 1980.[41] It is unlikely in the extreme that these figures relate to communal riots. If so, this information is consistent with the fact of relatively high participation of women, over the last two decades, in various social and political protest movements.

In addition, both the female and juvenile criminality appears to be on the increase too. In the period 1971-1981 the percentage increase in female criminality has been "phenomenal": 78.56% — especially when recalling that the "female population has increased by only 11.83%". The incidence of female criminality is estimated at 51.55% (for 1980 as compared with the base year of 1971) and the share of crimes, relative to the total, has risen by 56.8%.[42]

Similarly, the percentage of juvenile crime has increased, in 1970-1980 period, from 2.04% to 4.0%. Its incidence per million of population has increased from 5.1% to 8.3%. The percentage of juveniles sent to prison during this period registered a decrease from 19.9% in 1970 to 13.9% in 1981. The Juvenile Justice Act — 1987, implementig most of the Beijing Rules, now altogether outlaws imprisonment of juveniles. However, provision of alternate and meaningful custodial centres will demand substantial allocation of resources to the juvenile justice system which, so far, has not been done.

Dimensions of Organized Crime in India:
an Impressionistic Survey

The Indian criminal justice system, both normatively and institutionally, has displayed a live concern with the problem of organized crime. The images of organized crimes vary; distinct legislative regimes deal with, for example, "dacoity", *goondaism* (gangsterism), laws against "anti-social" elements, food and drug adulteration, tax evasion and fraud, smuggling, hoarding and blackmarketearing, foreign exchange evasion, trafficking in women and children, and drug trafficking.

248

Over the decades, difficulties of enforcement in some of these arenas has led to the institutionalization of preventive detention, which are already authorized by Article 22 of the Indian Constitution. Where the National Security Act (a lineal descendant of the earlier Preventive Detention and Maintenance of Internal Security Acts) has proved less efficient to cope with organized crime, special preventive detention legislation, such as the Conservation of Foreign Exchange and Prevention of Smuggling Act, 1974, have conferred vast powers of detention for limited periods with the assurance of minimal review by detention boards. Valid detention orders under the latter enactment make the property of the detainee liabe to confiscation under the Smuggler and Foreign Manipulation (Forfeiture of Property) Act — 1976. A law also provides that the periods of limitation for prosecution prescribed by the Criminal Procedure Code shall not extend to economic offences.

The preventive detention laws have spawned a civil-rights oriented "detention jurisprudence" under the auspices of the Supreme Court of India. To some extent, adversarial vindictive and political uses of detention laws, especially archived during the emergency regime, have led courts and lawyers to place under forensic microscope the validity of procedures, grounds and nature of detention orders. Yet, the overall concern for maintenance of strict standards of constitutionality and legality has provided a valued resource for the leaders of organized crime in India. Following is a brief look at some data on organized criminality.

Smuggling

Extensive smuggling of gold into India provides a thriving black market. During the period 1970-1986 at least 100 metric tons of gold (equal to Rs. 2,926 crore — a crore is a unit of ten million rupees) were smuggled into India. Depending on the international price of silver, contraband export of silver in "good" years amounts to twenty five million ounces *per annum*, equivalent to the annual production of silver in Mexico.[43] Other items of contraband import include watches, synthetic fibres and electronic goods, whose rupee value is yet to be fully estimated. Despite all the antismuggling drives, it has been acknowledged officially that the seized contraband constitutes annually no more than 5% of smuggled goods imported into India.[44]

As a complex operation, involving multivarious agents and transactions (principally oral), smuggling has to rely on techniques of intimidation, terror and assassination. Mystery murders, by hired assassins, are now quite common. Conflict of territoriality and of loyalty among various "gangs" of smugglers often lead to large scale violence, amply documented in routine police communiqués and the national press. The surplus money generated by smuggling operations is channeled into other extortionate activities (suc as gambling, trafficking in women, kidnapping, extortionate fund raising from businessmen). The surplus is also "productively" channeled as patronage funding to sections of law enforcement officers, political bosses and often dedicated to party campaign funds.

Bootlegging

After decades of experimentation, prohibition of liquor survives stringently only in two Indian states — Gujarat (the birth-state of Mahatma Gandhi and Tamil Nadu). The universally noted criminogenic consequences of prohibition regimes are also witnessed in the Indian experience. But in India the (also noted) axis between some politicians, enforcement officials and bootlegger barons assumes a rather sinister dimension where their criminal skills are placed at the service of communal violence, atrocities against untouchables and "management" of fledgling trade union movements. The Gujarat state prohibition inquiry commission, headed by an incumbent High Court Judge,

250

was constrained to acknowledge that "... there are materials to show that these baron bootleggers ... play an important part in political life, especially during the elections".

Drug Trafficking and Addiction

A comprehensive national legislation (broadly implementing the narcotic traffic conventions) — known as the Narcotic Drugs and Psychotropic Substances Act — came into force in November 1985. Still the long lack of such a legislative regime made possible the entrenchment of patterns of trafficking and addiction. At present there are an estimated 500,000 drug addicts and future estimates indicate that by the year 2000 this number will have risen to 5 million. Sociological surveys indicate a high proportion of heroin addicts (68.6% in a Delhi survey) among the high-school students and the youth ranging from 21 to 30 years.

The extent of the market may be inferred through fragmentary statistics made available by the Director of Revenue Intelligence: to take just one example, 2,280 kgs. of heroin were seized in 1987 — an increase of about 300% over the figure for 1986! Regulatory measures in cultivation of opium have brought down its annual licensed production to 673 tons in 1986-1987 as compared with 1,646 tons in 1977-1978; nevertheless, extensive leakages persist.[45] Already, considerable dissatisfaction is being expressed concerning the judicial enforcement of the narcotic drugs law: of the 4,503 prosecutions launched throughout India since 1985, convictions have resulted in 525 cases, with acquittals places at 145, and a large number of cases still exposed to long pendency. An eminent, now retired Indian police official, observes that "it would be naive to expect that our prevailing law of evidence and judicial procedures would help enforcing the drug laws properly and promptly".[46]

251

The drug trafficking problem in India has already assumed international dimensions. An assessment presented at the United Nations Fund for Drug Abuse Control Meeting (Vienna, June 1987) suggests that, because of stricter controls in Thailand, Burma and Iran 80% of the heroin that circulates "in the streets of the United Kingdom and Western Europe goes via Bombay". The Indian government also perceived a strong connection between illicit drug trafficking and acts of terrorism ravaging Punjab.[17]

Black Money

Apart from violence, the most pertinent effect of organized crime is the expansion of "black" or "secret" money, resulting in a "parallel economy" and in an escalation of "privileged class deviance".[48] The phenomenon of "secret money" is of course universal;[49] nevertheless, in India it assumes rather poignantly disruptive proportions that thwart efforts at planned democratic development.

According to the most recent report on the subject, commissioned by the Ministry of Finance of the Government of India, the proportion of black money estimated at 6.5% in 1960-1961 and 11.4% in 1975-1976, has grown to between 18% and 21% of the GNP of India as of 1985. Among the sources of black money (apart from smuggling and narcotics trafficking) is bureaucratic and political corruption; of the Rs. 27,133 crores entailed in public expenditure in 1981-1982, 'leakages' of the magnitude of Rs. 5,427 crores have taken place. The report, in addition, states that tax evasion is "not only higher in absolute terms but also as percentages of the GDP (gross domestic product) and income assessed to tax".[50]

Conclusions

The foregoing, rather non-rigorous survey, suggests at least the following conclusions:

First, both "ordinary" (individualistic) and "organized" crime in India is on the increase. Second, the Indian experience privileges some forms of criminality by *de facto* decriminalization, and combats others, thus illustrating the dialectic between the "progressive" and "regressive" forms of criminality. Third, toleration of certain types of criminality is at times regime-sponsored and at others produced by an operative consensus among the dominant interest formations in civil society as well as the state. Fourth, this consensus is particularly jeopardized in the arena of legitimation and valorization of patriarchal violence by insurrectionary feminist consciousness and movement. Fifth, privileged class deviance and organized crime demonstrate the inimical impact of the present practice of democratic poltics. Sixth, privileging of standardless use of force in security and law and order operations, while serving the reason of the state in the short run, carries the potential, in the long run, of shaking the very foundations of democratic legitimation of power and a rule of law society. Seventy, India, overall, emerges as a very violent society despite the gospel of Mahatma Gandhi. It would appear that if India achieved freedom from colonial yoke through preeminently non-violent struggle, she now seeks to sustain it by increasing toleration of violent means, within and outside constitutional/legal frameworks.

All these distinct but related, conclusions suggest more specifically the dynamics of accumulated contradictions; the changing forms of criminality help us somewhat in deciphering both the nature of state-formative practices (in moments of their consolidation as well as of their crises) and the structural changes in Indian society.

As to the nature of state-formative practices, the prevailing regime style, and criminal justice policies in particular, reflect growing contradictions of wielding power and authority. Privileging of corruption creates an enduring contradiction between the colonial/mercantilist state-formative

253

practices as opposed to the constitutionally-mandated democratic, republican practice of politics. Similarly, privileging of criminogenic use of force, including fatal force, while in the short run serving regime needs, inclines political culture to increasingly authoritarian and autocratic mould, contradicted at every stage by the endless normativity of the Indian Constitution having the potential for delegitimating practices of power at their very moment of triumph. Privileging of communal violence is at odds with promotion of secular images of politics, which are at the same time essential for the pursuit of power within the constitutional organization of the Indian state and society. There is also the insuperable difficulty of ensuring such planned development as would disproportionately benefit the impoverished masses without, simultaneously, waging a war against black money, parallel economy and organized crime. In the absence of such constitutionally-inspired belligerency, the emerging politics of crime has an immanent tendency of converting practices of politics into forms of privileged criminality.

This last dimension was poignantly summed up by Rajiv Gandhi, addressing the Congress Centenary celebrations in 1985. Castigating "the brokers of power" in the Party who have "converted a mass movement into a feudal oligarchy" by their "grasping mercenary outlook", and "shallow ideological roots", Prime Minister Gandhi lamented the

> "self perpetuating cliques who thrive by invoking slogans of religion and by enmeshing the living body of the Congress in the net of avarice ...; their life-style, their self aggrandizement, their corrupt ways, their linkages with vested interests in society".

He also lamented "business and industrial establishments which shelter battalions of lawbreakers and tax evaders, the bureaucracy ... like a fence that ate away the crop, ... government servants who do not uphold the law but shield the guilty...". This anguished introspection by a national leader extends not just to his party but holds true of all major political formations in India today.

The travails of politics, so poignantly presented by the young Indian Prime Minister, also symptomatize rapid structural changes in the Indian society, especially the growth of the middle classes and within these of the merchant capitalist class. The latter untempered by the "spirit of national movement" or by the "ratonality of industrial capitalism", "conformity to civic norms", and in cultural terms by its "non-cosmopolitanism,... ruthless opportunism,... (and) by a gaucherie of cultural style" marking "conspicuous consumption and waste...".[51] This class registers, in its rapid growth, an intersection between the civil society and the state and poses, through the medium of organized crime, the gravest possible threat to India's democratic sustenance.

Additionally, of course, the changing social structure is characterized by the mobilization and stuggle of the disadvantaged classes and by deep antagonisms between culture and technology. Thus, overall, the governing elites and dominant interests in state and society stand confronted by growing contradictions and have begun to appreciate, in Rajiv Gandhi's words, that if "...we are to demonstrate that we are an ungovernable people in a democratic way, we are succeeding uncommonly well".

Put another way, the legitimation of power requires a rehabilitation of legality among the "classes" as well as the "masses" at the very time when the belief spreads that the modern Indian state can only cohere through continually privileging certain forms of deviance.

References and Notes

[1] U. Baxi, *Inconvenient Forum and Convenient Catastrophe,* Indian Law Institute, New Delhi, 1986.

[2] D. N. Dhanagare, "Green Revolution and Social Inequalities in Rural India, *Economic and Political Weekly,* 1987, XXII, An-137; Dinesh Mohan, "Food vs. Limbs; Pesticides and Physical Disability in India", *Economic and Political Weekly,* 1987, XXII, A-23.

[3] T. R. Gurr, "A Comparative Study of Civil Strife", in H. D. Graham and T. R. Gurr, Eds., *Violence in America,* 1969, New York, Bantam, p. 544.

[4] U. Baxi, *The Environment Protection Act: An Agenda for Implementation,* New Delhi, Indian Law Institute, 1987.

[5] The incidence of non cognizance of offences, which the enforcement officials are under a legal duty to investigate, is not easy to qualify. But, obviously, the growth of organized crime in India must depend on significant non-cognizance behaviour. The cruelest manifestation of the readiness to take no steps against criminal behaviour occurred in November 1984 when, in the wake of Indira Gandhi's assassination, mobs went around killing, maiming, raping Sikhs and systematically damaging their property in Delhi. The enforcement personnel stood by helplessly and hopelessly witnessing the carnage. The exceptional nature of paralysis needs to be more closely understood in terms of political economy of regime and society-sponsored collective violence which we examine in this paper.

Non-prosecution may be considered an important strategy for law enforcement, crime prevention and treatment of offenders, only when crimes are cognized, arrest and investigations made. When priviliging of certain forms of criminality leads to strategies of non-enforcement, obviously considerations other than efficient and equitable criminal justice administration predominate. The same needs to be said when withdrawals from prosecution in the "public interest" become synonumous with that notion of public interet which merely serve the needs of a particular regime (see, on this situation, U. Baxi, *Liberty and Corruption: The Antulay Case and Beyond,* Lucknow, Eastern Book Co., 1989; P. R. Rajgopal, *Violence and Response: A Critique of Indian Criminal Justice System,* New Delhi, Uppal Publishers, 1988, pp. 60-63).

India has developed, on matters involving questions of public importance, the device of Commissions of Inquiry. Under the Act of 1952, Commissions may be appointed by both the federal and state governments. The commissions are usually appointed to examine charges of corruption in high places or large scale violence. Event after the eminent, sometimes incumbent, Supreme and High Court justices leading the commissions report finding of high culpability, further action remains the prerogative of the executive. Inaction has been the norm. (A. G. Noorani, *Ministers' Misconduct,* Delhi, Bell Books, 1974; U. Baxi, *Liberty...*, *op. cit.,* 1989).

Amnesty for serious economic offences, resulting in non-prosecution, is a frequent occurrence; while executive or legislative provision for amnesty (the latter in terms of voluntary disclosure scheme for tax offenders) make salient the strategies of incentives as positive sanctions, the fact that no such sanctions are available to the victims of impoverishment who are punished for far less structurally significant transgressions of the law reinforces the perception that the criminal justice system is itself wholly unjust (W. Dhagamwar, "Prisoner at the Bar: Are you Rich or Poor?", in *Law and Poverty: Critical Essays,* 1988; K. D. Gaur, "The Poor as the Victims of Uses and Abuses of Criminal Law and Process", in *Law and Poverty: Critical Essays,* 1988, p. 63).

The state of arrears in courts is indeed alarming. No judicial person-power planning forms an aspect of national planning: nor is expenditure on administration of justice a 'plan' subject which means that provision of budgetary allocation and priorities is *ad hoc.* Significant delays characterize judicial consideration of serious criminal charges; there is good reason to believe that delay in trial affects seriously the rate of acquittals (R. P. Rajgopal, *Violence...*, *op. cit.,* 1988, pp. 245-289). The human rights costs are, of course, staggering (U. Baxi, *The Crisis of the Indian Legal System,* New Delhi, Vikas, 1982, pp. 209-243). As at 1984, to invoke gross statistics, 147,040 criminal cases were pending before Indian High Courts; the total pendency of civil and criminal matters, at appellate level, for the period was 1,251,045. The crisis of the judicial system is institutionalized as an unwritten aspect of national planning and is a resource for the organization of privileged criminality in India.

[6] U. Baxi, "Legislative Reservation for Social Justice", in J. B. Goldman and J. Wilson, Eds., *Managing Ethnic Conflicts in Five Asian and African States,* London, 1984; M. Galanter, *Competing Equalities,* Berkeley, University of California Press, 1984; P. N. Singh, "Equality, Reservation and Discrimination", in *In India,* New Delhi, Deep and Deep Publications, 1982.

[7] U. Baxi, *Law and Poverty: Critical Essays,* V-XXIV, Bombay, Tripathi, 1988, pp. 182-185; and materials cited.

[8] M. Weiner, *India's Preferential Policies: Migrants, the Middle Class and Ethnic Equality,* Delhi, Oxford, 1981.

[9] U. Baxi, *Law and...*, *op. cit.,* p. 387.

[10] U. Baxi, *The Crisis...*, *op. cit.*

[11] A. R. Desai, Ed., *Violations of Democratic Rights in India,* New Delhi, Oxford, 1986.

[12] U. Baxi, *Liberty and ...*, *op. cit.*

[13] U. Baxi, *The Crisis ...*, *op. cit.*

[14] U. Baxi, *Liberty and ...*, *op. cit.*

[15] U. Baxi, *The Crisis ...*, *op. cit.*

[16] M. K. Singh, "Economic Development and Crime", in K. S. Shukla, Ed., *The Other Side of Development*, New Delhi, Sage, 1987, p. 192.

[17] G. Shah, *Ethnic Minorities and Nation Building: Indian Experience*, Varanazi, Benares Hindu University, 1983, p. 35.

[18] M. J. Akbar, *Riots*, New Delhi, Penguin, 1988.

[19] V. Das and A. Nandy, "Violence, Victimhood and languages of Silence", *Contributions to Indian Sociology*, (N. S.), 1985, pp. 19, 177.

[20] A. A. Engineer, "The Guilty Man of Meerut", *Economic and Political Weekly*, XXVII, 1982, p. 1803.

[21] P. R. Rajgopal, *Violence ...*, *op. cit.*, 1988, p. 164.

[22] D. G. Mandelbaum, *Society in India*, Berkeley, Berkeley University, California Press, 1966; Y. Singh, *The Modernization of India: A Systematic Study of Social Change*, New Delhi, Thompson Press, 1973.

[23] G. Shah, *Ethnic ...*, *op. cit.*, p. 33.

[24] W. Dhagamwar, *Uniform Civil Code*, New Delhi, The Indian Law Institute, 1989.

[25] Y. Singh, "Development in India: Continuities and Contradic-tions", in K. S. Shukla, Ed., *The other Side ...*, *op. cit.*, p. 65.

[26] U. Baxi, "Violence, Dissent and Development", in R. B. Meagher, Ed., *Law and Social Change: Indo-American Reflections*, New Delhi, Indian Law Insitute, 1988; M. Galanter, "Compensatory Discrimination in Political Representation ...", *Economic and Political Weekly*, XIV, p. 435.

[27] India, *Atrocities of Harajans*, New Delhi, Bureau of Police Research, Home Ministry, Government of India, 1979.

[28] U. Baxi, "Violence ...", *op. cit.*, pp. 183-184.

[29] U. Baxi, "Reflections on the Reservation Crisis in Gujarat", *Mainstream*, Issues dated June 8, 15 and 22, 1985.

[30] D. Seth, "Politics of Class Conflict", *Seminar*, 1979, No. 233, p. 29.

[31] A. Sinha, "Class Wars, not 'Atrocities' against Harijans", *Journal of Peasant Studies*, 1982, No. 9, p. 148.

[32] For a rigorous dual ruling class analysis — bourgeois and feudal — see S. Lyn, "Theory of a Dual Mode of Production in Post-Colonial India", *Economic and Political Weekly*, 1980, XV, p. 515; and for its extension to atrocities, see U. Baxi, "Violence ...", *op. cit.*, pp. 182-185.

[33] B. Joshi, "Whose Law? Whose Order?: Untouchables, Social violence and State in India", *Asian Survey*, 1982, XXII, p. 676.

[34] India, *Towards Equality: Report of the Committee on the Status of Women*, New Delhi, Government of India, 1974.

258

[35] U. Baxi, et al., "An Open Letter to the Chief Justice of India", *Supreme Court Cases Journal,* 1979, I, p. 17.

[36] Y. Singh, "Development ...", *op. cit.,* p. 60.

[37] M. K. Singh, "Economic ...", *op. cit.,* p. 93.

[38] *Ibidem,* p. 102.

[39] *Ibidem,* p. 102.

[40] M. K. Singh, "Economic ...", *op. cit.,* pp. 18-19.

[41] R. S. Shukla and R. Saxena, "Women and Crime", in K. S. Shukla, Ed., *The other Side ..., op. cit.,* p. 135.

[42] M. K. Singh, "Economic ...", *op. cit.,* pp. 104-105.

[43] P. R. Rajgopal, *Violence ..., op. cit.,* p. 148.

[44] *Ibidem,* p. 150.

[45] *Ibidem,* pp. 173-174.

[46] *Ibidem,* p. 182.

[47] *Ibidem,* p. 175.

[48] B. B. Pande, "The Nature and Dimensions of Privileged Class Deviance", in K. S. Shukla, Ed., *The other Side ..., op. cit.,* p. 135.

[49] I. Walter, *Secret Money,* London, Unwin Paperbacks, 1985.

[50] India, *The Report of Black Economy,* New Delhi, National Institute of Public Finance and Policy, Ministry of Finance, Government of India, 1985.

[51] Y. Singh, "Development ...", *op. cit.,* p. 58.

RELIGIOUS TRAINING AS A METHOD
OF SOCIAL CONTROL

The Effective Role of Shariah Law in the Development of a
Non-Criminal Society in the Kingdom of Saudi Arabia *

*Sam S. Souryal***

Introduction

Students of comparative criminology have been reminded over and over again of the low level of criminality in the Kingdom of Saudi Arabia. Many of them accepted this notion but discarded its significance on the basis of a "horrendous" system of punishments totally unacceptable in the Western world. A few, including myself, were further skeptical of the use of official crime statistics as a basic fo such assumptions. My skepticism diminished slightly when I became aware of the first major project conducted by the United Nations Secretariat, in 1975, to measure the dimensions of criminality on a world-wide basis.[1] In that world crime survey, official figures from sixty-four countries were collected and compared; countries were ranked in order of levels of overall "criminality." On the basis of the survey,

---

* The author, who is Christian, had the unique opportunity of spending part of his sabbatical leave in the Kingdom of Saudi Arabia and other Middel Eatern countries (December 20, 1983 – March 11, 1984), where he pursued social and criminal justice research. For several weeks he travelled to many cities in the Kingdom. He had the privilege of meeting with numerous leaders in Islamic jurisprudence. More importantly he met with lower-level police officials, clergymen, and laymen at large. Information collected from these sources constitute the main body of this paper and form the grounds upon which conclusions are made.

** Professor, Sam Houston State University, USA.

the Kingdom of Saudi Arabia unsurprisingly made the list of "nations not obsessed with crime," along with Bulgaria, Peru, Nepal, and a few others.[2] Nevertheless, my basic "police" skepticism continued on the grounds that inaccuracy of official crime statistics is a foregone conclusion; in Middle Eastern data the question is, "by what margin?" The problem of dishonesty or lack of professionalism on the part of crime-reporting officers at local, provincial, and national levels, is a more serious one. Figures are usually deflated for a variety of reasons and the resulting differences in reported crimes could destroy comparability. As a plausible remedy, Adler reported conducting a process of informal peer-group evaluations within regions. In discussions with government leaders, administrators, and scholars she discovered "surprisingly little disagreement as to which countries had the lowest crime rates."[3] Once again Saudi Arabia stood out as a country with the lowest crime rates, at least in the region of the Middle East.

Two main difficulties appear in Adler's work: one procedural, and the other theoretical. On the procedural side, Adler seems to have conducted her process of "informal peer-group evaluations" by asking the wrong sources. She precisely cited "government leaders, administrators, and scholars." Needless to say these sources represent a higher likelihood of bias. In the objective reality of policing, for instance, when one wants to know the true extent of crime in a neighbourhoods, one does not ask the mayor, the police chief, or the local teacher. One asks the beat patrolman. The mayor would be too embarassed to show his town in a bad light for political reasons. The chief of police would be reluctant to expose his department's inefficiencies. The teacher, finally, would normally tend to reiterate what the newspaper has reported the other two to have stated.

On the theoretical side, Adler's work did not reach beyond the official data or investigate the reasons behind the reported low criminality in these nations. In the case of the Kingdom of Saudi Arabia, she scantly described "The" criminal justice system which may not in fact exist as we know it in the Western world, nor might there be any endogenous reasoning for its existence.[4] While she confirms that "[the] Saudis credit the Shariah law with their low crime rate," she fell short of explaining the system's role in the dynamics of social order and organization in the Kingdom of Saudi Arabia.

The purpose of this paper is fourfold: a) to examine the reality of criminal behaviour in Saudi Arabia by validating the official crime rates in the Kingdom; b) to delinate the Saudi rates by comparing them to six Islamic countries which do not apply Shariah law; c) to observe the role of Shariah law in action; and d) to attempt to explain what might be learned in terms of contemporary criminological theories. An important caveat, however, must be mentioned here. The reader should not fall in the trap of "over-expected claims." This manuscript does not claim the discovery of a theory of Islamic criminality or a comprehensive study of crime patterns in the six Moslem nations. There exist demographic differences, particular variations in the distribution of wealth in each, and delicate "twists" in the overall socio-political accommodations, among other intangible characteristics. Nevertheless, given all of these, the empirical findings regarding criminal behavior under Shariah law as practiced in the Kindgom of Saudi Arabia remain unimpeachable and practically confirm Adler's figures. The focus of the study will, therefore, be the dynamic role of Shariah in Saudi Arabia. Reference to the other six Moslem countries should be kept in its incidental perspective.

Overview of Shariah Law and Shariah Crimes

In recent criminological literature, there seems to be growing recognition among researchers that the central questions in understanding crime may not be the study of

263

criminals, the strategies of the police, or court procedures, but rather the encompassing effects of the law and its potential to realizing justice through its role as a moralizing and deterrent agent.[5] Consequently, contemporary research may begin by asking how many citizens choose not to engage in criminal behaviour and why. What is the role of homogeneity, religiosity, and social reinforcement in criminal behaviour? Such an expanded view of socio-legal inquiry seems most conducive to examining the phenomenon of societies "not obsessed with crime," as in the case of Saudi Arabia today or among Orthodox Jewish communities. In these communities social goodness is claimed to be sustained and social evil resisted through a *nomos* based on divine law and a spiritual commitment to social decency.[6]

Islamic law, like Jewish law, is a theocratic legal system which rests on the concept of a divine law revealed to a prophet in a scripture. In Islamic legal tradition, there is only one lawgiver—God—and Shariah law is God's command which regulates human conduct by demanding, authorizing, or prohibiting human behaviour, "Shariah," which is the Arabic word for "law" and literally means "a pathway," became the standard of right and wrong in Saudi culture, providing an all-inclusive scale of religious evaluation of conduct. The crux of Islam is submission to the will of God, through which universal order and peace can be brought about. Furthermore, it is believed that only through the harmonization of man's will and the will of God can the perfect actualization of human life be achieved under an all-embracing divine guidance. On the other hand, a departmentalization of human conduct into religious and secular, sacred and profane, spiritual and material, is contrary to Islamic doctrine since man's limited judgment will always fall short of God's plan for creation. In Islam, religion and behaviour cease to be autonomous categories; they become two sides of the same coin. Each human act must reflect God's will, and at the same time is regulated by

264

His guiding rules. All human activities, therefore, receive a transcendent dimension: they become purposeful and sacred, earthly and heavenly, for this day and for the herafter. Good deeds earn man righteousness with God and bad deed take away in the same manner.

The assumption underlying Shariah is that men are incapable of discriminating right and wrong by their own unaided power. It was for this reason that guidance was sent to them through prophets. God has decreed a pathway for men based upon His sovereign will. Such decrees are not subordinated to rational considerations, nor are they to be judged by a standard of human reason.

The perpetual task of Shariah law is to create and sustain a state of social bonding committed to the preservation of religious beliefs, social organization, and proper conduct. This task is entrusted not only to elders of the clergy and officials of the government, but also to each and every believer in the commonwealth. The bond that results technically imposes a dual social responsibility on Moslems: the believer's obligation always to do what is good and to abstain from what is blameworthy, and one's responsibility for directly or indirectly correcting corrupt behaviour by non-conformists.

Compared to the neatness and precision of Western penal philosophy which must legislate morality through an exhaustive enumeration of prohibitions, Shariah law merely presents a resume of obligatory rules and prohibitions which should formulate the working of a benevolent society and its principal social practices. Theoretically speaking, when these rules are internalized in the psyche of believers, they produce a collective moral conscience by which the society can distinguish between right and wrong, deter criminal behavior, and adequately respond to criminal activity. Reprehensive acts, therefore, do not shock this collective conscience because they are criminal, but rather are considered criminal because they shock this collective conscience. Consequently, obligatory duties thus perceived are seldom ignored and it does not become necessary to make them manifest.

In order to establish justice in accordance with Islamic doctrine, the head of the Islamic state has a judicial responsibility consisting of two functions, one positive and the other negative. His positive function relates to the establishment of peace in the state, maintenance of concord among the various sections of the people, and the protection of the weak against the strong. His negative function concerns punishment of evil-doers and the restitution of the rights of the injured. For the dispensation of justice, the head of the state has to appoint Qadis (judges), well-versed in Shariah law, God-fearing, and of irreproachable character and sterling piety. The Qadis, who apply Divine Law, consider themselves responsible only to God Almighty and, as such, should dispense justice equitably and speedily.

Human behaviour falling under the prescription of Shariah law includes all religious and secular conduct, without exception. Aspects of this behaviour are classified as: obligatory (fard); meritorious or recommended (mandub); indifferent, that is, bringing neither reward nor punishment (mubah); reprehensive, that is not punishable but disapproves (makruh); and forbidden (haram). The main body of Shariah's law deals with serious crimes and basically constitutes the Shariah's penal code. The code is explicitly presented in a special section generally known as "Huddud Allah," or divine limitations. Punishment for these crimes is severe and includes, for example, eighty lashes for public intoxication, hand amputation for theft, stoning to death for adultery, and beheading for murder and robbery. All such penalties are carried out expediently and in public.

Some major differences, however, exist between the Western application of criminal law and the Islamic practice. Shariah, as mentioned earlier, is primarily designed and used as a moralizing instrument as well as a preventive agent. It is effective by the use of a five-projng approach: (a) it constantly endeavors to reform the individual and purify his or her conscience with sublime Islamic ideals and lofty morals; (b) it adequately warns people against committing offenses and admonishes the offender with dreadful punishment in this world and in the herafter; (c) it commands Moslems to assist one another "on the path of righteousness and piety" by offering counsel, moral support, and the exchange of religious coaching; (d) it prevents crime by blocking the way leading to its commission by, for example, prohibiting the use of intoxicants and minimizing possible encounters between the sexes; (e) it prepares Moslems, in anticipation of man's moral fallibility, by urging marriage at a young age, condoning controlled polygamy, and requiring the well-to-do to contribute to the needs of the less fortunate in accordance with the concept of Zakah (paying alms).

While in countries with positive law, one is usually struck by the frequency of street violence, brawls, and business altercations, in the streets of Saudi cities such infractions seem to be an aberration. The streets are usually quiet, the markets businesslike, and people soft-spoken. Also, since firearms, alcohol, and drugs are strictly banned, the opportunity for violence is further reduced, and an atmosphere of genuine tranquillity always looms. When a dispute inevitably erupts, it is swiftly settled on an informal basis by passersby. These arbitrators are usually affronted by the event, but more so are motivated by the religious reward of acting as peacemakers.

Nevertheless, this preventive role of Shariah law ceases once spiritual heed is ignored and serious violations are inevitably committed. The law is then applied formally and forcefully, and penalties are meted in a certain, swift, and severe manner. Also, since severe punishment has a definite tangible impact, its effectiveness is maximized by public execution of criminals. Such executions underscore society's deep abhorrence of disorder and moral corruption and its innate affection for spirituality and conformity. Nevertheless, and perhaps surprisingly, these harsh penalties are rarely imposed due to a strict law of evidence that serves as a human rights delimitation in the rigors of a seemingly unalterable law. Shariah law also maintains the ultimate weapon of compassion and mercy by encouraging the foregoing of punishment altogether if the mischievous person came forward and repented before he was apprehended by the authorities.

Crime Rates in Saudi Arabia Compared to World Rates and to Six other Moslem Countries[7]

The English anthropoligist Bronishlaw Malinowski stated that social science is an institution with "strong coloration," and that comparative research makes it a "perilous undertaking".[8] His concerns were primarily with the Western scientist's inability to read "in the lines of alien people," and his or her inability to gather appropriate data. Two additional caveats must be stated here at the outset. First, as most international comparative researchers have already discovered, cross-cultural data could be.[9] This is due to the obvious difficulty of testing for casualty or manipulation in the reporting and recording of statistics, but more so to the problems of ascertaining the presence or absence of plea bargaining and of determining whether the law is applied equally. Such major distractions obligate the researcher to make every effort possible to validate the data prior to making informed opinions on their basis. Secondly, comparative researchers, especially when dealing with third world countries, become aware of the "nationalism factor" which many foreign officials seem unable (or unwilling) to control. This factor can be even more visible in Middle East countries, African countries, and many countries in South America. Officials in these countries seem committed, as an act of patriotism (or more likely of loyalty to the ruling regime), to impress foreign researchers by playing down official figures that might present their country in an unfavorable light, or by qualifying them in such a manner so as to justify, and often glorify, their political or ideological doctrines. Given these shortcomings, the figures that will be cited in this article must be interpreted to indicate rough relationships among Saudi Arabian crime rates, world rates, and the official rates of six other Moslem countries, and not to mean firm quantitative differences.

Table 1 provides a summary of unvalidated official crime rates in the Kingdom of Saudi Arabia as submitted by the officials at the Ministry of Interior. It will be followed by Table 2 which shows the United Nations world crime rates referred to earlier in Adler's work. In the world crime survey the problems of variation in the use of legal terminology and classification were ensured to have been largely overcome. Participating countries were asked to fit their crimes into broadly defined categories which had been established for purposes of insuring comparability. According to Adler, the imprecision resulting from generalization did not detract from the usefulness of the data in identifying countries with low (or high) crime rates; indeed, it made such a task possible. The purpose of this comparison is to show the "dramatic" difference between crime rates in the Kingdom and the combined rates of the world in genral.

With a current population of eleven million people, including an estimated five million foreign ex-patriots who are generally attributed with a higher crime rate than native Saudis, the Kingdom shows official crime rates as listed in Table 1:

Table 1
Official Crime Rates in the Kingdom of Saudi Arabia

Year	Population	Number of Murders	Rate Per 100,000	Number of Property Crimes	Rate Per 100,000	Number of Sexual Offenses	Rate Per 100,000
1966	5,662,000	169	3	879	1.6	380	7
1967	5,815,000	154	3	905	1.6	459	8
1968	5,973,000	74	1	905	1.6	300	5
1969	6,135,000	40	1	791	1.3	321	5
1970	6,301,000	49	1	854	1.4	392	6
1971	6,472,000	41	1	791	1.2	345	5
1972	6,647,000	54	1	980	1.5	346	5
1973	6,827,000	39	1	973	1.4	323	5
1974	7,012,000	54	1	948	1.4	239	4
1975	7,201,000	70	1	873	1.2	328	5
1976	7,600,000	49	1	853	1.2	327	5
1977	8,011,000	58	1	726	1.1	330	5
1978	8,500,000	70	1	520	1.0	546	9
1979	8,940,000	46	1	671	1.1	346	5

Source: *The Effect of Islamic Legislation on Crime Prevention in Saudi Arabia*, Ministry of Interior, Riyadh, 1976, pp. 500-504.

Given the available categories of crime (murder, property offenses, sex offenses) cited in the Saudi Arabian crime statistics, comparison with world crime rates is made in the same categories and over the same period of time (1970-1975). In the first category (murder), the combined world rate is about four times the rate in the Kingdom (3.9:1). In the second category (property crimes), the combined world rate is about six hundred fifty times the rate in the Kingdom (908.5:1.4). In the third category (sex crimes), the combined world rate is about five times the rate in the Kingdom (24.2:5). Any hasty or simplistic attempt to explain the reasons behind this considerable difference in criminality in Saudi Arabia *vis-à-vis* the combined rates of the world will be unreasonable (if not foolish), given the wide variety of social, political, economic, religious, and cultural differences among the member nations in the survey. A question that cannot be ignored, nevertheless, is the fact that the official crime rates in the Kingdom (however reliable they are) indicate a much lower level of reported crime than the average official rates of the world (however reliable they are), during the years of comparison.

Table 2

World Rates of Reported Offenses (per 100,000)
1970-1975

Intentional homicide (murder)	3.9
Assault	184.1
Sex crimes	24.2
Kidnapping	0.7
Robbery and theft (property crimes)	908.5
Fraud	83.3
Illegal drug traffic	9.8
Drug abuse	28.9
Alcohol abuse	67.8
Total offence rate	1,311.2

Source: From *Report of the Secretary General on Crime Prevention and Control*, U.N. Report A/32/199, September 22, 1977, p. 9.

In the following section, crime rates from the Kingdom of Saudi Arabia will be further compared with six neighbouring Moslem nations which do not use Shariah law. The Arab crime survey was conducted by the Arab Organization of Social Defense. Variations in the definitions of crimes and

271

in the method of counting and coding them were similarly reduced through the broadening of criminal categories and the utilization of a central transnational synchronization mechanism. The selection of countries surveyed was based primarily on their cultural similarity, common social and religious beliefs, and the availability of data. Expanding the data to include crime rates from the State of Israel, which would admittedly make this study more interesting, was advisably ruled out for fear that it might blur the focus of this paper on Shariah law. Thus, studied here are the Arab Republic of Syria, The Republic of Sudan, The Arab Republic of Egypt, The Arab Republic of Iraq, the Republic of Lebanon, and the State of Kuwait. All six nations are considered Arab (with minor variation as to the ethnic composition of Lebanon and Sudan) and Moslem. While Saudi Arabia has been a monarchy since 1935, all others are republics with the exception of Kuwait, which is ruled by a constitutional Amir. The Sudan applied Shariah law in 1983[10] but recently abolished it after the removal of President Numirie in 1985. Egypt has been debating the introduction of Shariah law but is faced with strong opposition by its Coptic minority.[11] Otherwise, all six countries applied state law during the ten years of comparison.

The Kingdom of Saudi Arabia, on the other hand, is the leader in the use of orthodox Shariah law today. All criminal behaviour, except in minor offenses like traffic enforcement and zoning regulations, is identified by Shariah law and punishments are meted by a clerical judge in accordance with its provisions. No statutory legislation exists (except in minor offenses) and Saudi justice, which precludes the jury system and the use of lawyers, continues to apply the 1353-year-old Divine Law.

Tables 3, 4, and 5 show crime rates in the Kingdom of Saudi Arabia as compared with the six Moslem nations in the categories of murder, property crimes, and sexual offenses, respectively.

Table 3

Number of Murders in the Kingdom of Saudi Arabia
Compared to Six Arab Countries Which Apply State Law*

Country	Present Population*	1970	1971	1972	1973	1974	1975	1976	1977	1978	1979	Average For 10 Years	Rate Per 100,000
Saudi Arabia	11 Million	61	41	54	39	54	70	49	58	70	46	53	.4818
Syria	11 Million	314	—	351	355	324	381	481	482	488	455	403	3.6636
Sudan	22 Million	773	938	1009	967	988	1128	1089	877	949	1074	979	4.4500
Egypt	44 Million	1224	—	1229	1241	—	1289	1348	—	—	1583	1319	2.9977
Iraq	14 Million	1136	1303	1243	867	1026	890	—	1028	994	1584	1119	7.9929
Lebanon	3.5 Million	643	203	324	121	191	—	—	—	—	1187	439	12.5429
Kuwait	2 Million	51	49	59	57	57	70	69	73	58	70	61	3.0500

Source: *Arab Crime Statistics*, Arab Organization for Social Defense, Bagdad, Iraq, 1981, p. 55.

* Since no reliable data are available regarding the increase in population in any nation on an annual basis, and assuming the rate in population increase is approximately the same within the region, present population will be used as a base for all the countries. The rate per 100,000 will also be computed on the basis of an average of crimes reported over the 10 years.

273

Table 4

Number of Property Crimes in the Kingdom of Saudi Arabia Compared to Six Arab Countries Which Apply State Law

Country	Present Population*	1970	1971	1972	1973	1974	1975	1976	1977	1978	1979	Average For 10 Years	Rate Per 100,000
Saudi Arabia	11 Million	854	791	980	973	948	873	853	726	520	671	818	7.4364
Syria	11 Million	5538	—	3017	4667	7084	6385	9029	8562	8804	6318	6,599	59.9909
Sudan	22 Million	40603	42304	65611	49125	57367	67425	53042	69430	60376	57141	56,242	255.6455
Egypt	44 Million	45415	39288	3339	30588	26597	—	—	—	46404	39944	33,088	75.1886
Iraq	14 Million	1788	—	2358	2427	2136	2267	2286	3515	2691	12238	3,522	25.1571
Lebanon	3.5 Million	4618	—	—	4240	3855	—	—	2099	8515	8189	5,252	150.0571
Kuwait	2 Million	1739	—	2545	4613	2125	3207	1042	2592	1178	1109	2,238	111.9000

Source: *Arab Crime Statistics,* Arab Organization for Social Defense, Bagdad, Iraq, 1981, p. 68.

* Since no reliable data are available regarding the increase in population in any nation on an annual basis, and assuming the rate in population increase is approximately the same within the region, present population will be used as a base for all the countries. The rate per 100,000 will also be computed on the basis of an average of crimes reported over the 10 years.

Table 5

Number of Sexual Offenses (including rape) in Saudi Arabia Compared to Six Arab Countries Which Apply State Law

Country	Present Population*	1970	1971	1972	1973	1974	1975	1976	1977	1978	1979	Average For 10 Years	Rate Per 100,000
Saudi Arabia	11 Million	392	345	346	323	239	328	327	330	546	346	352	3.2000
Syria	11 Million	333	474	426	330	578	637	596	677	701	785	553	5.0273
Sudan	22 Million	774	829	904	968	951	2364	1844	2020	1910	2678	1,524	6.9273
Egypt	44 Million	3789	—	1682	1113	—	2006	2265	—	—	—	2,171	4.9341
Iraq	14 Million	1483	1487	1569	1402	1525	1556	1549	2054	2813	2882	1,832	13.0857
Lebanon	3.5 Million	569	709	564	607	1207	901	—	—	—	—	759	21.6857
Kuwait	2 Million	373	—	389	612	699	406	711	505	682	673	561	28.0500

Source: *Arab Crime Statistics*, Arab Organization for Social Defense, Bagdad, Iraq, 1981, p. 58.

* Since no reliable data are available regarding the increase in population in any nation on an annual basis, and assuming the rate in population increase is approximately the same within the region, present population will be used as a base for all the countries. The rate per 100,000 will also be computed on the basis of an average of crimes reported over the 10 years.

Data Summary

Table 3 indicates that the murder rate in the Kingdom of Saudi Arabia is the lowest among the seven nations surveyed. The murder rate (per 100,000 population) is less than 1/6 the second lowest rate in the countries of Egypt and Kuwait; less than 1/7 the rate in Syria; less than 1/9 the rate in Sudan; less than 1/16 the rate in Iraq; and less than 1/25 the rate in Lebanon. Eschewing the highest rate in Lebanon, a country which has been afflicted with unusual political and religious strife throughout the comparison years, the murder rate in the Kingdom stood about 1/9 the median rate of murder among the other five nations. Criminologists in the countries of Syria, Sudan, Egypt, and Iraq can forward their own explanations of the higher rate of murder in their respective societies. But it remains most intriguing to note that the murder rate in Saudi Arabia is 1/6 the rate in Kuwait, an adjacent Islamic Arab nation which is ethnically and culturally indistinguishable from the Saudi society. With a few intangible differences both societies have recently experienced great economic wealth, both share the Sunnite version of Islam, and both employ about the same ratio of foreign workers. The Kingdom, nevertheless, strictly applies Shariah law while Kuwait uses an adapted version of Egyptian criminal laws.

On the subject of property crimes in the Kingdom of Saudi Arabia, an examination of Table 4 shows that the rate is the lowest among the seven nations. It ranked less than 1/3 the rate in Iraq; less than 1/8 the rate in Syria; less than 1/10 the rate in Egypt; less than 1/13 the rate in Kuwait; less than 1/20 the rate in Lebanon; and less than 1/36 the rate in Sudan. Eschewing the highest rate in Sudan on the basis of the widely reported faminelike conditions caused by prolonged drought periods during the 70s (which may or may not be true reason for a higher rate in property crimes), the rate of property crimes in the Kingdom stood 1/12 the median rate among the other five nations. The

276

same reason for intrigue described earlier in relation to the higher murder rate in Kuwait still persisted in the category of property crimes, at an even higher ratio (1/6 to 1/13). The state of Kuwait, a nation with the highest *per capita* income among the seven countries surveyed, had a property crime rate second only to those in Lebanon and Sudan. While admittedly Kuwaitis may be responsible for a smaller share of their country's crime, due to the presence of a large foreign work force, the claim has little validity since the Saudis consistently invoke the same claim. Neither claim has been conclusively substantiated.

On the subject of sexual crimes, Table 5 indicates that the crime rate in Saudi Arabia is still the lowest among the seven nations but at a lower ratio of difference than in the other two categories. It stands less than 7/10 the rate in Egypt; less than 7/10 the rate in Syria; less than 1/2 the rate in Sudan; less than 1/4 the rate in Iraq; less than 1/7 the rate in Lebanon; and less than 1/8 the rate in Kuwait. In the aggregate, the rate of sexual offenses in Saudi Arabia stood only as 1/4 the median rate of sexual crimes among the other six nations. It was puzzling to note that the ratio of difference between the rate of sexual offenses in the Kingdom and the median rate for the same category in the six nations surveyed is over twice the ratio in the murder category (1/4 to 1/9), and three times the ratio of property offenses (1/4 to 1/12). This might indicate a clear case of displacement in criminal activity in Saudi Arabia, from the violent to the subtle, from the visible to the hidden, and perhaps, from the easy to prove to the harder to prove.

Attempts at Data Validation

Upon initial examination it became apparent that the low crime rates presented by the officials of Saudi Arabia seemed "too good to be true" and could hardly be taken at face value, especially since victimization surveys in the

Kingdom are not conducted and corroborative sources are lacking. Attempts to validate the data through a field survey instrument or a mail opinion poll were shunned by the officials on the grounds of stirring public doubt, and several ride-along exercises in police squads proved meaningless. Some of these shortcomings were later ameliorated when the author traveled to several Saudi cities and associated himself with many ordinary citizens. Given these difficulties, this author had no alternative but to conduct a quasi-Delphi approach by which controlled interviews were held with selected resource panels. While this approach may admittedly fall short of the scientific method ordinarily used in the United States and Western countries, it was deemed most conducive to exploring the true role of active Shariah law.

The chosen methodology called for the selection of three self-reporting panels representing the government, the clergy, and the society at large in order to serve as validation resources. The first panel consisted of low-level police official representing the arm of government most involved in criminal issues. The second consisted of low-level clergymen, who also are government officials. The third consisted of lay members who have had no official function in the government. Each panel consisted of three members. The selection of each member was based on three criteria: a) knowledge and ability to articulate the issues, b) reputation for honesty and good judgment, and c) interest in unbiased research.

For over six weeks private sessions were held with panel members, often on an individual basis, but not infrequently with two members in attendance at the same time. Questions were normally asked in a formal manner but answers often followed in an informal way, especially after a preliminary agreement was reached among panel members. A notebook documentary was used during each session to record the main comments presented by the participants.

The use of a tape recorder was not deemed prudent for its obvious negative effect.

The purpose of the interview sessions was to ask two categories of questions: procedural and substantive. The first category sought input pertinent to the validation of the following procedural issues:

a) the reliability of crime rates as publicized;

b) the amount of unreported offenses;

c) the amount of unrecorded offenses;

d) the presence of (or lack of) plea bargaining; and

e) the applicability of criminal law equally to all citizens.

Findings pertinent to the category of procedural validation will be presented in this section. Similar arrangements to validate crime data in the other six countries were not possible since limitations of the research did not allow for on-site visits to those countries. Thereupon, the official figures published by these governments will be arbitrarily treated as valid.

The second category of questions formed a substantive inquiry into the role of Shariah law as it pertains to the dynamics of social order and social organization in Saudi Arabia. Findings pertinent to this category will be infused in the following discussion at the point they become relevant.

Reliability of Official Saudi Crime Rates

Responses by panel members concerning the reliability of Saudi official crime rates varied appreciatively among the three panels, but slightly so among individual respondents on each panel. The consensus of members on the police panel, perhaps as expected by virtue of their bureaucratic nature, was in strict support of the official line. They seemed unable, and frequently unwilling, to admit the possibility of data manipulation or even of "casualty" in the gathering of, or in the computation of, crime figures. Like most police-men in traditional countries, the members of the panel emphasized that every police department in the Kingdom is strictly required to submit crime figures to the central bureau of statistics at the Ministry of Interior immediately upon the confirmation of a crime report, regardless of whether a suspect was in custody.

The consensus of the clergy panel, however, was less com-mittal. Panel members admitted the possibility of a certain amount of negligence and/or self-interest on the part of "low-level station personnel." When asked how much of this occurs and how it could affect the reliability of the overall official figures, their general estimate was around 10%.

The consensus of the lay panel was considerably dif-ferent. Panel members, with significant variance among them, indicated that data inaccuracy is much more common in minor crimes which are not Huddud crimes. In the latter category, manipulation is more likely to occur by high of-ficials at the ministry level. When asked as to the manner in which such manipulation could take place, the laymen's re-sponse focused on: (a) the use of modern definitions (or interpretation) of criminal activity which allows more crimes to be recorded as non-Huddud crimes or as civil matters; (b) the common practice by the police of resolving criminal complaints through the medium of arbitration (therefore their exclusion altogether from police records), especially if such complaints were levied against "prominent personalities;" (c) the tendency among "higher authorities" in the Ministry to omit crimes of a political nature, the recording of which (and thereupon their becoming public) may undermine the country's national security or its image of domestic tranquility; and (d) the difference in compu-tation that results from transferring the number of crimes committed in a Hijri year — the Arabic lunar calendar year, which consists of 354 days — to a number corresponding with the Gregorian calendar. For a more accurate comparison this group suggested that crime figures must be converted to the Gregorian calendar by adjusting them upwardly by 11/365. When asked to identify the group of "prominent personalities," panel members politely chose to ignore the question. When they were further queried as to the estimated amount of overall negligence and/or manipulation in the official figures, the consensus of the panel was 20%. Consequently, and on the basis of the estimates by both the clergy panel and the layman panel, it appeared logical to suggest that the overall official data should be adjusted upward by 15%. This figure constitutes the average of the 10% under-estimation factor by the clergy group and the 20% under-estimation factor by the layman group.

Unreported Offenses

Furthering the same line of questioning, each member of the three panels was asked about the extent of unreported crimes as best as they were able to estimate.

The police group, behaving uneasily and rather skeptically, unsurprisingly pleaded ignorant to the question. One of the panel members, a graduate of a major American university, responded in a confrontational manner. He reminded this author that according to his old class notes, unreported offenses in the United States are over 50% of all crimes committed. Nevertheless, the panel members, as a group, estimated that unreported crime in the Kingdom is "much, much, much smaller" than that in the United States. When pressed to identify the types of criminal behaviour that are more likely to go unreported, they offered the general categories of juvenile offenses, larceny committed by unknown persons, minor business crimes, and intoxication committed within private homes (which in itself is a Huddud crime in Shariah law). When asked for a precise figure that could indicate the panel's estimation of such unreported crime, the police officers simply reiterated the same phrase, "much, much, much smaller" than in the United States.

When the members of the clergy group were asked the same question, they were unable to offer a numerical estimate but were more forthcoming in their responses as to the types of crimes more likely to go unreported. Perhaps, because of their older average age and their freer access to more intimate family affairs the clergy members were able to confirm, and to further add to, what the police officers had mentioned. Members of the panel reported a category of unreported crimes known as "honor killing." These offenses are committed by husbands — and very infrequently by wives — who suspect infidelity on the part of their spouses, or by fathers or brothers who discover their daughter or sister pregnant out of wedlock.

When the lay members were asked to respond to the same question, they, like the other two groups, were unable to reach a numerical estimate. They, nevertheless, agreed with the previous views.

Unrecorded Offenses

Pursuing the same line of questioning, each member of the three panels was asked about the amount of unrecorded crime which might be omitted from the official data.

The police group responded to that question by sticking to the official line indicating that police officials "everywhere" must enjoy a margin of discretion by which they can choose to handle certain cases informally in conjunction with local community leaders. They, nevertheless, hastened to assure that in Saudi Arabia such cases are predominantly of a civil nature, committed by juveniles, or of a "forgivable nature." Such crimes are not included in the crime statistics and are better classified as social torts which Islamic teachings have recommended to be resolved by social arbitration. Group members further indicated that social arbitration in these cases has been most effective and restitution has always provided a fair and acceptable remedy. On the other hand, serious crimes (e.g., murder, rape, and robbery) are always recorded in the Ministry's crime statistics since, by their nature, they are henious crimes and must be disposed of in a formal proceeding in accordance with the provisions of Shariah.

The consensus of the clergy group and the lay group regarding the recordability of serious crimes did not vary appreciably from that of the police group. They further emphasized that Huddud crimes are crimes against God's rights and their commission without the severest punishment ordained by God could shake the foundation of an Islamic community. Consequently, non one can change the nature of their charge, the process of their prosecution, or the outcome of their adjudication. Once guilt has been proven in accordance with Shariah rules of evidence, the penalty must be imposed and carried out swiftly. No appeals are allowed and no probation or pardon can be offered. Political or administrative meddling with the application of Shariah law is prohibited since it could constitute a Huddud offense in itself, namely the seventh.

Based on this discussion, it appeared safe to conclude that while a number of lesser crimes in Saudi Arabia are handled through the mechanism of informal arbitration, all the crimes cited in the official rates fall within the serious category of Hudduds and no significant reason remains to doubt their proper recordability. As to the other part of the question dealing with the overall accuracy of recording crimes, the previously suggested adjustment (official data x 15%) continued to provide a "fair estimate."

The Presence of Plea Bargaining

In responding to this issue, the three panels concurred, with unanimous agreement among their members, that plea bargaining as practiced in the American judicial system, enabling a defendant to plead guilty in a court of law to a lesser crime, is unknown in Islamic jurisprudence. This is explained in a three-prong argument. First, Huddud crimes, they reiterated,cannot be seen as transgressions against individuals or against the society as a whole; rather, they are offenses against God's sovereignty and, therefore, cannot be plead out by human judges. Secondly, Islamic law, unlike state law, does not provide for degrees of felonies or classes of misdemeanors. The law clearly identifies *corpus delicti* for each crime (murder, rape, theft, etc.) which either materialize in the alleged act within the rules of Islamic evidence, or do not. In the latter case, the suspect must be set free. Panel members further elaborated by stating that this should not be confused with the judge's right, in certain Quissas crimes (crimes against individuals) and Ta'azir crimes (crimes against society), to consider a lesser penalty based on the offender's age, competence, or on the victim's willingness to forego maximum punishement (i.e., acceptance of blood money). Thirdly, given the strict categorization of crime under Shariah law, judges cannot allow admission for an offense in one category to qualify for another category. Panel members summed up the obligations of a Shariah judge as first and foremost applying the letters of Shariah law, then in satisfying the victim's right to restitution, and lastly in accommodating the intersts of the accused.

The Applicability of Criminal Law Equally to All Citizens Alike

This question was naturally the most sensitive and perhaps the least fair to the three groups. The question could admittedly cause equal discord if it were asked to an informed citizen in the United States or in any other Western nation. Nevertheless, answers by members of the three panels did not vary significantly. The clergy members, who are appointed to their position by the government, strongly affirmed that Shariah law is applied equally to all citizens alike. To support this position they reiterated the Quranic verse, "Lo! The noblest of you, in the sight of Allah, is the best in conduct." They als quoted two Hadith: "The Arab is not more worthy than the Persian, and the red is not more deserving than the black, except in godliness." The second related to a saying by the prophet in which he stated that if his own daughter, Fatima, committed theft, her kinship ties to him would not save her the legal punishment. They, furthermore, recounted the recent incident of a Royal princess in the Kingdom who was convicted of adultery and executed with her lover in 1981. The case was later made into the widely known movie feature, *Death of a Princess*.

The other two panels had slightly different views. While both groups spoke eloquently of the absence of "absolute justice" anywhere in the world, they indicated that, in lesser offenses and civil matters, judges are naturally influenced by Islamic social custom favouring old age, piety, honour, remorsefulness, and knowledge. Nevertheless, if one is accused of a serious crime that violates the Huddud law, the "sword of Shariah must take priority over social custom," litigants must be treated alike, and Shariah judgment is rendered equally. In another attempt to inquire about the category of the so-called "prominent persons," the youngest of the lay group responded that such a term has consistently been used to refer to members of the Royal family. He quickly retorted, however, that small as that group may be, its members rarely involve themselves in serious criminal acts that warrant a trial. If they do, the panel member added, they are treated no differently under Shariah law from other citizens in the Kingdom.

The question of foreign workers in the Kingdom of Saudi Arabia raised a special concern. It should be noted that since the mid-1970s the population of foreign workers in the Kingdom has been considered approximately equal to the number of native Saudis. Members of the work force, who are predominantly employed from Asian countries, could not be expected to be well-informed of — or capable of comprehending — the strictness of Shariah law and might unknowingly end up being offenders in a proportionately higher number of crimes. And since the official crime rates did not distinguish between native and foreign offenders, the issue was raised with members of the three panels. Consensus among the respondents was diffult to reach, except in the category of murder since the name of the offender executed would normally be advertised in the newspapers. Only on this basis did panel members concur with the notion and estimated that about 60% of all executed murders in the Kingdom were of the foreign work force.

Major Findings

For the purpose of validating crime data in the Kingdom of Saudi Arabia and for further comparing them with world rates and rates from the six Moslem nations which apply state law, it appeared safe to conclude the following on the basis of the interviews held with the three self-reporting panels:

(1) The official crime rates in the Kingdom, in as much as they pertain to serious crimes, seemed to be "reasonably" reliable.

(2) Due to a substantial perception of possible laxity in recording crime rates by lower-level police functionaries as well as to offset the possible effect of the "nationalism factor" on the part of high ministry personnel, the overall official Saudi crime rates should be adjusted upward by 15%. However, this will by no means change the overall results of the study.

(3) The issue of unreported crimes in Saudi Arabia will have no bearing on comparability since the phenomenon is

universal and no amount of extensive scrutiny— within the limitations of this research project — could objectively discern it.

(4) The questions relating to the possibility of plea bargaining or to the non-enforcement of the law to particular groups, seem to have no bearing on the published figures. This is due to lack of adequate substantiation and to the fact that the rates under study pertain only to the category of Huddud crimes which were deemed by panel members to be too "serious" to be tampered with at the judicial stage.

(5) The official rates for the crime of murder in the Kingdom might be slightly higher due to the higher probability of committing such crimes by foreign workers. Nevertheless, the difference might, in turn, be offset by the "dark figures" of honour killing.

Discussion

Based on the information offered by the three panel groups over a six week period, but more importantly after having the opportunity to travel extensively to several cities (Jedda, Taif, Hoffuf, Dhahran, Al-Khobor) and after having been acquainted in an ethnographic sense with so many ordinary citizens and their interpretation of events, two basic assumptions will have to be rejected and some informed speculations about possible explanations for the apparent low criminality in Saudi Arabia will be made.

The first assumption to be rejected is the notion of homogeneity in Saudi society and, therefore, the postulation that the low crime rates are expected from such a highly integrated society. A careful investigation of the anthropological and cultural background of the Saudi society reveals the opposite. The fact that the Kingdom is widely considered a traditional society does not necessarily confirm its homogeneity. Except when considered in a religious framework, the Kingdom seemed no more homogeneous than other Moslem nations previously visited by this author, particularly Kuwait, Egypt, and the Sudan. Until King Abdel Aziz Al-Saud unified the realm in 1932, the country was composed of entirely self sufficient Sheikdoms (including Kuwait) with very few bonds to tie them together into an enduring association. The only possible interest among them related to power balances. But since power constellations always changed because they lacked a firm "subcultural base" the association also shifted constantly.[12] As a result, the country at the present time is distinctively divided geographically into four regions (Najd, Hijaz, Asir, and Al-Hasa) with separate vivid subcultural norms; 10% of the present population belongs to the Shiite faith; clans are subtly recognized by their foreign origin; an economic middle class stratum does not seem to exist; and people continue to identify first and foremost with their tribal lineage.

The second assumption to be rejected is the notion that the severity of punishment in the Shariah system is a more likely reason behind the lower crime rates since people would avoid committing crime out of fear of sanctions rather than abidance with the law. While the idea of severity is clearly a relative issue which could be raised with equal reasoning among all nations that apply capital or corporal punishment, the issue becomes purely academic unless it troubles the particular society that practices it.[13] To understand properly the perception of severity of punishment by the Saudis, one must consider it in the historical context of its divine revelation in the Quranic principle of Quissas or *Lex talionis*, and in its social impact. Given the Quranic emphasis on equal retaliation, the ordinary Saudi citizen seems unbothered with its severity since it ensures the equivalency of pain and loss inflicted on the victim. Also, given the old tribal practice of raids and counter-raids over trivial matters, Quissas came to be seen

288

as a reasonable alternative to a greater retribution against the offender or his family and tribe. In terms of its social impact, there is consensus that capital punishment is not to be perceived as a means of frightening the believers, but rather as a necessary by-product of an effective justice mechanism ordained to suppress a climate conducive to the existence or spread of social disruption. Tangible and severe as it may appear, many citizens found in corporal punishment what amounts to an act of mercy to those who have a strong tendency to commit crime. These argue that when compared with long term prison sentences, which in time lose their effectiveness, the execution of "bodily penalty" (e.g., flogging and cutting the hand) offers obvious advantages. Serving as an act of penance and remission, it can allow the criminal to resume his work almost immediately and to continue to support himself and his family. As to its application as a symbolic tool rather than a practical policy, the consensus of opinion focused on the need to apply Shariah law in a manner that more or less best fits the needs of a changing society. When the society is experiencing some radical changes due, for instance, to the sudden affluence of its members or the influx of too many foreign workers, there would be more need to apply Shariah laws much more literally. Otherwise, the selective application of the law was deemed adequate for the preservation of an orderly society.

Two major sociologica theories might help explain the unique phenomenon of low criminality in Saudi Arabia: the theory of social disorganization to articulate the current structure of the society; and the theory of social learning to elucidate the processes of social development and maintenance. Simply stated, the theory of social disorganization [14] suggests that a society is well organized if ample consensus exists regarding common norms and values, and if strong ties among its members flourish. In the absence of consensus, normative behaviour diminishes, social anomie increases, and individuals resort more often to violating social norms. Maintaining a desirable level of social organization depends, however, on the efficacy of two elements: epidemiology or social ecology, and individual conduct or psychological tendency.[15] The first relates primarily to the directive role of government in engineering and maintaining, on behalf of society, a hygienic social climate. The second is the obligatory role of individuals in espousing — or ignoring — a high standard vf proper conduct. In Saudi Arabia, unlike secular societies in which the two elements may be independent, the two roles are integrated through the catalyst of puritanical faith. The divine Shariah not only strengthens each element individually, but also galvanizes them in a hughly potent religious amalgam.

This amalgam in Saudi society can also serve an indirect function: it bridges the conventional gap which separates the entity of government from the masses and thus furthers social bonding within the nation. For instance, despite the traditional monarchical system of government in Saudi Arabia, the King's role is popularly perceived as the entrusted custodian of the faith, a duty without which "Islam would certainly suffer." This perception of the King's role by his faithful community of believers is constantly reinforced on a daily basis. Whether in person, or when viewed on television (which covers almost every remote village in the realm), the King is seen praying with his followers, washing the walls of Mecca's Haram, presiding over the council of elders, and handing out financial assistance to the indigents, among other religiously symbolic duties.

The directive role of government in maintaining a puritanical social climate in Saudi Arabia is of critical importance to social organization. For instance, the government requires all employers, public and private, to make available a prayer hall in every building where Moslems work so they can make their regular prayers on time without leaving the building. It employs an army of retired clergymen (Mutaween) to walk the streets in towns and villages at prayer time to direct shoppers and passersby to enter promptly the nearest mosque and pray. It allows paid-for vacation time to all employees during the pilgrimage season to attend to this holy duty. It appoints all judges in the realm from among the clergymen or graduates of the Shariah College in Mecca. It monitors all T.V. and radio programs lest they include theologically unacceptable scenes or themes. It censors all newspapers lest they publish pictures or articles in violation of the Islamic code of proper conduct. The government, needless to say, pays for the entire cost of building, maintaining, and staffing of public mosques and religious schools in the country.

Perhaps the most graphic display of the government's endorsement of a puritanical social climate in the Kingdom is its role when capital punishment is administered on behalf of the community. While such exercises are carried out on much fewer occasions than the Western reader is led to believe (given the small number of serious crimes committed in any given locale per year), the performance is usually perceived as a sobering and a purifying occasion. Unlike the carnival-like scenes depicted in English history books, the occasion represents a welcomed solance in which the forces of religion, government, and of society climax in a live experience of Islamic justice, social deterrence, and popular relief. The scene, and the memory of such an exercise, serves to reinforce in the conscience of believers the net value of conformity and the horrible cost of criminal life.

Now, to understand the role of individuals in support of proper conduct, it must be remembered that the Saudi com- -munity can be considered a highly united community only in a religious sense. In that sense alone the Saudi community sees its social deliverance. But since most social values, manners, and rules of ethics are rooted directly or indirectly in Quranic teachings, an image of religiosity is often reflected. Thus, for example, while tribal and regional differences among the Saudi population are plentiful, public expression of prejudice seldom surfaces since such sentiments are expressively prohibited by Shariah. In order to strengthen an emerging community that encompassed converts from many lands, the Quran specifically denounced nationalism, elitism, and a classist society. It advocated, instead, a community of do-gooders ranked solely on the basis of their piety. Furthermore, outside influence by foreigners, who are not members of the foreign work force, is almost nonexistent. The government does not allow tourism and visas are only issues on the basis of a certified invitation. Except for the necessity of sending large numbers of students abroad, the Saudi society remains well-insulated from Western influence.

In order to articulate those factors behind the premise of popular support for proper conduct in the Saudi society, the tenets of the social learning theory (and instrumental conditioning theory) seem most valuable to draw upon.[16] The heart of the theory advocates that one chooses to commit crime because one's accepted definitions of the law as principles to violate are in excess of one's accepted definitions of the law as principles that can, must, or should be obeyed. Wilson later added to this theory the construct of instrumental stimuli or "conditioning." He argued that actors exposed for a prolonged period of time to an excess of positive definitions of the law would become conditioned to resist the temptation of criminal acts by the development (within the actor) of a "conscience sufficiently capable" of restraining one's desire to commit crime.[17]

The predominant source of social learning in the Kingdom is the Quran. Reverence of the Quran is the *conditio sine qua non* in the life of the Saudi. The Quran is perceived by Moslem believers not only as a divine book of scriptures, but literally as a total guide for the total life in this world and the hereafter. Therefore, every social practice, every intellectual thought, and every psychological disposition must conform to its teachings. Any knowledge which had no source in the Quran is likely to be discarded as unimportant since the omniscient book is believed to contain all knowledge including, for instance, detailed predictions of man's explorations of space.[18]

Shariah law can be learned either directly or indirectly. Direct learning occurs through the day-to-day exposure to an orthodox Islamic environment. The call for prayer is the first sound heard every day at sunrise and the last one hears before going to bed. In the meantime, one is constantly exposed to religious symbols in the streets (the Saudi national flag basically portrays a single verse from the Quran), Quranic recitation at the mosque and at school, lengthy readings from the Quran on the radio several times a day, Quranic contests for children on television, and the constant display of religious literature in public places and in store windows. Furthermore, the Kingdom requires Islamic studies as part of the educational curriculum at all school levels (grade, junior high, high school, college, and graduate levels), with a passing grade as a requisite for graduation. This variety of reinforcers, continuously heightened by government and social forces, produce an overpowering effect on the minds and hearts of the Saudi youth, resulting in a strong, hard-to-change set of beliefs.

The indirect learning of Shariah occurs through the absorption of tradition. As such, learning is not necessarily the product of rewards one receives for one's actions but, rather by watching a model's behaviour being rewarded, one learns through vicarious reinforcement.[19] The earliest stage of indirect social learning in a Saudi community occurs at childhood. Children watch the regularity of their fathers' routine trip to the mosque several times a day; of their mothers performing prayer at home; of abstention from eating during daytime throughout the month of Ramadan; of segregation by gender — in a scramble — when guests ring the door bell; and of listening to Quranic chanting over the radio almost constantly.

After the age of ten, boys are normally expected to dress in the native dress and to accompany their father on his trips to the mosque. They are rewarded for their regularity and promptness in making the prayers. They learn to imitate the preacher at the mosque, in performing ablution, in praying reverently, and in memorizing the 6342 verses in Quran. But more importantly, adolescents in a Saudi community are rewarded for polite manners, deference of parents, obedience to authority, disinterest in material things, and conformity with the rules of Islamic piety.

Islamic tradition has been equally effective in suppressing and deterring decadent behaviour within the community. The Shariah prohibits Western-style amenities including the use, sale, or importation of liquor, movie houses, dances, country clubs, or the appearance of females in cultural and social events. While such an environment would be considered a "no-fun culture" by Western standards, Saudi youth — with perhaps the exception of an emerging group of modern jet-setters — find it natural and spiritually rewarding.

The behaviour of adult males in Saudi Arabia is, unsurprisingly, highly structured. They are strongly encouraged to marry at an early age. Early marriages serve the primary function of preserving one's piety through sparing young adults the hardship and temptations of prolonged celibacy. At work, Saudi employees are expected to be congenial, egalitarian, and soft spoken. After work, adult Saudis, undistracted by worldly pleasures and fun activities, spend their long evenings reading the Quran, coaching the children, visiting with relatives, and perhaps once a week arranging a setting for playing cards or watching a soccer match at the local stadium.

Another factor that is privately appreciated by the Saudi community, but is seldom mentioned in the company of foreigners, is the popular view relating piety to the present state of prosperity in the country. Most Saudi citizens — especially among the unsophisticated groups — believe that the present oil prosperity has been a reward from God for their long dedication to piety and to Shariah teachings. Should the nation relent its central concern for puritanism, either by the government becoming less protective of the Islamic structure, or by individuals becoming less supportive for proper Islamic conduct, God will "pull back his generous hand," and the vast depositories of oil in the land will dry up.

From the previous discussion, one cannot escape the prominent and most pervasive role of Shariah law in the Saudi Arabian society. While the law clearly does not seem to embrace a uniquely identifiable "behaviour purificant element" (at least when compared with Talmudic law), its unsual impact on crime in Saudi Arabia must derive from the way it is applied. Furthermore, the evidence that the other six Moslem countries which do not apply the law suffer from a substantially higher crime rate might lend more credence to these speculations. As a personal note, the impact of the study was invaluable; it further reduced my skepticism of crime rates in the Kingdom but demonstrably heightened my inquisitiveness about Shariah law and the role similar instruments could play directly or indirectly in social structuring and in the deterrence of crime.

Summary

Compared to world crime rates, the Kingdom of Saudi Arabia has a rate which is demonstratively lower. Even when compared with surrounding Moslem countries which do not apply Shariah law, the Kingdom shows a crime rate considerably lower. It appears fair to assume that the role of Shariah law makes the difference. Shariah law is the divine law of Islam revealed to prophet Mohammed in the Seventh Century along with the teachings of the prophet himself. Unlike Western-style positive laws, Shariah reflects an expanded view of socio-religious rules based on the principles of prevention, conditioning, bonding, moralizing, and punishment. While Shariah does not present an enumeration of all crimes, it relies primarily on a category of prohibitions knows as Huddud Allah (God's limitations). When these are invoked, along with their mandatory severe punishments, they come alive in the conscience of believers and strengthen their tendency to pursue a non-criminal life. While Shariah law does not appear to embrace an identifiable "crime purificant element," the way it is aggressively practiced in the Kingdom seems to be the foremost factor contributing to its effectiveness. Its application is carried out in a dual endeavor: the role of government, on behalf of society, in instituting a tight social structure in the Kingdom; and the role of a spiritual community bent on piety and the pursuit of proper conduct. Both roles are amalgamated, thus reinforcing each other under the hegemony of puritanical orthodoxy. The impact of such an amalgam seems most instrumental in maintaining the low level of crime in the Kingdom.

References and Notes

[1] F. Adler, *Nations Not Obsessed With Crime,* Littleton, Colorado, Fred B. Rothman and Co., 1983.

[2] *Ibidem.*

[3] *Ibidem.*

[4] W. H. Nagel, "Structural Victimization", *International Journal of Criminology and Penology,* 1974, No. 20: 2, pp. 71-84.

[5] J. Andeneas, "The General Preventive Effects of Punishment", *University of Pennsylvania Law Review,* May 1966, No. 114, p. 949; R. Quinney, "The Idealogy of Law: Notes for a Radical alternative to Legal Oppression", 1972, pp. 30-40 in C. E. Reasons and R. M. Rich, Eds., *The Sociology of Law: A Conflict Perspective,* Canada, Butterworth; M. Feeley, "The Concept of Laws in Social Science", *Law and Society Review",* May 1976, No. 10, pp. 497-523; G. Newman, *Comparative Deviance, Perception and Law in Six Cultures,* New York, Elsevier, 1974; F. Adler, *Nations Not Obsessed...,* op. cit.; J. Q. Wilson and R. Hernstein, *Crime and Human Nature,* New York, Simon and Schuster, 1985.

⁶ Conflicting results have characterized research in the area of religiosity and criminality. In a famous study by Hirshi and Stark (1969), the authors concluded that religion and delinquency were unrelated. Over almost 10 years these findings have been debated by one study after another (Albrecht et. al; Benson; Fitzpatrick; Knudten and Knudten; Peek et. al.). In fact, there is a total of 65 published studies which report some actual and original evidence concerning the relationship between a measure of religiosity and some indicator of lawbreaking (Tittle and Welch, 1983). Among these studies, some significant ones (e.g., Burkett and White, 1974; Higgins and Albrecht, 1977; Albrecht et al., 1977) have confirmed a negative relationship. In a recent study by Elifson, Petersen, and Hadaway, it was further shown that religious salience, belief in the efficacy of personal prayer, and orthodoxy are generally more substantial correlates of delinquency. This assertation should not be surprising given the close conceptual links among salience, orthodox religious beliefs, and the internalization of religious moral values. It should not, on the other hand, undermine the findings of Charles Tittle and Michael Welch (Social Forces, Vol. 61, 1983), who showed that the religiosity-deviance relationship can vary predictably across sociodemographic contexts and not always in directions suggested by extant theories.

⁷ Sections III, IV, and V, which provided the quantitative data of crime rates in Saudi Arabia and attempts at its validation through a quasi-Delphi approach, have been used in a different conceptual framework focusing on the role of religiosity in Saudi Arabia in a paper that appeared in the *Journal of the Scientific Study of Religion*, December 1987.

⁸ J. Q. Wilson, *Crime and Human ..., op. cit.*

⁹ D. J. Black, "The Production of Crime Rates", *American Sociological Review*, 1970, No. 35, pp. 733-748; J. E. Price, "A Test of the Accuracy of Crime Statistics", *Social Problems*, 1966, No. 14:2, pp. 214-221; A. Reiss, "Public Perceptions and Recollections About Crime", *Law Enforcement and Criminal Justice*, Washington D. C., Government Printing Office, 1967; E. Vetere and G. Newman, "International Crime Statistics: An Overview from a Comparative Perspective", *Criminology and Penology*, 1977, No. 17: 4, pp. 251-252; S. Wheeler, "Criminal Statistics", *Journal of Criminal Law and Criminology*, 1967, No. 58, pp. 17-24.

¹⁰ G. N. Gordon, "The Islamic Revolution: The Case of Sudan", *The International Lawyer*, 1985, No. 19: 3, pp. 793-794.

¹¹ American and Canadian Coptic Association, *Coptic Newsletter*, Jersey City, New Jersey, The American and Canadian Coptic Association, 1985.

¹² N. Safran, *Saudi Arabia: The Ceaseless Quest for Security*, Cambridge, Maryland, Belknap Press, 1985; F. Adler, *Nations Not Obsessed ..., op. cit.*

[13] N. Christie, "Comparative Criminology", *Canadian Journal of Corrections,* 1970, No. 12: 1, pp. 40-46.

[14] R. Cloward and L. Ohlin, *Delinquency and Opportunity,* 1961, Glencoe, Illinois, Free Press; A. K. Cohen, *Deviance and Control,* Englewood Clifs, New Jersey, Prentice Hall 1966; R. E. Hilbert and C. Wright, "Representation of Merton's Theory of Anomie", *American Sociology,* 1979, No. 14; R. K. Merton "Social Structure and Anomie", pp. 185-214 in R. K. Merton Ed. *Social Theory and Social Structure,* New York, Free Press.

[15] R. Akers, *Deviant ..., op. cit.*; D. Cressey "The Application of the Theory of Differential Association", *American Journal of Sociology,* 1955, No. 61; J. D. Orcutt, "Self Concept and Insulation Against Delinquency", *Sociological Quarterly,* 1970, No. 11.

[16] R. Akers, *Deviant ..., op. cot.*; E. Sutherland and D. Cressey, *Criminology,* Santa Barbara, California, 1970.

[17] J. Q. Wilson and R. Hernstein, *Crime and Human ..., op. cit.*

[18] M. Bucaille, *The Bible, The Quran and Science,* Indianapolis, American Trust, 1978.

[19] R. Akers, *Deviant ..., op. cit.*

DEVELOPMENT AND CRIME IN YUGOSLAVIA

Results of the preliminary analysis *

Uglješa Zvekić **

Introduction

Background

The United Nations has in the past paid considerable attention to the crime and development question, and the Organization's engagement in this area is growing. Indeed, it has by now acquired a very high referential significance for the whole range of activities and in particular at the quinquennial United Nations Congresses on the Prevention of Crime and the Treatment of Offenders. This was highlighted in the Milan Plan of Action, the preeminent document adopted by the most recent congress, namely the Seventh, held in Milan, Italy in 1985. The same concern is being frequently reflected in the preparatory activities now

---

* This paper is based on the material elaborated by a joint United Nations Interregional Crime and Justice Research Institute (UNICRI) / Institute of Criminological and Sociological Research (IKSI) research team composed of:

Project Directors:	U. Leone (Director UNICRI)
	D. Radovanović (Director IKSI)
Project Co-ordinator:	U. Zvekić (UNICRI)
Research Experts	
UNICRI:	N. Queloz, A. Rzeplinski, T. Kubo
IKSI:	D. Cotić, K. Momirović, S. Hrnjica, V. Korać, E. Kupek, N. Pavić, N. Mrvić, V. Nikolić-Ristanović and K. Savin.

** Research Co-ordinator, United Nations Interregional Crime and Justice Research Institute (UNICRI).

underway for the forthcoming Eighth Congress to be held in Havan, Cuba in 1990.

The United Nations Interregional Crime and Justice Research Institute — UNICRI (formerly UNSDRI) also reflected these concerns in its programmes and activities. The abovementioned concerns lead to the launching of this action-oriented pilot project in Yugoslavia.

For reasons of technical feasibility the project in Yugoslavia focused on a limited period of time (1966-1986) and on a selected aspect of the subject matter. Limits are also set by the type and form of information used in the analysis, namely statistical secondary data, available from official recording systems.

It is standard UNICRI practice, for activities at country level, to work very closely with national research structures and institutions. This project explifies complete partnership between the Institute of Criminological and Sociological Research in Belgrade (IKSI), the Yugoslav Government and UNICRI. Financially, organizationally and substantively, the partnership in this instance is one of full equality and reciprocity.

Objectives

This study is of national character but its objectives are partially directed to an international context. It may be characterized as an action-oriented pilot research. Its action-oriented characteristics mark the emphasis on a sequential approach, that is "the initial priority of research is to advance an overall understanding of the phenomenon in its socio-legal context, realizing that there is a direct link between understanding and the formulation of (preventive) policies" (Resolution 20 of the Seventh UN Congress, 1985). It being characterized as pilot project sets limits to the depth and direction of the exploration; it is directed more towards outlining possible fruitful research paths rather than providing definite answers or paving rigid tracks for research.

A complementary objective is that of providing research-related technical assistance and training. These two types of assistance exemplify the often requested practical achievements of the UN services in the field of research. In a concise mode this joint endeavour reflects the UNICRI's mandate, philosophy, approach and potentials in delivering services within the context of international co-operation in crime prevention and criminal justice.

As regards these characteristics, the objectives were identified as follows:

i) research-related objectives

— identification of the adequate methodological design and approach;
— identification of the most significant types, directions and strength of association between development and crime;
— integrated political, economic, penal and criminological interpretation of the identified associations;
— testing the explanatory and predictive potential of the identified methodological design.

ii) technical assistance and training-related objectives

— collection of significant and reliable developmental and criminal justice data;
— creation of developmental and criminal justice database;
— identification of the minimum requisites for the developmental and criminal justice data-base model;
— promotion of methodologies relevant for the data-base model;

— training of personnel in the field of developmental and criminal justice statistics;
— training of the researchers in the use of developmental and criminal justice data-base;
— training of researchers in models and methods of dimensional and comparative data analysis.

Progress and Problems

The project started in 1987. The Project Document was prepared in the first half of 1988 identifying the main directions of research and its structures, and outlining the methodological design. The next phase consisted in the collection of data and the creation of data base. Then, the analysis of the test year (1980) was carried out which identified major problems with data, their interpretation, and further analyses needed to supplement the adopted methodological model. The preliminary analysis based on 1973, 1980 and 1986 was carried out. This paper will present major findings of the preliminary analysis. The results of the preliminary analysis served as a basis for the elaboration of further data analysis and the adoption of the structure of the final report. It is expected that the final report will be completed and ready for publication by the end of 1990.

A number of problems were encountered in each of the phases of the project. These problems may be classified into three distinct but related categories.

The first category of problems concerns conceptualization and interpretation. Development is a case at point. Despite numerous attempts to define it, there is no consensus regarding the concept of development. For a long time, both in science and commonsensically, development carried positive connotations. It underlined affirmative aspects of social change, mostly of economic growth. In science, it was also connected with the notion of progress, linearity, accumulation and continuity, although there were attempts to move away from the exclusively positive loadings. UNESCO's definition is an attempt to depart from the "affirmative backlog": "Development, in short, is an integral and integrating process, both requiring and precipitating far-reaching social, political and economic changes. It is by no means a unilinear process that moves steadily and smoothly towards some predetermined set of models and values ... it is typically turbulent, often a downright disorderly and painful process".

Apart from the complexity of the definition of development, another complication lies in the internal conceptual structure of development. Is it a singular, undifferentiated process or does it consist of a number of such processes? Thus, some speak of global development and types of development, like: economic, industrial, political, educational and social. For some, global development is the result of its composite processes; for others, it is totality *per se*. The unitary concept of development suggests a singular indicator or singular index of development; the differentiated concept suggests multiple indicators, themselves in different degrees of mutual association and of different direction of relationships.

The substitution of development with social change does not present an adequate solution either. Although social change seems to be of a more neutral connotation, it does not reduce the ambiguity of the concept. It is of great importance to use coherently the concept of development and to define it as precisely as possible, since the conceptualization of development has definite consequences for the adoption of the theoretical interpretative framework.

The situation with the crime component — in the crime and development phrase — is also complicated but somewhat to a lesser degree since the research is of national character. Yet, some complications regard the theoretical concept of crime; is it an ontological concept or a social construction? If so, in what sense and how is one to talk about crime? What is the relationship between the criminal justice system and criminal behaviours? What are the indicators of crime and in what way should they be socio-culturally and politically interpreted?

The theoretically conceived position of crime *vis-à-vis* development determines its position in the analytical process (dependent or independent variable). For those who regard crime as a dependent variable, time sequence is of crucial importance and therefore appropriate methods for analysis must be selected. On the other hand, some authors regard crime as a social activity with its own internal logic and historical developments, thus, essentially, as an independent variable. Others claim that crime is an integral part of social processes and talk not only about modernization of society but also about modernization of crime. The concepts of societal and crime modernization is not quite clear although it points out the adaptive capacities of social patterns of interaction and their interpretation within the framework of a determined set of goals and means. But these concepts cannot easily confront themselves with the reality of development, which is far from being unidirectional.

This research project adopted the concept of development as an integral process which allows the existence of different development profiles. Each developmental profile describes a discrete configuration. Therefore, the project's concept of development is basically an empirical concept, established within the limits set by the nature and type of available developmental parametres.

The most serious problem concerned the collection of data and the creation of data base. It stem from the fact that the project covers a twenty-year period, that the basic unit for data collection was the municipality (on an average 500 municipalities for each year) and that data base contains 67 developmental variables and 20 criminal justice variables (10 for adults and 10 for juveniles) for each

304

municipality and for each year. The main difficulty emerged from the fact that data were recorded following different methodologies, in different forms, in different media; furthermore, they had to be searched for in different sources.

The next problem is related to the fact that not all the data were available for each basic unit. Therefore, some data were missing for some municipalities which created a problem of data systematization and in particular their sequential ordering.

Data analysis was carried out according to the methodological model containing several techniques:

— descriptive statistical parametres on a level of discrete variable;

— linear correlation within and between the sets of variables;

— multiple regression analysis for (i) each singular developmental and criminal justice variable; (ii) latent developmental variables (factors of development) and each singular criminal justice variable; (iii) singular and latent developmental variables and the first major component of the criminal justice variable set;

— factor analysis of developmental and criminal justice variables by the methods of major components and their rotation in the ortoblique position;

— canonical and quasi-canonical analyses on the level of singular developmental and criminal justice variables and within the factor solutions;

— taxonomic analysis;

— methods for the analysis of rhythm and disproportions in development and its relation to crime.

Bearing in mind the volume of data and complexity of analyses, a number of technical problems arose for which

305

relatively satisfactory solutions were found. Two such problems, however, need to be pointed out. The first refers to the already mentioned lack of certain data. In some small-sized municipalities certain forms of crime were not registered at all. This was particularly the case with certain forms of serious offences and juvenile offenders. This situation led to an attempt to group singular criminal justice variables into larger categories. Such a solution resulted in criminal justice categories identical to the categorization adopted by the Yugoslav Criminal Code. However, a certain amount and quality of significant information for criminal policy analysis was lost.

The second problem refers to the analysis of rhythm and disproportions in development and their relationship with crime. The problem is not technical but rather of interpretative nature. One of the main hypothesis contained in the Project Document was that faster rhythm of development and marked disproportions in development lead to marked increase in crime rates, and that the relationship between development and crime varies according to the abovementioned characteristics of developmental process. Preliminary analysis showed that this is not so, that is to say, the coefficients of determination between certain developmental factors and certain forms of crime are at approximately equal level throughout the twenty-year period and that these coefficients do not reflect a developmental curve. This seems to be an interesting finding from the theoretical point of view but it needs further testing with different models of analysis in order to increase its reliability (or to dispel it).

Development and Crime: Trends and Characteristics

A Short Note on Yugoslavia's Economic and Legal History

Yugoslavia was created in 1918 after the First World War and, following the Second World War (national liberation struggle against fascism and the socialist revolution), was constituted a federal socialist state. It is a multi-ethnic, multi-lingual and multi-religion federation made up of six republics and two autonomous provinces. Its basic political principles are self-management, monaparty system and non-alignment in foreign policy.

Post-war development in Yugoslavia followed quite closely the Soviet economic model up to 1948 after which it initiated a number of economic and political reforms. Yet, in the fifties it still relied on the model of centrally-planned economy.

The economic situation over the twenty-year period under consideration (1966-1986) can be characterized as follows:

1965-1972: This period was initiated by the economic reform of 1965, a reform with an emphasized market orientation. This period ends with constitutional amendments inserted in the Constitution of 1974. The major idea of the reform consisted in giving enterprises a more independent role which should, in turn, lead to a more efficient allocation of resources and higher productivity. Social tensions, strife between the republics and provinces in the process of decentralization, etc., caused a shift away from a distinct market orientation towards the end of the period. The major economic indicators show still high growth rates of industrial production, a doubling of the rate of inflation, higher unemployment, a high growth of productivity and a stable increase in real wages. Export growth lagged behind import growth, but the migration of labour to the West and resulting workers remittances eased the pressure on the balance of payments and unemployment levels.

In a broader sense, this period can be regarded as a turning point, not only in terms of the economic system, but also from the point of view of a deeper social reorientation in terms of social values. This was caused not only by a

307

pronounced market orientation, but also by an opening-up to the rest of the world (migration abroad, freedom of travel abroad, development of tourism, etc.).

1972-1980: This period was characterized by the establishment of a system of "social agreements" as a regulating mechanism within the economy and an import substitution strategy with high foreign lending in order to cover the gap in domestic savings. Borrowing on the financial world market was pronounced after 1976, resulting in a huge foreign debt and the undertaking of huge investment projects. The growth of industrial production in this period is still impressive, but the rate of inflation was doubled. As a result of a sharp fall in the standard of living, the growth of productivity and the average growth rate of real incomes were dampened over the last two years of this subperiod. The rate of unemployment was doubled while growth rates of export and import were reduced to half.

1980-1986: This period is characterized more by macro-economic tendencies that took a turn for the worse as compared to the preceeding period, than by any type of institutional reform. The growth rate of industrial production fell to only 2.8% on the average. There were marked declines in the absolute standard of living, a galloping inflation, a further increase in unemployment, negative rates of productivity growth in industry, while a drop in the growth of exports was accompanied by import restrictions. While there was a lack of institutional reform, this period was marked by a broad debate on the nature of and remedies for what has been openly called a "major crisis" in Yugoslav society.

The whole period under consideration is furthermore characterized by rapid urbanization and related rural/urban migration. Yet, nowadays, more than 50% of the population in Yugoslavia (out of approximately 22 million) still lives in rural areas, which means that the level of urbanization is low, as compared to other European countries. Nevertheless, only 20% of the active population works in the agricultural sector. Of course there are marked differences between regions in this respect. In fact, disagrarization is quite marked despite the fact that the majority of the people still live in the country; this can be explained by the high daily migration to industrialized centres (comuters), and slower urbanization — in terms of spatial concentration and sectoral occupational allocation — than disagrarization.

The development of the Yugoslav penal system can also be divided into three distinct periods:

1945-1951: This period is characterized by the passing of a number of individual penal acts in order to regulate and protect the economic and political bases of the new socialist system. The Constitution of the Federal People's Republic of Yugoslavia was passed in 1946 as well as the General Part of the Criminal Code (1947) and the Code of Penal Procedure (1948). These two were the first systematic penal legislative acts. It should be noted that the Criminal Code was, to a great extent, inspired by the theory and experience of the Soviet Union. At the same time a number of individual legislative acts were passed, thereby expanding the penal legislation's special sections and creating solid basis for the formulation of a unified and comprehensive criminal legislation.

1951-1977: The new criminal code was passed in 1951 and it is considered the most important instance in the development of a democratic penal system. Progressive principles contained in the penal systems of some European countries were adopted, with emphasis on the principle of Legality and negation of the principle of analogy. The Criminal Code underwent several revisions during this period. The 1959 reform introduced a number of important changes in the juvenile justice system inspired by the social defence movement. In the early sixties, types of punishment were reduced to five and security measures and judicial reprimand were also introduced. The new Constitution was passed in 1963. Further reforms took place in 1965, 1967 and 1969, while the reform of 1973 already paved the way to a new phase in the development of the penal system.

1977 to date: The new Constitution of the Socialist Federal Republic of Yugoslavia was passed in 1974 and as a result of adjustments, the unified Criminal Code ceased to exist on 1 July 1977. In fact, the Federal Criminal Code was passed on 28 September 1976 while the Criminal Codes of the Republics and Autonomous Provinces were adopted on 1 July 1977. This meant that federal jurisdiction included the general part of the Criminal Code and a limited number of federal crimes. All other criminal offences are contained in the criminal codes of each constitutive unit of the Federation. Still, the unified Code of Penal Procedure is retained.

Main Characteristics of Socio-economic
Development: 1973-1986

Socio-economic and cultural development are represented by the sets of variables. Their values are given for three points in time: 1973, 1980 and 1986. At a descriptive level the following characteristics are noted:

Demographic change: It is represented by a number of indicators all of which point out a relatively slow demographic growth on average, however, with drastic variations between regions; a slight trend towards decrease in fertility rate, infant mortality rate and number of registered marriages, and an increase in mortality rate.

Income and investments: The index of active basic assets at purchase value per inhabitant grew in the period 1973-1980 approximately three times faster than in the 1980-1986 period. A more drastic fall is registered in a latter

310

period regarding the coefficients of growth in values. National income per inhabitant also registered drastic growth in the 1973-1980 period (2.82 times) and then a slight tendency towards decrease. The same tendencies are found in industry, mining and agriculture although the increase in agriculture was significantly lower. In the individual (private) sector of agriculture there was an increase in income per inhabitant, but two times lower than in the public sector of agriculture in the same period (1973-1980), followed by the downward trend in both sectors in the subsequent period. Investments in economy showed a high rate of increase in the first period (3.5 times) and then rapid fall in the 1980-1986 period, so that the value of investments in the basic assets of the public sector in 1986 dropped to only 71% of their real value in 1980. In addition, it is noted that both yield of wheat and maze showed slight but constant increase in the whole period under consideration (an average of 2% yearly) although there were no substantial changes in terms of the areas of arable land.

Traffic and communication: The number of railway stations, the value of transport of goods by railway and the number of passengers showed a slight decrease in the 1973-1980 period and then an opposite trend in the period that followed. The number of post offices increased slightly over the fifteen year period (10%). Only the number of passenger cars registered constant and drastic growth from 42.67 per 1000 inhabitants in 1973 to 112.92 in 1986.

Supply of goods: This activity was measured on the basis of the number of stores and turnover. In the 1973-1980 period the turnover increased much faster (about three times) than the number of stores; in the following period, the turnover decrease on an average of 0.5% real value per year.

Tourism: The number of beds, domestic and foreign tourists grew constantly at an yearly average rate of approximately 3% with, nevertheless, differences between regions.

311

Housing construction: In the 1973-1980 period there was a significant growth in public and total housing construction, while both investments in housing and number of houses decreased significantly in the 1980-1986 period.

Medical care: All parametres of medical care registered increased in the period under consideration, although it should be noted that the number of physicians grew much faster (6% annually) with respect to the number of hospital beds (1% annually).

Education: There were no substantial changes in all parametres of education in the period under observation, except for the significant increase in number of pupils in the secondary schools in the 1973-1980 period.

Culture: Developments in the sphere of culture were measured by a number of variables indicating cinema attendance and radio and TV subscribers. While there was constant although slight decrease in the number of cinemas and in the attendance, the number of TV and radio subscribers rapidly increased in the 1973-1980 period following which the achieved level was maintained over the 1980-1986 period.

This summary presentation of the selected developmental variables highlights the existence of two clear trends. In the 1973-1980 period growth continued in almost all developmental parametres with respect to the preceeding period. For some of them, the rate of increase was highly marked. On the other hand, over 1980-1986 the effects of economic crisis is clearly demonstrated by the downward trend in almost all developmental parametres except private transport.

Trends in Crime: 1973-1986

In the period under consideration, the number of final sentences passed in criminal proceedings in Yugoslavia more or less stagnated, showing a decrease in the rate of persons convicted, as compared with the 1960-1974 period. After a considerable fall in the number of final sentences recorded in the period 1978-1981, the number of persons convicted began to rise in 1982, primarily as a result of an increase in some forms of property, economic and traffic offences. In addition, there were some changes in substantive and procedural penal legislation that may have to some extent influenced the general crime picture. Thus, as of 1 July 1977, six republican and two provincial criminal codes have been inforced together with the Federal Criminal Code, all of which have introduced some new forms of economic offences and criminal violations of self-managing rights; there were also some changes regarding private penal action and obligatory conciliation proceedings.

The dynamics of adult crime in terms of the total number of adult persons convicted of criminal offences showed decrease up to 1979, followed by minor fluctuations until 1981, and a considerable increase after 1981, especially in 1984 (Table I in Annex).

The participation of women in the total number of persons convicted declined steadily throughout the entire period considered. However, in the last three years of the period, the number of women convicted increased but, in relative terms, less than the number of men.

The structure of crime by kind of offence change (Table II in Annex). Thus, in 1975, the largest number of adults were convicted of offences against property (about 22 percent of the total number), followed by offences against life and limb (about 19 percent) and public transport safety (about 17 percent). Also in 1985, the largest number of convicted persons were found guilty of offences against property (about 30 percent of the total figure), followed by offences against public transport safety (about 18 percent), while the proportion of those convicted of offences against life and limb decreased (to approximately 14 percent of the total number).

The rise in the overall number of persons convicted over the last few years of the period under consideration was due to an increase in the number of offences against property; there was also an increase in the number of persons convicted of offences against the national economy. The number of persons convicted of offences against official duty and the general security of people and property also increased. On the other hand, there was a marked decrease in the number of persons convicted for offences against honour and reputation. This was, it is presumed, to a large extent due to obligatory conciliation procedure before conciliation councils for perpetrators of offences on the basis of private action.

The period under survey also saw a decrease in the number of persons convicted for offences against civil liberties and human rights, and in the number of offences against public order and legal transactions.

In the total number of persons sentenced, the proportion of those convicted for political offences was small and, in addition, kept declining, thus continuing the downward trend for this kind of criminality that began in the mid-seventies. Persons convicted for such offences accounted for approximately 0.5 percent of the total number of persons sentenced in 1975, and for approximately 0.2 percent of those sentenced in 1985. From 1977 to 1979 the number of persons convicted declined considerably. However, this figure increased suddenly in 1982, especially the number of those convicted for counter-revolutionary activities against the social order, hostile propaganda and association for purposes of hostile activity, as a result of unrest in the province of Kosovo.

The proportion of persons convicted for violent crime from among the total number of persons sentenced, declined steadily. In 1975 it amounted to about 20 percent and ten years later to about 15 percent of the total figure. This decline was the result of a decrease in the number of persons convicted for light bodily injuries (approximately 32 percent), which otherwise accounted for the bulk (approximately 70 percent) of the total number of persons sentenced for offences against life and limb.

In addition, the number of persons convicted for the most serious offences falling within this group — such as: murder, voluntary masnlaughter and grievous bodily injury — also decreased but to a lesser extent.

The number of persons convicted for economic offences increased in the period under survey both in absolute (44 percent in 1985 as compared to 1975) and relative terms (from 1/5 in 1975 to 1/3 of the total figure for 1985). Until 1978 this number declined steadily, but it increased considerably after that year. There was, in fact, an increase in the number of adults convicted for offences against social property and national economy, while the number of sentences for offences against official duty varied negligibly. Among criminal offences against the national economy, "issuing and passing of a bad cheque" and "forest theft" predominated (65%). The incidence of criminal offences against social property increased steadily. After a decrease in 1977 and 1978, the number of persons convicted for theft of social property rose steadily topping, in 1985, by 83 percent the figure for 1975. The number of persons convicted for offences against official duty, which are also considered to be a form of economic criminality was, in contrast with the two former groups, rather stable until 1982, following which it increased in 1983, 1984 and 1985. There was, in fact, an increase in the number of persons convicted for abuse of official position, while the number of adult persons convicted for embezzlement in offices remained the same.

The marked increase in the number of various types of vehicles resulted in a considerable rise in the incidence of traffic offences. In 1953, for example, there were approximately 50,000 automobiles, buses and other motor vehicles on the Yugoslav roads as compared to over 3,4 million vehicles thirty years later. In addition, it should be borne in mind that Yugoslavia is an open-frontier country and transit territory for the Middle East countries and vice versa. All this has contributed to a rise in the number of traffic offences. The proportion of persons convicted for traffic offences, from among the total number of adult perpetrators, increased steadily until 1980 and then slightly declined. However, the consequences of such offences were considerable. Thus in 1954 a total of 429 persons were killed in traffic accidents, as compared to 4,105 in 1984. On the other hand, in 1984, approximately 500 persons died a violent death.

Penal policy is best illustrated by data on convicted persons by type of final sentence (Tables III and IV in Annex).

In the Yugoslav criminal law death penalty is, according to the Constitution, applicable only for very serious forms of some of the most grievous crimes. In the period under consideration, altogether 39 death penalties were imposed, and the largest number of murders were committed out of greed or blood vengeance, followed by murders committed in a cruel and perfidious manner, and multiple homicide.

Throughout the entire period under consideration, 1/5 of the total number of persons convicted were sentenced to immediate prison. Most frequent were the lowest sentences — up to 12 months imprisonment (73% in 1977 to 81% in 1984; the largest number were sentenced to three/six months imprisonment).

There were negligeable changes in penal policy concerning the imposition of fines. Thus, in 1975, fines accounted for about 29 percent and in 1985 for approximately 37 percent. The proportion of reduced punishments amounted to 1/4 and about 50 percent of this was accounted for by traffic offenders.

Suspended sentences accounted for almost 40 percent of the total number of sentences imposed, and suspended fines for 15 percent thereof.

The use of judicial admonition declined steadily while the number of educational measures (imposed upon young adults), although increasing, was quite small.

The proportion of security measures was rather small and ranged from about 4 percent in 1975 to about 5.5 percent in 1981. The most frequent security measure imposed on convicted adult persons was the withdrawal of the driving licence (63%); the second most frequent being prohibition from exercising a certain occupation, activity of duty, which is explained by the increase in the commission of economic offences.

In the period under consideration there was an increase in the number of measures calling for the compulsory treatment of alcoholics and drug addicts which shows the increased danger of this category of perpetrators, and also a rise in the number of alcoholics and drug addicts.

The table that follows summarizes the abovementioned information using the mean (XA), standard deviation (SD) and the registered maximum in the population.

Table 1 reveals the already noted trends in crime. Thus, offences against life and limb show constant decrease, while property crimes increase constantly. Both economic crime and traffic offences vary but in opposite directions: traffic offences increased while economic crime decreased between 1973 and 1980; the reverse trends (although slight) are noted in the 1980-1986 period. Only sexual offences exhibit constant rates throughout the period of examination. Finally, there is an increase in recidivism rate which can be attributed to its high association with property crime (0.77) and traffic offences (0.70).

Table 1

Crime Category		1973	1980	1986
Offences against life and limb	XA	9.86	7.56	6.55
	SD	6.58	4.50	4.53
	max	43.25	25.70	31.50
Property crime	XA	8.62	9.22	14.58
	SD	7.55	6.67	13.39
	max	77.03	38.90	67.18
Economic crime	XA	5.25	4.59	7.88
	SD	5.18	3.84	9.51
	max	44.74	48.26	40.73
Sexual offences	XA	0.39	0.38	0.37
	SD	0.52	0.47	0.49
	max	2.80	2.88	2.87
Traffic offences	XA	7.32	11.11	8.66
	SD	7.31	7.66	5.72
	max	45.79	51.87	70.32
Other offences	XA	13.50	10.71	9.56
	SD	10.65	6.98	6.95
	max	101.87	62.54	50.16
Recidivism	XA	6.54	7.41	9.80
	SD	6.60	6.34	9.41
	max	51.35	33.64	102.07

Development and Crime: Interrelations

Examination of interrelationships between crime and individual developmental variable and prediction of certain crimes on the basis of development parametres.

As can be noted in Table 2, developmental variables are most significantly linked with property crime, with a predictive value as high as 70-79%. The trend is that of relatively mild stagnation during the period when developmental parametres increase, followed by the increase of property crime during the period of development recession. Developmental variables have a relatively strong predictive value for traffic offences and recidivism. Economic crime in both

Table 2

Multiple Correlation and Coefficients of Determination: Development and Crime

Crime category		1973	1980	1986
Offences against	Rm	0.49	0.55	0.56
life and limb	D	25%	30%	31%
Property crime	Rm	0.86	0.84	0.88
	D	74%	70%	79%
Economic crime	Rm	0.47	0.49	0.54
	D	22%	24%	29%
Sexual offences	Rm	0.58	0.51	0.48
	D	34%	26%	23%
Traffic offences	Rm	0.79	0.72	0.65
	D	62%	52%	42%
Recidivism	Rm	0.79	0.71	0.78
	D	62%	51%	61%

developmental periods shows solid links with parametres of development.

The association between discrete developmental variables and selected crime categories provides a more detailed information on the abovementioned trends. These results are presented in Tables V, VI, and VII in Annex.

Offences against life and limb are positively associated with just a few developmental variables that characterize rural areas (e.g. income) while developmental variables indicating standards of living typical of urban environment are negatively correlated with this crime category.

Property crime is more strongly associated with a number of develpmental variables. Almost 50% of discrete developmental variables are significantly associated with property crime while some twenty developmental variables have, on average, above 0.50 correlation with property crime for all three years under consideration. From among discrete developmental variables, positive and significant correlation show, in particular, parametres of income, individual standard of living, social standard of living and intensive touristic activities. It should be noted that there is no single negative association between any developmental variable and property crime. In addition, only a few developmental variables have significant partial coefficients of correlation which indicate indirect links even for property crime which in turn, as noted, is most reflective of trends in development. This, of course, highlights the limits of macro-social explanation of the criminal justice phenomena.

Sexual offences which show almost a constant rate throughout the period under consideration are related to developmental parametres characterizing sites with intensive industrial development, but at the same time, located in a predominantely agricultural environment.

Traffic offences, as expected, are most significantly related with developmental parameters of social and individual standard of living. It is worth noting that the association between traffic offences and developmental parametres steadily decline over the 1973-1986 period; thus, for example, the correlation between number of cars and traffic offences decreased from 0.69 in 1980 to 0.48 in 1986. Similar to property crime, none of the partial correlations was greater than 0.25, and the majority were of zero order, indicating indirect links.

The abovepresented findings may be summarized as follows:

— some crime categories "follow", to a certain extent, trends in development but exhibit also opposite variations. For example, during the period of upward trend in developmental parametres, property crime registered a slight increase which then became quite significant in the period of downward trend in development; decrease in economic crime during the former pattern of development and a signicant increase over the latter one;

— some other crime categories exhibit more autonomy with respect to development, as exemplified by offences against life and limb and sexual offences;

— practically all links are indirect including those between property crime and development, which is otherwise most contingent, indicating the limits of a macro-social level of explanation;

— coefficients of association and prediction are lower on the level of discrete developmental variables with respect to the joint effects indicating the higher explanatory and predictive power of development as an integral process rather than its singular aspects. Yet, a particular configuration of developmental parameters (developmental profile) seems to possess some explanatory potential for particular crime categories.

These findings directed further analysis towards the structural level. Factorial analysis of developmental variables revealed the existence of several factors of development.

General factor of development comprises variables indicating standard of living and it is defined by marked income, investments in health care, education, cultural institutions and employment in sectors of education, medical services, financial and trade agencies.

Factor of agricultural development describes typical agricultural environment defined by the size of land ownership, yields of agricultural products and income from agricultural activity in the private sector. In addition, lower natality rate and higher divorce rate also characterize this developmental profile. However, the structure of this factor appears to be differentiated in two additional subtypes. The first refers to the public sector agriculture and the second to rather passive agricultural regions.

Development of tourism and urban development were also identified as distinct developmental factors. Urban development also had a differentiated structure comprising centres with developed health and cultural institutions network, those characterized by intensive housing construction, and finally, those which are also important transport and traffic sites.

The analysis of correlations (linear and partial) between developmental factors and crime indicates that only the general factor of development is significantly and meaningfully associated with certain crime categories. These associations are revealed in Table 3.

The association between the general factor of development and property crime is most significant and high as compared with other crime categories save traffic offences. Furthermore, partial correlation indicates direct links with property crime. This association decreased in the period 1980-1986 although, as noted, there was rapid increase in

Table 3

Crime category	1973		1980		1986	
	R	PR	R	PR	R	PR
Offences against life and limb	−.14	−.01	−.25	−.16	−.19	−.14
Property crime	.68	.46	.69	.40	.69	.27
Economic crime	.04	.14	−.02	−.05	−.13	−.17
Sexual offences	.19	.03	.13	−.01	.19	.04
Traffic offences	.45	.14	.48	.24	.37	.16
Recidivism	.49	.22	.50	.32	.26	.19

R = linear correlation
PR = partial correlation

property crime in the period of development recession. This finding is strongly supported by trend analysis (for each separate year over the twenty-year period under consideration).

In addition to property crime and traffic offences, the general factor of development is also highly associated with recidivism, which, as already noted, is in itself highly correlated with property crime and traffic offences. Therefore, the general factor of development has significant predictive potentials *vis-à-vis* property crime, traffic offences and recidivism with coefficient of prognosis of 47%, 23% and 25% respectively.

The explanatory and predictive power of the general factor of development are negligible as regards offences against life and limb, sexual offences and economic crime, with either negative or insignificant coefficients of correlation.

323

Due to the differentiated structure of the agricultural development factor, its explanatory potential is reduced. Areas with developed agriculture in the private sector tend to be associated with property crime (R = 0.26; PR = 0.27, sexual offences (R = 0.24; PR = 0.19) and traffic offences (R = 0.20; PR = 0.21). On the other hand, in regions characterised by developed agriculture in the public sector, negative low but significant association is found with offences against life and limb (R = 0.22; PR = 0.25) and, inversely, positive with property crime (R = 0.18). Other crime categories are not significantly associated with this developmental factor.

Table 4

Multiple Correlation and Coefficients of Determination between Factors of Development (Orthoblique Solution) and Crime
(RM – multiple correlation, DP-prognostic value of factors)

Crime category	1973	1980	1986
Offences against life and limb	RM 0.39 DP 15%	0.40 16%	0.36 13%
Property crime	RM 0.82 DP 67%	0.77 60%	0.83 63%
Economic crime	RM 0.32 DP 12%	0.23 5%	0.34 11%
Sexual offences	RM 0.43 DP 18%	0.32 10%	0.32 10%
Traffic offences	RM 0.60 DP 36%	0.68 47%	0.47 19%
Recidivism	RM 0.66 DP 44%	0.60 36%	0.44 19%

Factors coined "development of tourism" and "urban development" are significantly but mildly associated with property crime and traffic offences.

The advantage of factorial structural analysis seems to be reflected more in terms of the characterization of different developmental profiles and their links with certain forms of crime rather than in terms of prediction. This is revealed in Table 4.

By comparison of prognosis of crime on the basis of discrete development variables and sets of variables (OBQ factor) a systematic reduction in prediction is noted. One of the possible explanations could be that a number of significant developmental variables are excluded from the separated sets, which lead to a decrease in the predictive capacity of the system. Nevertheless, the general factor of development has a much higher predictive potential than any other factor.

An attempt towards exploration of predictive potentials of the developmental variables lead to a canonical analysis of factors for 1980. While seven pairs of factors were identified, only the first pairs provided significant results, as presented in Table 5.

Table 5

First Pair of Canonical Factors, 1980

Variables of development	loading	crime variables	loading
Income	.82	property	.92
Turnover in trade	.85	recidivism	.71
Number of automobiles	.77	traffic	.63
Number of radio apparatuses	.75	conditional sentences	.61
Number of TV appliances	.82	security measures	.61

The developmental component of the first pair (on the left hand side) refers to development defined in terms of the parameters of standard of living. This may be identified as predominantely of economic nature although, for the lack of better indicators, the use of radio and TV sets contains elements of cultural life. The crime component (on the right hand side) refers to crime categories which are most significantly connected with the developmental set. Again, property crime, traffic offences and recidivism associate with development; furthermore, the possibility of property crime prognosis on the basis of the given configuration of developmental variables is as high as 85%. In addition, both offences against life and sexual offences are absent, indicating their possible linkage with different configurations of developmental variables.

The second pair of canonical factors indicates a developmental configuration comprising parameters of demographic growth, developed agriculture in the public sector and developed transport. However, all links with crime categories are low, save negative association with offences against life and limb.

Other canonical pairs present a variety of developmental profiles with rather low projections on crime categories.

Concluding Remarks

The preliminary analysis and presentation of the results thereof are primarily of descriptive character. Moreover, the analysis aims at outlining certain major trends and characteristics of the interrelation between development and crime. Thus, through description and noting of trends it directed both further data analysis and its integrated interpretation. In fact, the preliminary analysis is more exploratory than explanatory.

This is so because of its preliminariness and because of the limits set by the type of data used and models of data analysis applied. An integrated interpretative reading must be based on a number of additional information coming from the economy, social policy, crime policy and penal law. This integrated interpretation cannot be based solely on quantitative data and quantitative type of data analysis. Furthermore, limits stem also from the fact that the preliminary analysis considers only three points in time (1973, 1980 and 1986) over the twenty-year period. Another limit emerges from the fact that one of the central hypothesis of the study regarding the relationship between development and crime in a more dynamic perspective (rhythm and disproportions), is not fully tested in the premiminary analysis. As noted in the introduction, further work is needed in order to elaborate and validate some of the otherwise interesting findings in this respect. Perhaps the most serious shortcoming of this preliminary analysis is the lack of clear empirical references as to the concrete municipalities which exhibit distinct developmental profiles and/or levels of corollary crime types. Only such concrete empirical references would enable meaningful integrated interpretation of the results. Finally, some of the problems noted at the beginning of this paper also set limits not only to the preliminary analysis but to the whole research endeavour.

Although the primary goal of the preliminary analysis was to explore the capacities of the methodological model adopted for this study, some significant tendencies regarding the relationship between development and crime can be noted.

The general picture of this relationship in Yugoslavia shows that neither intensive development (upward increase of developmental parameters) nor recession in development (downward trend of developmental parameters) have, in general, lead to significant increase of or decrease in crime. This is supported by the preliminary results regarding rhythm and disproportions in development and their effects on crime; a trend only noted and still requisting further investigation.

327

However, a more detailed analysis indicated significant variations within this overall picture.

With regard to crime, it is demonstrated that property crime is increasing while offences against life and limb are decreasing. Recidivism, which is closely connected with property crime, is also increasing. Traffic offences and economic crime show different patterns in different time periods — the former increasing and then decreasing, the latter decreasing and then increasing. Sexual offences have kept constant and low rates throughout the period under observation.

The interrelation between development and crime is not universal nor unidirectional, at least not in terms of direction of trends in development and crime. Some crime categories "follow", to a certain extent, the trends in development but also exhibit significant variations in direction. Thus, during the period of intensive upward trends in development (1973-1980), property crime has registered a slight increase, followed by significant growth in rates over the period of socio-economic crisis (1980-1986); economic crime showed a reverse trend in the former developmental period and then the same upward trend as property crime in the developmental period characterized by socio-economic slow down and crisis. Other crimes exhibited more "autonomy" in their trends with respect to trends and characteristics of development, as exemplified by offences against life and limb and even more so by sexual offences. Similarly, but to a lesser extent, such "autonomy" is present with traffic offences, although, while the association between these offences and development declined over time, traffic offences are most significantly related with developmental parameters exhibiting social and individual standars of living.

Notwithstanding these significant variations in direction, it is important to keep in mind that the preliminary analysis seems to support the hypothesis that the determination of the relationship between development and crime is at approximately the same level throughout the whole period. While, as already mentioned several times, this indication needs further methodological elaboration, it also requests significant interpretative efforts. At present it certainly indicated at least the limits of the macro-social analysis applied to the relationship between development and crime, and consequently, the "autonomy" of criminal justice phenomena with respect to social change processes, particularly when the latter are methodologically treated in such a way as to exclude the impact of changes in the criminal justice system's behaviour. The dicourse on the autonomy is also complicated by the consideration that "crime" cannot be explained away solely, nor predominantly, on a macro- level; *inter alia* evidentiated by the indirect links between macro-social processes of change and the criminal justice phenomena.

Analysis of developmental variables either in a discrete form or as factors of development and their relationship with crime categories revealed convergent results. While the predictive potentials of developmental categories are higher when the joint effects of all discrete variables are measured, the reduction of variables in the form of developmental factors did not significantly lower the system's predictive capacity. Thus, the general factor of development seems to be appropriate for the analysis of the macro-social level influences. Yet, this appears to hold true only for some crime categories, and in particular, property and economic crime, which, anyhow stand in a "dependency" position vis-à-vis developmental profiles, as compared to other more "autonomous" crimes. However, the identification of developmental factors indicates the possibilities of taxonomisation of concrete territorial units (municipalities) on the basis of the level, and the socio-cultural and economic structure of the factors. This, it is expected, could enable identification of distinct developmental profiles and corollary crime types. Furthermore, it would provide a concrete empirical reference and meaningful basis for integrated interpretation.

329

The results of the preliminary analysis indeed provide important insights into the complexity of the subject matter. Some of the indicated findings have quite interesting theoretical implications and are in need of further reflection. Similar considerations apply to the methodological model adopted although its basic explanatory potentials and limits were already tested.

In addition to response to the research-related objectives, as indentified by the Project Document, the work carried out so far also fulfilled some of the objectives pertaining to the field of technical assistance. These mainly consist in the collection and systematization of an enourmous quantity of developmental and criminal justice information, which lead to the creation of a specific developmental and criminal justice data-base for the twenty-year period. Such data-base did not exist in Yugoslavia before this research project started and its research and policy use potentials are, without any doubt, of great significance. Moreover, this project brought together experts from different fields and sti-mulated the identification and adoption of an appropriate methodology for the systematic collection, evaluation and analysis of developmental and criminal justice data. In itself, this may be considered an important achievement of this joint research endeavour. It is also an example of research- related technical assistance between the UN body (UNICRI) and national research and governmental authorities within the context of international co-operation in crime prevention and criminal justice.

ANNEX

Table I*
Adults Convicted

	Total number			Of which women	
	Number	Chain indices	Rate per 1,000 adult population	Total	Percent-ages
1975	115,649	100	7.8	17,989	15.6
1976	113,576	98	7.6	17,163	15.1
1977	107,398	94	7.1	16,309	15.2
1978	93,880	87	6.1	14,078	15.0
1979	94,395	101	6.0	13,311	14.5
1980	98,865	105	6.3	13,533	13.7
1981	98,213	99	6.2	13,078	13.3
1982	104,317	106	6.5	13,980	13.4
1983	107,759	103	6.7	14,454	13.4
1984	113,655	106	6.9	15,406	11.5
1985	107,593	95	6.5	14,808	13.8

* Tables I to IV reproduced from: D.Cotic, S. Mrkic, "Criminality and Basic Characteristics of Penal Policy, 1975-1985", *Yugoslav Survey*, 1987, pp. 41-62.

Table II

Adults Convicted, by Kind of Offence, 1975-1985

	Total	Offences against										
		State order and security	Life and limb	Civil liberties and rights	Honour and reputation	National economy	Property	General safety of persons and property	Public traffic safety	Public order and transactions	Official duty	Other
1975	115,649	543	22,835	3,399	17,705	9,355	26,275	1,119	20,096	6,065	3,958	4,299
1976	113,576	589	21,466	3,078	16,476	8,002	28,129	1,156	19,803	6,085	4,284	4,508
1977	107,398	398	19,621	2,818	14,798	7,406	26,538	1,171	20,188	5,481	4,464	4,515
1978	93,880	119	16,540	2,087	13,401	6,613	20,780	1,099	20,438	4,976	3,937	3,890
1979	94,395	114	15,690	2,089	12,059	6,643	20,854	1,194	23,021	4,601	4,063	4,067
1980	98,865	177	15,605	2,089	10,428	7,803	23,143	1,311	24,996	5,049	4,036	4,201
1981	98,213	202	14,353	1,790	9,405	10,109	23,848	1,405	24,235	4,752	4,083	4,031
1982	104,317	431	14,409	2,005	9,829	12,291	26,336	1,478	24,207	4,649	4,109	4,373
1983	107,770	255	15,233	2,231	10,164	12,420	28,655	1,645	23,435	4,975	4,532	4,225
1984	113,655	295	15,749	2,260	9,938	13,125	33,046	1,638	23,209	5,115	4,821	4,459
1985	107,593	199	15,209	2,271	9,391	12,798	32,338	1,536	19,384	5,153	4,941	4,373
					— Percentage composition —							
1975	100.0	0.5	19.7	2.9	15.3	8.1	22.7	1.0	17.4	5.2	3.5	3.7
1980	100.0	0.2	15.8	2.1	10.5	7.9	23.4	1.3	25.3	5.2	4.1	4.2
1985	100.0	0.2	14.1	2.1	8.7	11.9	30.1	1.4	18.0	4.8	4.6	4.1

332

Table III
Adults Convicted by Kind of Sanction

	1975	1976	1977	1978	1979	1980	1981	1982	1983	1984	1985
Total	*115,649*	*113,576*	*107,398*	*93,880*	*94,395*	*98,865*	*98,213*	*104,317*	*107,770*	*113,655*	*107,593*
Death penalty	3	1	4	7	6	4	5	—	3	1	3
Unsuspended imprisonment											
Total	*26,901*	*28,071*	*25,009*	*20,621*	*21,271*	*21,211*	*21,520*	*20,892*	*23,943*	*24,778*	*23,067*
20 years	20	16	23	20	24	23	10	11	17	24	19
15 years	10	29	...	18	21	8	3	4	5	8	18
10 to 15 years	187	208	227	160	172	141	160	131	165	131	132
5 to 10 years	545	606	624	470	454	458	455	447	503	466	423
2 to 5 years	1,991	2,225	2,272	1,753	1,788	1,672	1,900	1,738	1,806	1,842	1,775
1 to 2 years	2,905	2,936	3,605	2,229	2,394	2,319	2,498	2,286	2,412	2,453	2,393
6 to 12 months	4,983	5,038	3,681	3,639	4,020	3,956	3,979	3,719	4,156	4,028	3,981
3 to 6 months	6,371	6,973	6,140	4,723	6,419	5,730	5,690	5,634	6,652	7,075	6,643
2 to 3 months	4,215	4,488	3,871	3,103	3,414	3,393	3,551	3,709	4,342	4,532	3,874
1 to 2 months	2,278	2,824	2,403	2,034	1,977	2,077	1,780	1,820	2,242	2,503	2,275
Up to 30 days	2,887	2,728	2,163	3,472	1,588	1,434	1,494	1,393	1,643	1,716	1,534
Unsuspended fine											
Total	*33,156*	*32,053*	*30,957*	*28,098*	*30,068*	*32,060*	*31,523*	*35,948*	*37,719*	*40,949*	*39,666*
Suspended sentences											
Total	*52,481*	*50,768*	*48,744*	*42,681*	*40,712*	*43,250*	*43,103*	*45,945*	*44,088*	*45,956*	*42,727*
Imprisonment	44,399	43,651	42,078	35,889	35,279	38,346	38,903	40,960	40,293	42,031	38,742
Fine	8,082	7,135	6,666	6,792	5,433	4,904	4,200	4,985	3,795	3,925	3,985
Judicial admonition	3,050	2,632	2,642	2,362	2,207	2,177	1,838	1,822	1,821	1,681	1,890
Found guilty, punishment remitted	51	18	34	88	116	138	200	137	147	218	202
Educational measures	6	9	6	26	16	26	26	26	49	72	38

Table IV

Adjudicated Adults by Kind of Measure Administered

	1975	1976	1977	1978	1979	1980	1981	1982	1983	1984	1985
Total	*4,097*	*4,337*	*5,143*	*4,194*	*5,017*	*5,218*	*5,309*	*5,525*	*5,682*	*5,233*	*4,577*
Compulsory psychiatric treatment on an outpatient basis	...	...	6	48	73	61	45	24	53	57	42
Compulsory psychiatric treatment in an institution	23	32	42	37	40	47	47	31	39	46	33
Compulsory treatment of alcoholic and drug addicts	361	348	373	317	318	437	485	515	515	543	523
Prohibition from exercising an occupation, activity or duty	753	991	1,048	790	835	697	764	690	864	802	765
Withdrawal of driving licence	2,146	2,170	2,421	2,204	2,871	3,197	3,305	3,635	3,479	3,260	2,672
Prohibition from appearing in public	3	10	4	5	3	6	10	4	5	5	5
Expulsion of foreigners from the country	40	39	63	22	67	32	21	24	77	44	39
Confiscation of objects	771	747	1,186	771	810	741	632	603	650	476	498

Table V

Correlations between Variables of Development and Crime Variables (Statistically Significant Coefficients) 1973

(R = linear correlation, PR = partial correlation)

Offences against life and limb		Property crime		Economic crime		Sexual offences		Traffic offences		Recidivism	
	R / PR		R / PR		R		R / PR		R / PR		R / PR
OSNAC	r −.24 / PR −.12	TRGPRO	.75 / .14	OSKUC	.23	PRIPSN	.23	AUTI	.69 / .26	AUTI	.61
DOHSEL	R .21 / PR	DOHDRU	.73 / .15	OSNAC	.22	PRIKUK	.24 / .14	DOHDRU	.61	DOHDRU	.61 / .17
POVVOC	R .19 / PR −.14	DOHTRG	.70	RADIO	−.21	ZANRAD	.27	TRGPRO	.57 / .19	TRGPRO	.60 / .19
AUTI	R −.17 / PR −.12	AUTI	.63	TV	−.16	DOHIND	.16 / .32	RADIO	.55	RADIO	.52
DECA	R −.22 / PR	TV	.63	MRTVI	−.21	INRAD	.28	TV	.54	TV	.49
POSBIO	R −.16 / PR	TRGRAD	.68	MRODOJ	.18	AUTI	.27	DOHIND	.48	DOHTRG	.51
STANOV	R −.16 / PR	OSSSRD	.62	OSSKOL	.16	RADIO	.27	DOHTRG	.47	DOHIND	.46 / .13
PROPUT	R .12 / PR	OSSPR	.62	PRIKUK	−.19	TV	.26	INVPR	.45	INVPR	.46 / −.11
		INVPR	.58 / −.13	PRIPSN	−.17	OSKUC	−.26	ZANRAD	.43	TRGRAD	.44 / −.14
		RADIO	.60			PRODAV	.17	SAORAD	.42	INRAD	.43
		TURUK	.47 / .15			MRODOJ	.12 / −.17	TRGRAD	.41		
		DOHIND	.46 / −.13			DJECA	−.16	INRAD	.44		
Multiple correlat.	.55		.84		.49		.51		.72		.71
Determin.	.30		.70		.24		.26		.52		.51

Table VI

Correlations between Variables of Development and Crime Variables (Statistically Significant Coefficients) 1980

(R = linear correlation, PR = partial correlation)

Offences against life and limb

Variable	R	PR
POVVOC	.28	.19
HOTELI	-.27	—
DOHDRU	-.25	—
TRGPRO	-.24	—
AUTI	-.23	—
TELEV	-.22	-.13
OSSSRD	-.22	—
DOHTRG	-.21	—
VANPRO	-.21	—
POSBIO	-.21	—
GRADNJA	-.20	—
INRAD	.13	-.12

Multiple correlation .55 — Determin. .30

Property crime

Variable	R	PR
TRGPRO	.69	.17
DOHDRU	.66	—
TV	.66	—
RADIO	.62	—
AUTI	.61	—
DOHTRG	.56	-.13
OSSSRD	.56	—
OSSPR	.53	—
DOHOST	.52	—
DOHIND	.51	—
HOTELI	.50	—
POSTO	.51	.15

Multiple correlation .84 — Determin. .70

Economic crime

Variable	R	PR
SAORAD	.15	.11
DECA	.11	.15

Multiple correlation .49 — Determin. .24

Sexual offences

Variable	R	PR
RAZBRA	.24	.11
POVVOC	.19	.16
BIBLIO	.19	.11
RADIO	.22	—
PRIPSN	.19	—
OSSKOL	-.19	—
STIZDR	.17	.13
ZUNRAD	.16	—
PRIKUK	.16	—
AUTI	.15	—
DOHPRV	.14	.12

Multiple correlation .51 — Determin. .26

Traffic offences

Variable	R	PR
DOHDRU	.47	.17
AUTI	.41	-.11
MRTVI	.35	.22
RAZBRA	.35	.12
DOHIND	.31	-.15
TV	.50	—
RADIO	.46	—
TRGPRO	.50	—
DOHTRG	.40	—

Multiple correlation .72 — Determin. .52

Recidivism

Variable	R	PR
TRGPRO	.53	.18
AUTI	.17	.48
PARZDR	—	.38
RAZBRA	.19	.37
PROPUT	.15	.29
LEKARI	.11	.24
INVPR	-.14	.20
TURUK	.14	.17
NOCSTR	.14	.12 .10

Multiple correlation .71 — Determin. .51

336

Table VII

Correlations between Variables of Development and Crime Variables (Statistically Significant Coefficients) 1986

(R = linear correlation, PR = partial correlation)

Offences against life and limb			Property crime	R	PR	Economic crime	R	PR	Sexual offences	R	PR	Traffic offences	R	PR	Recidivism	R	PR
POVVOC	R .26	PR .13	TRGPRO	.78	.15	SREUC	.25	.11	TRGRAD	.24	—	TRGPRO	.34	.12	TRGPRO	.64	.12
DJECA	R −.21	PR −.12	DOHDRU	.73	—	OSKUC	.22	.11	DOHDRU	.24	—	MRTVI	.25	.13	DOHDRU	.58	—
TV	R −.20	PR −.13	VANPRI	.71	.17	LEKARI	.17	.14	DOHTRG	.24	—	DOHIND	.25	−.13	LEKARI	.49	−.13
OSSKOL	R .18	PR .10	PARZDR	.71	.21	DJECA	.17	—	TRGPRO	.22	—	OSSSRD	.21	−.17	PARZDR	.57	.19
OSSSRD	R −.18	PR —	DOHTRG	.69	—	AUTI	−.16	−.10	TURUK	.21	—	OSSPR	.20	.17	VANPRI	.55	—
OSSPR	R −.18	PR —	RADIO	.57	—	OSNAC	.15	—	RADIO	.21	—	PARZDR	.18	.13	AUTI	.52	—
DOHDRU	R −.18	PR —	LEKARI	.66	—	SESUM	.12	.19	POSSIO	.20	—	STIZDR	.15	−.13	DOHTRG	.49	—
AUTI	R −.18	PR —	POSSIO	.61	—				AUTI	.19	—	NOČUK	.12	.15	RADIO	.47	—
OSKUC	R −.18	PR .10	ZANRAD	.58	—				IZSTDR	.19	—	OSSKOL	−.08	.15	PROPUT	.44	—
STIZDR	R −.17	PR —	TRGRAD	.52	—				OSSSRD	.18	−.12	NOČSTR	.07	−.16	ZANRAD	.44	—
DOHTRG	R −.16	PR —	TV	.54	—				PARZDR	.18	.17	PRODAV	.03	−.16	INRAD	.33	.10
DOHSEL	R .15	PR —	INRAD	.37	.12				OSSPR	.17	.12				MRTVI	.28	.19
Multiple correlation	.56			.88			.54			.48			.65			.78	
Determinat.	.31			.79			.29			.23			.42			.62	

337

Legend for Tables V, VI and VII

I ECONOMIC VARIABLES:

Number of workers in public sector (per 1000 inhabitants):

INRAD	v1	– industry and mining
POLJRAD	v2	– agriculture, forestry and water resources
GRARAD	v3	– construction
SAORAD	v4	– traffic and communications
TRGRAD	v5	– trade and hotel business and catering
ZANRAD	v6	– crafts and communal activities
FINRAD	v7	– financial and other services

Active basis assets at purchasing value (1000 din. per inhabitant):

OSSSED	v8	– total
OSSPR	v9	– activities in economy

National income (1000 dinars per inhabitant):

DOHDRU	v10	– public sector
DOHPRV	v11	– individual sector
DOHIND	v12	– industry
DOHAGR	v13	– agriculture
DOHTRG	v14	– trade and hotel business and catering
DOHOST	v15	– other activities
DOHSEL	v16	– individual sector in agriculture

Realized investments in basis assets of public sector (100 dinars per inhabitant):

INVPRV	v17	– economy
INVRDU	v18	– non-economy
PRIPSN	v19	– yield of wheat per hectare in tons
PRIKUK	v20	– yield of maize per hectare in tons
DRVO	v21	– volume of wood in 1000 m³ per km² of surface area
SECSUM	v22	– felling of woods in m³ per hectare of surface area
GRADNJ	v23	– accomplished construction works in 1000 din. per inhabitant
	v24	– number of freight vehicles per 1000 inhabitants

338

Sale of agricultural products in 1000 din. per inhabitant:

OTPOLJ   v25 – total
              v26 – sales

Hotel business and catering per 1000 inhabitants:

HOTELI   v27 – business units
HOTKRV   v28 – number of beds
HOTPRO   v29 – turnover in mil. of dinars

II ECOLOGICAL VARIABLES:

POVRS   v30 – surface of municipality in km^2
POVORA   v31 – agricult. surf. – plough fields and gardens in hectares/hectares of municipality surface
POVVOC   v32 – agricult. surf. – orchards in hec/hec municipality surface
POVVIN   v33 – agricult. surf. – vineyards in hec/hec municipality surface
POVLIV   v34 – agricult. surf. – meadows and pastures in hec/hec municipality surface
              v35 – surface under woods in hec/hec municipality surface

III TRAFFIC AND COMMUNICATIONS (per 1000 inhabitants)

STANIC   v36 – number of railway stations
ZEPROM v37 – turnover of goods in railway stations in 1000 tons
POSTE   v38 – number of post offices
PROPUT   v39 – turnover of passengers in railway stations (departed)
AUTI   v40 – number of passenger cars

IV TOURISM (per 1000 inhabitants)

TURUK   v41 – number of tourists (total)
TURSTR   v42 – number of tourists (foreign)
NOCUK   v43 – number of lodgings (total)
NOCSTR   v44 – number of lodgings (foreign)

V EDUCATION (per 1000 inhabitants)

OSSKOL	v45 – number of elementary schools
OSUC	v46 – number of pupils in elementary schools
OSNAS	v47 – number of teachers in elementary schools
SEEUC	v48 – number of pupils in high schools
VANPRI	v49 – budget expences of non-economic activities (education)

VI CULTURE

BIBLIO	v50 – number of peoples' libraries per 1000 inhabitants
BOOKS	v51 – number of books in libraries, per 1000 inhabitants
BIOSK	v52 – number of cinemas per 1000 inhabitants
POSBIO	v53 – number of cinema visitors per inhabitant
RADIO	v54 – number of radio subscribers per inhabitant
TV	v55 – number of TV subscribers per inhabitant

VII MEDICAL AND SOCIAL CARE (per 1000 inhabitants)

BOLPOS	v56 – number of patients' beds
LEKARI	v57 – number of physicians and dentists
	v58 – number of independent medical organisations (without pharmacies)
PARZDR	v59 – budget expences for health care
	v60 – budget expences for social assistance

VIII HOUSING AND LEVEL OF URBANIZATION

Accomplished construction works (1000 dinars per inhabitant):

STANOV	v61 – public sector (Total)
STAIZG	v62 – housing construction
STIDR	v63 – housing construction in public sector

Number of constructed apartments (per 1000 inhabitants):

UKIZDR	v64 – total
IZSDR	v65 – public sector
PRODAV	v66 – number of shop
TRGPRO	v67 – turnover in retail trade (in mil. of dinars)

340

IX DEMOGRAPHIC VARIABLES

PEOPLE	v68	– number of inhabitants in total (evaluation)
SKLBRA	v69	– number of registered marriages per 1000 inhabitants
RAZBRA	v70	– number of divorces per 1000 inhabitants
CHILDREN	v71	– number of live births per 1000 inhabitants
DEEADEAD	v72	– number of deaths per 1000 inhabitants
MRODOJ	v73	– infant deaths per 1000 live born births

DEVELOPMENT AND CRIME IN THE CONTEXT OF THE UNITED NATIONS CONGRESSES ON THE PREVENTION OF CRIME AND THE TREATMENT OF OFFENDERS *

Ugo Leone **
Uglješa Zvekić ***

Introduction

Over the past forty years, our superficial, and therefore optimistic, knowledge and evaluation of development problems have given way to a rather more disturbing awareness of the complexity of the realities and the techniques of development. It has now been ascertained that the problem of economic development in any given country or society is more complicated and has more diverse implications than was supposed in the early years of development assistance. For reasons only partly understood, development is often accompanied by troubling deterioration in a society's capacity for peaceful co-existence, with a consequent striking increase in the shapes and severities of social problems.

It could almost be said that the problem of providing incentives for development grows more complex day by day. This is due not only to the evolution of politics and

* Revised version of the essay originally prepared for and published in Franco Ferracuti, Ed., *Trattato di Criminologia, Medicina Criminologica e Psichiatria Forense*, Vol. 2, "La dimensione internazionale della criminologia", Milano, Giuffrè, 1987, pp. 107-163.

** Director, United Nations Interregional Crime and Justice Research Institute (UNICRI).
*** Research Co-ordinator, United Nations Interregional Crime and Justice Research Institute (UNICRI).

economics to national, regional, and international levels but also to a deepening awareness of the complex mechanisms of chain reactions. Unpredictably, these reactions occur in the wake of any action which changes the *status quo*, even if in a positive direction.

Such complexity raises, in turn, the question of analysis and synthesis which will lead to appropriate approaches. In other words, there is a great temptation to compartmentalize the various questions, overlooking interrelationships occurring in different fields of action. The global approach requires a solid multidisciplinary structure and the financial means to make it work. But the multiplicity of the attendant variables may render it useless. Moreover, the very complexity and delicacy of the global approach may lead to the choice of policies which lack a specific basis created by precise regional needs, and which are therefore paradoxically even more aberrant.

The aim of these warnings is to stress the fragility and instability of the balance between various approaches which must nevertheless co-exist to cope with the matter in order best to meet the immediate and long-term needs of the developing society.

Another factor often neglected in the past which is properly assuming increasing importance is the full understanding of the real situation on which an action is proposed. As in the early days, situations are still often reported only negatively as crises to which the *status quo* cannot respond. Such crises may still exist, but the static and dynamic consistency of every developing society must be acknowledged: static as regards its transitoriness in the evolution of its own civilization, responding to ethnic, environmental, historic, and economic factors; dynamic as a result of a series of delicate balances slowly but surely moving toward evolution. In this perspective, the social factor begins to show all its mass and volume in the evolutionary process of the community, however unsatisfactory this process may be.

Preliminary considerations on the relationship between development and crime

Public opinion and concerned statesmen in all countries are increasingly aware of the grave connotations of the relationship between development and crime. Neither internal systems for regulating socio-economic balances nor international co-operation schemes for the defence and support of these balances are prepared to deal with the issue.

Without going into detail, we have reasonably certain evidence that, although in different ways, more or less rapid economic development inevitably gives rise to phenomena of social maladjustment and grave malaise within a community or its fractions. Aberration and ultimate violence gradually lead from the most obvious manifestations of delinquency to petty or organized crime and to terrorism.

Outside intervention provokes a breakdown of social balances and may traumatically open the door to new problems. On the other hand, given the precise needs and the increasingly dramatic plights of the Third World, it would be profoundly unfair to withdraw into the easy attitude of doing nothing for fear of making mistakes.

Consciousness of the crucial importance of the quality of life in development work is an increasingly essential factor in any type of intervention. The topicality of the matter and the potential relationships between crime and development can be illustrated by the fact that the United Nations increasingly seeks explanations and solutions for this phenomenon. The subject of the Sixth United Nations Congress on the Prevention of Crime and the Treatment of Offenders, held in Caracas in 1980, was Crime Prevention and the Quality of Life.

Recognition of the need to act raises the issue of what action to take. In addition to the analysis and synthesis which precede a sophisticated combination of regional and global approach, the political options of the developing countries must be considered.

The harmful effects of rapid and insufficiently planned socio-economic development are understandable in the light of the traumatic changes to which contemporary communities are increasingly subjected. Traditional societies evolved slowly. Until the 19th century, their infrequent setbacks were mainly due to natural disasters or local conflicts. The spread of economic progress and industrial civilization undoubtedly awakened latent forces within these communities. On this already unstable condition came to be superimposed the movement toward development co-operation. Existing balances were badly upset, and a new and livelier mechanism came into effect, inevitably creating social ferment and dangerous cracks.

This could only directly influence the quality of life, the improvement of which remains the ultimate objective of any individual or collective action. This objective has already been defined in the United Nations Charter[1] which states: "We the peoples of the United Nations determined ... to promote social progress and better standards of life ... " and, later: " ... (to promote) the economic and social advancement of all peoples."[2] It is confirmed in Article 55, where we read: " ... the United Nations shall promote: a. higher standards of living ... ". There are also two significant Articles of the Universal Declaration of Human Rights adopted and proclaimed by the General Assembly of the United Nations on 10 December 1948: Article 22: " Everyone, as a member of society, has the right to social security and is entitled to realization, through national effort and international co-operation and in accordance with the organization and resources of each State, of the economic, social and cultural rights indispensable for his dignity and the free development of his personality; " and Article 25: (1) "Everyone has the right to a standard of living adequate for the health and well-being of himself and of his family ... ".

Despite this clear institutional vision, history shows that for too long purely economic and particularly industrial development has been favoured over any other approach. The basic error in this narrow viewpoint emerges dramatically when the results of this sort of development turn out to be quite different from those its planners had expected. This phase is characterized by multiple initiatives aimed at increased exploitation of resources and at industrialization and modernization of structures. Such factors are not necessarily negative, but they are incomplete if they lack careful and timely evaluations and social considerations.

Socio-economic planning and international co-operation

Later and occasionally cruel realities brought about a change of mind about such policies and schemes for development. They were threatened by a weakness in the social fabric demonstrated by serious tensions and conflicts which in turn brought halts or even regression in social development. The potential financial cost, not to mention the far graver risk to a whole philosophy and to the very objectives pursued, caused justified dismay. Rapid economic development has almost always brought about a breakdown in existing structures and their related balances, with severe human dislocation, a tendency toward limited concentration of development areas, and a high rate of urbanization of capital, of the labour force, and of services. Social problems became so urgent that once more hasty emergency action was taken for crime prevention and control. All too often this was repressive action aimed solely at keeping order and preserving some of the results achieved. The social approach should inspire development policy which includes adequate plans and resources to forestall the phenomena of maladjustment and social deviance. This would reduce to a minimum the causes of conflict and the traumas which result from sudden changes in living conditions and which

347

are injurious to the mental health of the most active and dynamic sectors of society.

It is fair to acknowledge that recently there has been a new awareness of this problem and that, on both bilateral and multilateral levels, social planning has received the attention it deserves. Precisely oriented policies and concrete actions are finally taking the right approach to the problem. More and more often, when social planning is sufficiently far-sighted, the specific problems most acutely manifest in certain parts of the world are dealt with individually, without overlooking the causes of those problems — effects and symptoms of profound social torment.

Although bilateral development programmes have increasingly social concerns, highest marks should be given to the actions of international organizations, particularly of the United Nations. Its specialized agencies and its special programmes have reacted most promptly to societal change, seeking to respond to the pressing needs of the international community and at the same time to cope with serious crises.

The most important element in any action is the choice of appropriate instruments. Many efforts have been made to identify ways of measuring the quality of life and to adopt basic social indices. One example of the international interest in indices and, more generally, in the identification of precise measures for the evaluation of criminal phenomena and of the efficacy of actions is the group work of United Nations experts[3] who met in Alghero (Sardinia) in February 1972 to examine methods for determining planning norms and standards and defining social policies. On that occasion, emphasis was once again put on the need for a cautious approach and on the variability from one situation to another of indices and of their relative importance. Actually this is rather treacherous ground because, apart from a few intuitive and fairly generalized concepts, such indices are identified on a case-by-case basis, taking account of specific situations and above all of the criteria appropriate to each society. In a consideration of the relationship between development and crime, the role of public perception is not negligible, and therefore the subjective social component should prevail over abstract objectivization and canonization of criteria which may be valid for some societies but which are not necessarily transferable to totally different communities. The system of interrelationships which forms the basis for co-existence within every social group varies from group to group, and observation of its workings is bound to reveal diversity from case to case, and a variety of internal stratifications due to different socio-cultural approaches.

Four factors must evolve as time passes and situations change: the individual consciousness, the collective consciousness, the phenomenon of development, and the rules of social co-existence. The purpose of social planning is to establish the most satisfactory relationships possible among groups and to create a balance of various human, financial, and structural forces and resources which can operate in different fields, particularly in crime prevention and in the war against crime. To the concept of social planning integrated with the country's overall plan, a constant flow of data, information, and verifications must be added, taking into account the global plan as well as the plans for various fields. This will create a balanced and organic operating structure to respond effectively to community needs and to control the rhythms of development so that the society will absorb rather than reject it.

The relationship between development funds and the quality of individual and community life is complex and delicate. It depends upon the state of the society's economy, even when, in the short term, national wealth is not equally distributed. Indeed, sudden massive doses of money can upset delicate social balances. In the broadest sense, the development mechanism favours economic growth, industrialization, urbanization, production or importation of

349

goods, increased consumption, and the creation of new needs not always of real importance. On the other hand, it also brings about an unfair distribution of income, the breakdown of some parts of the existing social fabric, and maladjustments ranging from aberration to violence, the danger to the hereditary cultural patrimony, and the breakdown of traditional values which had held the community together. When action takes place, even with the aim of improving the quality of life, the delicacy of the community's balances cannot be overemphasized. Development and improvement of the quality of life must continue to conform to peace and social justice and must not be confused with indiscriminate increase in goods and services.

Main characteristics of the development and crime issue

The contemporary world is divided into groups of countries which rotate around different axes. The distinction between developing and developed countries is only one method of classification. Yet this division shows what enormous differences exist today, in many respects, between countries that lie on one side or the other of the development axis. While social conditions in some regions have been profoundly changed since 1945 by technology and by decolonization, in other areas they stubbornly resist change, as the persistence of extreme tensions and mass poverty demonstrates[4]. Persistent and pronounced disparities in wealth and oportunities continue to prevail. Differences in levels of global development — wealth or poverty, economic strength, employment rate, educational and health conditions, for instance — illustrate these imbalances. The fruits of technological innovations and achievements, justly considered a major force for social change, often benefit only the privileged developed countries. Economic growth, the traditional index of development, has slowed down in many developing countries and, more important, many of

350

them are now undergoing severe economic crises. The development rate of much social mobilization is different in developing countries from that recorded in developed countries. The structure of employment is another example. In developing countries, a much smaller proportion of the work force depends for its income on employment than in developed countries. Another traditional measure of development, urbanization, which is indirectly considered a cause of increased crime, proceeds by different paths and at different rates, with social consequences which are much more burdensome to developing countries because they lack adequate resources to control them. This is not to overlook the fact that developed countries do face very serious problems, which, although they do not threaten survival, certainly tend to influence the quality of life. Moreover, despite their many barriers and divisions, the members of the international community are becoming more and more interdependent and, optimistically speaking, perhaps they share more benefits than problems.

Crime is one of today's problems that the whole world faces. The connection between development and crime is one of the continuous topics of interest and concern to both national and international communities. The last decade (1970-1980) saw a substantial increase in all types of crime. According to the Seventh United Nations Congress document[5], a report on the Second United Nations survey of crime trends, operation of criminal justice, and strategies for crime prevention, violent crimes have doubled and crimes against property have tripled. Even the homicide rate, which was low compared with rates for other crimes, increased from 3.9 to 5.7 per 100,000 population over the ten years under study.

Generally speaking, it seems that property crimes, particularly theft, are crimes typical of developed countries, while there seems to be a higher rate of violent crime in developing countries. Examination of particular types of offenses shows some similarities and at the same time differences in the patterns and evolution of crime in both deve loped and developing countries. For example, the comparatively high homicide and assault rates in developing countries continued through the decade 1970-1980. On the other hand, both theft and fraud showed higher rates in developed countries. The above-mentioned survey also touches on the distribution of crime, noting regional differences in the increasing total of reported crimes, which in 1975-1980 reached its peak in Asia and the Pacific. These data certainly do not reflect an accurate pattern, since they are based on only a few countries from each region. However, analysis of types of crime shows that, while reported crime was in general increase, there were pockets, areas, and types of crime with declining rates. If we consider theft, which represents 72 per cent of the total crime volume and which is in first place in most countries and regions, we can see that it went up in 20 countries and down in another 22, but that the global mean still rose by about 22 per cent. The trend in violent crimes was generally up in the Asian regions, down in the regions of Eastern Europe, and fluctuating in the other regions. On the other hand, the rates of drug-related crimes went up in a curve that bore no relationship to other types of crime. And although drug-related crimes are still much less frequent than thefts or assaults, the global average grew by 120 per cent.

Countries respond to this situation with a wide variety of crime-control and -prevention strategies. On the control side, since the measure refers to criminal-justice personnel, it can be generally noted that in developing countries 94 per cent of the criminal-justice personnel consists of police forces, as compared with 77 per cent in developed countries. Of total criminal-justice personnel in developed countries, judges constitute 1 per cent and prison staff 5 per cent. In developing countries, these figures are 4 per cent and 19 per cent. It can also be noted that the number of police per

100,000 population has increased more in developing countries than in developed countries, where it remained relatively stable.

Strategies for crime prevention — indirect or direct — differ from country to country. Indirect strategies, taken as a part of social-policy programmes, are measures intended to change living conditions perceived to be criminogenic. They include the provision of better housing, food, education, employment, social security, and so forth. Direct strategies include emergency procedures, techniques for reducing opportunities to commit crimes, citizen participation in patrolling, publicity campaigns, etc. Other types of crime-prevention and -control strategies are community participation, modification of penal legislation, and assistance to victims.

This summary of crime in the modern world substantiates the view that crime today is a major problem of society. This does not means, however, that it was not of real concern in the past to citizens, scholars, and policy-makers. Crime used to be examined and studied in terms of social interactions, but there seemed little need to deal with it as a factor in development. The relatively recent awareness of this approach is more than an evolution in schools of thought and research. Rather, this new tack and mounting interest grew out of the large-scale social changes, often paralleling development, which had crossed national boundaries to assume an international character. Despite the differences between countries, their increased international interdependence put crime and development in a stricter and more dynamic perspective and encouraged the search for new explanations and for adequate international action. This approach followed an evolutionary curve of its own within the framework of the United Nations. While it does not claim to be highly scientific or theoretical, the United Nations approach gave a boost to a factor neglected by traditional criminology, which had bothered little to see crime in a context of socio-economic development. Aware of the pressing needs of a world community undergoing large-scale change, the United Nations attempted to relate crime to the context of development and social justice, and the realities of the modern world. The activities of the United Nations may have been more pragmatically than theoretically oriented, but its interest has also made a notable theoretical contribution by focusing crime research on history and development.

The United Nations Congresses and the development and crime issue

The leadership role in social defence which was assigned to the United Nations in 1948 has been reaffirmed[6] several times. It cannot be denied that both national and international communities have long been deeply concerned about the problem of crime, its causes, and strategies for prevention and control. But, as it is increasingly viewed in the broader socio-economic context, crime is no longer dealt with as an isolated phenomenon. It is worthwhile, at least briefly, to examine the evolution of concepts, approaches, and actions with reference to the quinquennial United Nations Congresses on the Prevention of Crime and the Treatment of Offenders.

In historical terms, the topic of "development and crime" is relatively recent, especially if examined in its present-day form. The evolution of the concept of development, from economic growth to quality of life, is indicated in "development and crime" as a topic, but the interdependence of its two facets is not linked solely to the evolution of development. Crime, as such, has also evolved conceptually, at least in terms of structure. In a sense, this evolution can be seen as expanding from one dimension to many. Nevertheless, the conceptual definition of development has undergone more substantial and radical changes than has the concept

354

of crime. By comparison with development, crime carried with it more static biases, and its connotations have only recently been properly viewed as dynamic.

The First Congress, held in Geneva in 1955[7], touched only lightly on the topic of development and crime. There were some references to crime as a social phenomenon and to the need to deal with it in the context of other social problems. More explicit comments were made in the discussions on Topic E, "Prevention of Juvenile Delinquency," which raised the question of possible connections between juvenile delinquency and processes of social change. But these glancing references showed not the slightest intention of dealing either with the global processes of social change or with specific sub-processes. Special attention was paid to the role of institutions, like the family, in prevention and control. Thus, the Annex to Resolution E states "that industrialization and the growth of cities have been accompanied by an increasing measure of social, family, and personal disorganization. According to current opinion, delinquency appears to be intimately connected with the social and cultural changes that have operated through the family"[8].

The Second Congress[9] devoted more attention to the links between crime and social change. Once more, one of the topics was juvenile delinquency: "New forms of juvenile delinquency: their origin, prevention, and treatment," and allusions were made to the relationships between industrialization and new forms of juvenile crime. A report[10] prepared by the United Nations Secretariat noted that new forms of juvenile delinquency had been influenced by the evolutionary forces of social, economic, and cultural change in the countries concerned. The report went on to say that there was an increase in juvenile delinquency practically everywhere, although it seemed to have been less rapid in the less-developed countries and in those developed countries where there was a lesser degree of industrialization but greater emphasis on family ties. It added that more research was needed before significant comparisons could be drawn, but that data-gathering techniques and the development of recording systems presented obstacles. No clear links were affirmed between new forms of juvenile delinquency and social change or industrialization, but it suggested further research on the subject. The conclusions and recommendations of the Second Congress did not discuss methods of research, although the question was touched on in the topic "Prevention of types of crime resulting from social changes and accompanying economic development in less-developed countries."

It should be noted that this specific topic had already been identified in 1953 by the Social Commission and approved by Resolution 494 (XVI) of the Economic and Social Council on 23 July 1953. Two general reports[11] on this topic had been prepared for the Congress, as well as a report by the Secretariat[12] and a document prepared by UNESCO[13]. The reports and the ensuing discussions emphasized the novelty of the topic and the dearth of available information. Deliberations centered on three main points. First, the concept of "less-developed countries" was criticized for its ambiguity and for the difficulty of accurately measuring economic development. Second, it was pointed out that, since crime and its relationship to social changes was a problem of equal concern in highly developed countries, attention should not be focused only on developing countries. Third, after much discussion, the basic assumption that social change causes crime was challenged.

The importance of these discussions, conclusions, and recommendations lies in the fact that this was the first time a United Nations Congress had considered the subject of relationships between crime and development. Several of the statements made on that occasion can be considered basic to later developments of the topic, since it was generally agreed that criminality is not necessarily a consequence of

356

social changes accompanying economic development. The consensus was that "cultural instability, the weakening of primary social control, and the exposure to conflicting social standards, which have relationship to criminality, are intensified when social change is disorderly, when the degree of social change is high, and when the gap between the breakdown of old social institutions and the creation of new institutions is great." Specific processes of social change which are not *per se* conducive to criminality but which can nevertheless be linked to the increase in crime were identified as migration, urbanization, and industrialization. The Congress avoided discussion of types of crime associated with development and considered instead the question of the general increase in crime in relation to social change. Another important point was the call for more research into the many factors of social change which have a potential for encouraging crime, in order to develop solid bases for planning for crime prevention and control. Finally, while social change was acknowledged to be multidimensional, a one-dimensional approach was taken toward crime.

The Third United Nations Congress[14] devoted itself to the general topic of crime prevention. Two agenda items are of particular relevance: (1) Social Change and Criminality, and (2) Social Forces and the Prevention of Criminality[15].

Discussion on Item 1 revolved around two broad questions: whether and in what ways certain changes in a society may affect the incidence of delinquency and criminality; whether legal systems adequately reflect social changes in terms of modifications in institutional structure and behaviour patterns. Social change was considered as a ubiquitous process, implying the error of assuming that such changes are the prerogative of developing countries. There is ample indication that some types of change may be even more rapid in industrialized countries. Furthermore, it is politically and scientifically risky to assert that economic explanations for crime are valid or satisfactory in all cases. It was at last becoming clear that, in both industrialized and developing countries, the answer may lie primarily in factors other than economic, namely urbanization, changes in norms and moral values, and social controls. Crime occurs in varying degrees and in different forms in countries with different political structures, different levels of economic development, and different types of economic and social control systems. This Congress once again stressed the need for further research to define the dynamics of social change and crime as essential to programmes to control crime. Social change must also be taken into account in lawmaking and in litigation, especially since most countries have increasing recourse to social control through law to replace the vanishing, less formal controls once exercised by family, religion, tribe, caste, or village.

Item 2 of the Congress agenda dealt with the potential for crime prevention and control through such social forces as public opinion, the family, education, and employment opportunities. These forces were examined in the light of the changes they had undergone in the wake of industrialization, urbanization, and migration, all identified as having some relationship to crime. As at the previous Congress, it was re-emphasized that the use of social forces and their preventive potential must be incorporated into planning for economic development and for crime prevention.

Although the Third Congress dealt extensively with social change and crime, it clearly lacked perception of the multiple dimensions of both phenomena and of the immediacy and intensity of the various links between their different processes and the degrees to which they occur.

A step toward the recognition of this relationship was taken during the Fourth Congress[16], held in Kyoto in 1970, which actually took as its general theme "Crime and Development." This was the first United Nations Congress explicitly devoted to this topic, and two agenda items — (1)

Social-defence policies in relation to development planning, and (2) Organization of research for policy development in social defence — dealt extensively with the subject. The background material and the discussion focused on several important aspects of development and crime[17].

Because of the many variables linking crime to different social, cultural, and political structures, patterns in the relationship between crime and social change cannot be easily defined. The only categorical statement made by the Congress was that an increase in crime is often associated with rapid change. This implies that development does not cause crime but that the relationships between the two depend to a large extent upon the nature of the development process itself. It was explicitly acknowledged that both development and crime are words with many different meanings which vary according to the particular culture and interpretation concerned. For the first time, crime was considered not as a homogeneous concept but as a phenomenon which might be caused by the many dimensions of the processes of development: industrialization, urbanization, population increase, internal migration, social mobility, and technological change. Juvenile delinquency was specifically related to these aspects of development. In considering the relationship between law and social change, which had been tackled by the Third Congress, the Fourth Congress discussed the interesting question of the "creation" of crime or the inducement of crime-generating conditions by the criminal-justice system. Social change may indeed create problems which cannot be solved through legal action or by application of norms. In fact, legal intervention can sometimes bring about an increase in reported crimes. This might seem to indicate that a rising crime rate is the result of development, but there is, in fact, no exact correlation between legal action and other aspects of development.

Another topic was that of development planning and research. It was several times emphasized that social-defence planning must be aimed at more effective crime prevention as an integral part of national planning. Furthermore, social-defence planning should always be related to scientific research into the relationships between development processes and crime.

Development planning must include social-defence planning in order to deal adequately with all aspects of social development and to control the negative effects of social change. Crime should not be perceived as a separate problem, but as "part of the warp and weft of social development; and its remedies were to be looked for not only in specific measures but in the very processes by which the texture of society was woven."[18]

The general theme of the Fifth United Nations Congress[19] was "Crime Prevention and Control: the challenges of the last quarter of the century." This Congress was not specifically dedicated to the issue of crime and development, but three agenda items were discussed in the context of social change and crime: (5) Changes in forms and dimensions of criminality — transnational and national; (6) Criminal legislation, judicial procedures, and other forms of social control in the prevention of crime; and (9) Economic and social consequences of crime: new challenges for research and planning[20].

The Congress discussed the following aspects of change in the forms and dimensions of criminality: crime as business; offenses involving works of art and other cultural property; drug-abuse and alcohol-related crime; violence against persons; comparative transnational and international violence; crime related to moving traffic; crime resulting from migration, national disasters, and hostilities; and female crime. The many dimensions of crime in the context of development were acknowledged. Moreover, it was recognized that some new forms and dimensions of crime, such as crimes related to moving traffic and transnational crimes, tend to have closer relationships than others with the development process. In any case, organized crime, illicit drug traffic, forms of violent crime, etc., may have drastic consequences for the economic and other aspects of social development, as clarified by the working paper prepared by the Secretariat for Item 9[21] and by the subsequent discussions.

It was generally agreed that development has a decisive effect on the quality of life and that crime and other social problems are intimately related. The economic and social effects of crime on the evolution of the quality of life were highlighted. Particular attention was focused on the fact that, in appraising the economic, social, and humanitarian costs of crime, the dark or "hidden" cost is considerably higher than that of known crime.

An increase in crime forces communities to divert their energies and resources to seek its control. This is a particularly grave matter for developing countries since the resources thus diverted are urgently needed elsewhere. Besides, the social cost of crime creates great inequities in the burdens of different social groups.

Discussions at the Sixth Congress[22] focused on many pressing problems, all of which were considered from the perspective of the relationships between crime and development[23]. In discussion of agenda item 3, "Crime trends and crime prevention strategies," and item 8, "New perspectives in crime prevention and criminal justice, and development: the role of international co-operation," based on the working papers prepared by the Secretariat[24], special attention was given to the relationships between crime and development.

Crime prevention and criminal justice should be viewed in a development context and in their interrelationships with the various processes of development, particularly economic growth, social change, and the quality of life.

Crime and development are complex phenomena, at both the conceptual and the operational level, and, although their interrelationship is easy to see, it is difficult to define precisely. A better understanding of this relationship is needed for identification of appropriate options for development strategy. A very cautious and flexible attitude was taken to such matters as universally applicable definitions, statements, and policies about crime and development. Although crime and development should be considered in a transnational rather than simply a national context, it must be taken into account that both these phenomena are inseparably related to the economic, social, political, and cultural conditions of each country. Special attention should be paid to the role of scientific research, especially applied research. Similar ideas came up in the discussions on juvenile delinquency and criminal justice and in those on the abuse of power.

The Congress adopted the "Caracas Declaration,"[25] which explicitly recognizes the links between development and crime and which, among other things, states that:

"1. The success of criminal-justice systems and strategies for crime prevention, especially in the light of the growth of new and sophisticated forms of crime and the difficulties encountered in the administration of criminal justice, depends above all on the progress achieved throughout the world in improving social conditions and enhancing the quality of life; it is thus essential to review traditional crime-prevention strategies based exclusively on legal criteria.

2. Crime prevention and criminal justice should be considered in the context of economic development, political systems, social and cultural values and social change, as well as in the context of the new international economic order.

3. It is a matter of great importance and priority that programmes for crime prevention and the treatment of offenders

should be based on the social, cultural, political and economic circumstances of each country, in a climate of freedom and respect for human rights, and that Member States should develop an effective capacity for the formulation and planning of criminal policy, and that all crime-prevention strategies should be co-ordinated with strategies for social, economic, political and cultural development."

The significance of the Caracas Declaration resides in the fact that this document explicitly acknowledges the many dimensions of both crime and development. Particularly important from the viewpoint of action is the emphasis it puts not just on the structural interrelationship of these two phenomena but also on their interdependence in terms of planning activities and action-oriented measures. In other words, the Declaration poses the problem not only in the perspective of understanding the phenomenon itself but also in terms of actual, practical actions. Another significant feature is its recognition of crime as an essential component of social development with national and international dimensions.

The Seventh United Nations Congress[26] was devoted to the general theme: "Crime prevention for freedom, justice, peace, and development." The Congress raised many issues which come under the umbrella of crime and development. Actually, this Congress did little more than reflect the growing awareness of the close relationship between problems of criminality and development priorities. The problem was considered in the light of the Secretary General's message on the promotion of human rights.

Analysis of the proceedings of the Congress shows that all five items on the agenda[27] dealt organically and comprehensively with the problems of development, social change, and human rights. A new element was introduced by a precise reference, on the subject of crime prevention and control, to the International Development Strategy for the Third United Nations Development Decade[28], which states that "the ultimate aim of development is the constant improvement of the well-being of the entire population on the basis of its full participation in the process of development and a fair distribution of the benefits therefrom." This was a formal recognition of the fact that the increase in crime, especially in its new forms and dimensions, seriously impairs development, compromising the achievement of the objectives stated in the aforementioned document.

The links between crime and development are further demonstrated in many resolutions adopted by the Seventh Congress and in the documents prepared for the Congress. The working papers prepared by the Secretariat for Items I[29] and II[30], the report entitled "New Delhi Consensus on the New Dimensions of Criminality and Crime Prevention in the Context of Development"[31], and reports from the regional preparatory meetings[32] were the most significant. Other working papers and reports prepared for the Congress also dealt extensively with crime and development.

The crime side of the issue was carefully analysed, and specific manifestations of contemporary crime, both conventional and unconventional, were identified. While the correlation between development and crime was not defined, it was categorically reiterated that development *per se* does not cause crime, even though numerous links exist between development processes and crime. Most of the documents of this Congress clearly emphasize the effects of crime on development, while a more cautious and less incisive approach is taken to examination of the possible effects of development on crime. In this connection, paragraph 47 of the working paper prepared by the Secretariat for agenda Item I[33] notes, for example, that: "The deleterious impact of crime upon national development efforts is not, however, of a purely material nature. The damage inflicted upon certain human intangibles, such as dignity, spiritual well-being, optimism and hope, is as much a serious obstacle to socio-economic development as are other, more material factors ... ".

The significance of considering crime in the context of development and the importance of planning crime-prevention strategies in that context are, in fact, the major themes of two important documents approved by the Seventh Congress: "Milan Plan of Action" and "Guiding Principles for Crime Prevention and Criminal Justice in the Context of Development and a New International Economic Order." These documents, along with numerous resolutions, assign great importance to applied and action-oriented research and to the necessity for policy measures to be informed by such research. The resolution "Research on Youth, Crime and Justice," which emerged from the proceedings of the Research Workshop on juvenile delinquency and juvenile justice, organized during the Seventh Congress by the United Nations Social Defence Research Institute (UNSDRI)[34], is particularly relevant. As to the approach research should take on the issue, it states, in paragraph 7 of the Annex:

"Research on crime, including youth crime, should be undertaken in the context of socio-economic development and change with special attention being paid to the complex multifaceted relationship between:

— rates and directions of change in social structure, which may include urbanization, migration, modes of production and distribution, socio-economic status, family structure, and crime in general, as well as specific categories of crime;

— changes in value, and regulatory and control mechanisms, reflected in patterns of socialization, education, morals, religion, ideologies and law as each relates to crime."

The "Guiding Principles" paper, on the other hand, deals with the issue in relation to four areas: the new international economic order, national development, responsiveness of the criminal-justice system, and international co-operation. Thus the issue of crime and development is placed in a much broader context than in previous United Nations Congresses. Crime is at last linked not only to industrialization, urbanization, or migration but to the entire complex of expressions and actions directed at the objectives of human development, of which those technical processes are only a few aspects. At the same time, special attention is given to processes which characterize contemporary society. Growing industrialization and technological and scientific progress may affect and be influenced by the international economic order, public health, labour conditions, and exploitation of natural resources and the environment. The same sort of inter-relationship exists between criminal activities and crime prevention.

Aside from the call for a more systematic and co-ordinated approach to crime prevention, prevention and criminal-justice policies are seen in the context of development as instruments which should "not only reduce the human and social costs of traditional and new forms of criminality but should also, where appropriate, help provide safeguards to ensure equitable and full public participation in the development process..."[35] Furthermore, "legal systems, including criminal justice, should be instrumental in promoting beneficial and equitable development and due regard to human rights and social-justice considerations..."[36]

Finally, there is a recognition that changes in the processes of development and the internationalization of crime, particularly organized crime, drug traffic, economic crime, terrorism, etc., demand appropriate international efforts in legislative action, implementation of international instruments, and technical and scientific cooperation.

Conclusions

This brief analysis of the major views on the issue of crime and development expressed in the seven United Nations Congresses shows that, practically from the beginning of United Nations involvement in the subject of social defence, this issue was constantly discussed, even if it did not always receive the attention it deserved. The evolution of the approach to the issue and the subsequent action taken reflect an increasing awareness in the United Nations of its importance. Yet the initial assertion that the United Nations system, as such, devoted more attention and resources to development than to the issue of crime seems to hold true. This may be explained by the urgency of the problems of unequal development, hunger, and poverty which confront the developing countries. Moreover, the concept of development has undergone a more radical and swift evolution than has that of crime, even though the United Nations documents show that the concept of crime progressed from a limited legal scope to the broader one of social problems. Programmes for the prevention and control of crime are also receiving increasing attention in the United Nations.

Yet the relationship between crime and development remains an open question. On the level of scientific understanding as on the level of practical action, there are still many unknowns. The situation clearly calls for more research and a better use of existing knowledge to increase our comprehension of this complex relationship. To state that the relationship between these two phenomena is complex is only to make the first step toward avoiding the use of linear, mechanical patterns of interpretation and action. Sociologists, criminologists, and development specialists must delve deeper to analyse the complexity of the issue and its peculiarities.

But we must not forget that social change, when it is the result of calculated action, provides some leeway for its own control. Change will always produce unintentional and unforeseen consequences but, if the slow evolution of the issue through the United Nations Congresses is followed, it becomes apparent that neither a nihilistic attitude or explanation nor "a lesson in unintentional consequences" can usefully interpret the issue of crime and development, at least not today. To transcend these positions by considering the deliberate nature of change only opens up new challenges for those who would analyse the phenomenon. Despite the premises of those who believe that social changes are voluntary and can therefore be controlled, the ubiquity of crime cannot be overlooked. As the United Nations Congresses emphasized, the response of the legal system to such changes must be constantly kept in mind because, in terms of methodology, law is a particularly effective and useful factor for interpreting the relationship between crime and development. This role of the criminal-justice system has only recently, and in a limited way, been taken into account in United Nations documents. Its dimensions should certainly receive more attention and elaboration since, apart from changes in the indices of social and economic mobilization, one of the key variables of development is institutional ability to cope with social changes. But this variable is inconstant and unpredictable. Situations can arise, as they do in many developing countries, in which negative correlations emerge between the high level of development of various socio-demographic indices and the institutional capacity to sustain growth. The institutional ability to govern and control changes becomes less markedly dependent on the processes of development the more closely it is linked to the social, political, and cultural conditions of any given national system. If crime is seen in the context of institutional response to social unbalance — and crime is traditionally considered to be an index of the latter — it becomes evident that relationships between crime and development are in large part determined by the peculiar social, political, and cultural conditions prevailing in the countries concerned. This fact makes a sound examination of the global issue of crime and development difficult and directs research toward less macroscopic levels. Of course there are other methodological problems in studying these relationships, like the absence or dubious quality of quantitative data, but a systematic and exhaustive study of these obstacles would lead to a treatise on research methodology.

The United Nations Congresses dealt with the issue of crime and development by making a series of connections, like urbanization and crime, the role of the family, rural-urban migration, maladjustment of youth, etc., and seeking to provide partial explanations of these connections. Despite the lack of a sound theoretical or conceptual structure in this analysis of the phenomenon, the position of the United Nations has evolved from linear, mechanical treatment of the issue of crime and development to a more sophisticated, multidimensional approach. Lately there has been clear recognition that development is not merely an economic process of growth, and that it cannot be put into effect only in terms of expansion of the indices of economic and social mobilization. Certainly, a broader understanding of development creates methodological complications in the search for the interrelationship between crime and development, but at the same time it permits the issue to be considered as a significant one for both developed and developing countries.

The United Nations Congresses did not provide a conceptually clear or definitive approach to the issue of crime and development. Yet they certainly progressed to an awareness of its importance. They recognized the multiple implications of the relationship between the two phenomena and the need for a global approach, in research as in planning and political actions. Two important statements emerged. First, that development is a complex process which is not confined to the economic sphere, which is not harmonious, and which can be analysed and understood only by a concrete approach and within a particular frame of reference. Second, that crime is also a complex phenomenon which can be examined in relation to development only in the precise context of the particular and concrete social, political, legal, and cultural conditions of each system under study, paying special attention to the ability of institutions to cope with change and to respond to such consequences of change as social conflict, disequilibrium, and all other forms of deviance.

References and Notes

[1] United Nations, *Charter*, Preamble, para. 4.

[2] *Ibidem*, para. 8.

[3] European Social Development Programme, *Report of the Expert Group on Methods of Determining Norms and Standards for Planning and Policy-making in the Social Sectors*, SOA/ESDP/1972/1, Alghero, Italy, 13-19 February 1972.

[4] United Nations, *Survey of Recent and Prospective Trends and Fundamental Changes in the Field of Socio-economic Development: 1985 Report on the World Situation*, E/CN.5/1985/2, 23 January 1985.

[5] United Nations, *Report of the Seventh United Nations Congress on the Prevention of Crime and the Treatment of Offenders*, A/CONF.121/18, Milan, 1985.

[6] United Nations, Economic and Social Council, "Resolution", 731F, XXVIII, 1959 and 830D, XXXII, 1961; General Assembly, "Resolution", 415, V, 1950.

[7] United Nations, *Report of the First United Nations Congress on the Prevention of Crime and the Treatment of Offenders*, A/CONF.6/1, Geneva, 1955, (Sales No. 56.IV.4).

[8] *Ibidem*, p. 79.

[9] United Nations, *Report of the Second United Nations Congress on the Prevention of Crime and the Treatment of Offenders*, A/CONF.17/20, London, 1960, (Sales No. 61.IV.3).

[10] United Nations, Second United Nations Congress on the Prevention of Crime and the Treatment of Offenders. *New Forms of Juvenile Delinquency: Their Origin, Prevention and Treatment*, Doc. A/CONF.17/7, 1960.

[11] *Ibidem, Prevention of Types of Criminality Resulting from Social Changes and Accompanying Economic Development in Less Developed Countries*, Doc. A/CONF.17/3, General reports prepared by Messrs. J. J. Panakal and A. M. Khalifa.

[12] *Ibidem, Prevention of Types of Criminality Resulting from Social Changes and Accompanying Economic Development in Less Developed Countries*, Doc. A/CONF.17/4.

[13] *Ibidem*, UNESCO, *La prévention relative aux formes de criminalité résultant de changements sociaux et accompagnant le progrès économiques des pays peu développés*, Doc. A/CONF.17/12, 1960.

[14] Third United Nations Congress on the Prevention of Crime and the Treatment of Offenders, Stockholm, 1965.

[15] *Ibidem, Report*, A/CONF.26/7, (Sales No. 67.IV.1).

[16] Fourth United Nations Congress on the Prevention of Crime and the Treatment of Offenders, Kyoto, 1970.

[17] *Ibidem, Report*, A/CONF.43/5, (Sales No. E.71.IV.8).

[18] *Ibidem*, para. 287.

[19] Fifth United Nations Congress on the Prevention of Crime and the Treatment of Offenders, Geneva, 1975.

[20] *Ibidem, Report*, A/CONF.56/10, (Sales No. E.76.IV.2).

[21] *Ibidem, Economic and Social Consequences of Crime: New Challenges for Research and Planning*, A/CONF.56/7.

[22] Sixth United Nations Congress on the Prevention of Crime and the Treatment of Offenders, Caracas, 1980.

[23] *Ibidem, Report*, A/CONF.87/14/Rev. 1, (Sales No. E.1.IV.4).

[24] *Ibidem, Crime Trends and Crime Prevention Strategies*, A/CONF.87/4.

[25] See note 23.

[26] United Nations, *Report of the Seventh United Nations Congress on the Prevention of Crime and the Treatment of Offenders*, A/CONF. 121/22/Rev. 1, (Sales No. E.86.IV.1), Milan, 1985.

[27] I) New dimensions of criminality and crime prevention in the context of development: challenges for the future;

II) Criminal justice processes and perspectives in a changing world;

III) Victims of crime;

IV) Youth, crime and justice;

V) Formulation and application of United Nations standards and norms in criminal justice.

[28] United Nations, Annex to the General Assembly, "Resolution", No. 35/56, 1980.

[29] United Nations, Seventh United Nations Congress on the Prevention of Crime and the Treatment of Offenders. *New Dimensions of Criminality and Crime Prevention in the Context of Development*, A/CONF.121/20, 1985; *Second United Nations Survey of Crime*

Trends, Operations of Criminal Justice Systems and Crime Prevention Strategies, A/CONF.121./18, 1985.

[30] *Ibidem, Criminal Justice Process and Perspectives in a Changing World*, A/CONF.121/5.

[31] *Ibidem, Report of the Interregional Preparatory Meeting*, Topic 1, A/CONF.121/IPM/5.

[32] *Ibidem*, Report of the European Regional Preparatory Meeting, A/CONF.121/RPM/1/Corr., Sofia, 1983; Report of the Asia and Pacific Regional Preparatory Meeting, A/CONF.121/RPM/2, Bangkok, 1983; Report of the Latin American Regional Preparatory Meeting, A/CONF.121/RPM/3, San José, Costa Rica, 1983; Report of the African Regional Preparatory Meeting, A/CONF.121/RPM/4, Addis Ababa, 1983; Report of the Western Asia Regional Preparatory Meeting, A/CONF.121/RPM/5, 1984.

[33] *Ibidem, New Dimensions...*

[34] United Nations, Seventh United Nations Congress on the Prevention of Crime and the Treatment of Offenders. Research Workshop on "Perspectives in Action-oriented Research: Youth, Crime and Justice", Milan, 1985; see also document prepared by the United Nations Social Defence Research Institute; and Resolution 20 "Research on Youth, Crime and Juvenile Justice" adopted by the Congress, (Sales No. 86.IV.1), pp. 92-95. See also, U. Zvekić, Ed., *Action-oriented Research on Youth Crime: An International Perspective*, Rome, UNSDRI, Pub. No. 27, 1986.

[35] *Ibidem*, Report of the Seventh United Nations Congress... *op. cit.*, "Guiding Principles for Crime Prevention and Criminal Justice in the Context of Development and a New International Economic Order", para. 14.

[36] *Ibidem*, para. 24.

LIST OF UNSDRI/UNICRI PUBLICATIONS
AND STAFF PAPERS

1969 Publ. No. 1 TENDENCIAS Y NECESIDADES DE LA INVESTI-
GACIÓN CRIMINOLÓGICA EN AMERICA LATI-
NA[1]. *F. Ferracuti, R. Bergalli.*

1970 Publ. No. 2 MANPOWER AND TRAINING IN THE FIELD OF
SOCIAL DEFENCE[2]. *F. Ferracuti, M.C. Giannini.*

1971 S.P. No. 1 CO-ORDINATION OF INTERDISCIPLINARY RE-
SEARCH IN CRIMINOLOGY[1]. *F. Ferracuti.*

1971 Publ. No. 3 SOCIAL DEFENCE IN UGANDA: A SURVEY OF
RESEARCH[1].

1971 Publ. No. 4 PUBLIC ET JUSTICE: UNE ÉTUDE PILOTE EN
TUNISIE[1]. *A. Bouhdiba.*

1972 S.P. No. 2 THE EVALUATION AND IMPROVEMENT OF
MANPOWER TRAINING PROGRAMMES IN SO-
CIAL DEFENCE[1]. *R.W. Burnham.*

1972 S.P. No. 3 PERCEPTIONS OF DEVIANCE. SUGGESTIONS
FOR CROSS-CULTURAL RESEARCH[1]. *G. Newman.*

1973 S.P. No. 4 PERCEPTION CLINIQUE ET PSYCHOLOGIQUE
DE LA DÉVIANCE[1]. *F. Ferracuti, G. Newman.*

SEXUAL DEVIANCE. A SOCIOLOGICAL ANA-
LYSIS[1]. *G. Newman.*

ASPETTI SOCIALI DEI COMPORTAMENTI DE-
VIANTI SESSUALI[1]. *F. Ferracuti, R. Lazzari.*

---

[1] Out of print.
[2] Also published in French and Spanish.

1973 S.P. No. 5 PSYCHOACTIVE DRUG CONTROL. ISSUES AND RECOMMENDATIONS[1-2]. *J.J. Moore, C.R.B. Joyce, J. Woodcock.*

1973 Publ. No. 5 MIGRATION. Report of the Research Conference on Migration, Ethnic Minority Status and Social Adaptation, Rome, 13-16 June 1972.

1973 Publ. No. 6 A PROGRAMME FOR DRUG USE RESEARCH. Report of the proceedings of a workshop at Frascati, Italy, 11-15 December 1972[1].

1973 S.P. No. 6 UN PROGRAMMA DI RICERCA SULLA DROGA. Rapporto del seminario di Frascati, 11-15 dicembre 1972[1].

1974 Publ. No. 7 A WORLD DIRECTORY OF CRIMINOLOGICAL INSTITUTES[1]. *B. Kasme* (ed.).

1974 Publ. No. 8 RECENT CONTRIBUTIONS TO SOVIET CRIMINOLOGY[1].

1974 Publ. No. 9 ECONOMIC CRISIS AND CRIME. Interim report and materials[1].

1974 Publ. No. 10 CRIMINOLOGICAL RESEARCH AND DECISION-MAKING. Studies on the influence of criminological research on criminal policy in The Netherlands and Finland[1].

1976 Publ. No. 11 EVALUATION RESEARCH IN CRIMINAL JUSTICE. Material and proceedings of a Research Conference convened in the context of the Fifth United Nations Congress on the Prevention of Crime and the Treatment of Offenders[1].

1976 Publ. No. 12 JUVENILE JUSTICE. An international survey, country reports, related materials and suggestions for future research[1].

---

[1] Out of print.
[2] Also published in French and Spanish.

1976 Publ. No. 13	THE PROTECTION OF THE ARTISTIC AND ARCHAEOLOGICAL HERITAGE. A VIEW FROM ITALY AND INDIA [1].
1976 Publ. No. 14	PRISON ARCHITECTURE. An international survey of representative closed institutions and analysis of current trends in prison design [3].
1976 Publ. No. 15	ECONOMIC CRISIS AND CRIME. Correlations between the state of the economy, deviance and the control of deviance [1].
1976 Publ. No. 16	INVESTIGATING DRUG ABUSE. A multinational programme of pilot studies into the non-medical use of drugs [1]. *J.J. Moore.*
1978 Publ. No. 17	A WORLD DIRECTORY OF CRIMINOLOGICAL INSTITUTES (2nd edition) [1].
1978 Publ. No. 18	DELAY IN THE ADMINISTRATION OF CRIMINAL JUSTICE - INDIA. *S.K. Mukherjee, A. Gupta.*
1979 Publ. No. 19	RESEARCH AND DRUG POLICY [1]. *J.J. Moore, L. Bozzetti.*
1981	THE EFFECT OF ISLAMIC LEGISLATION ON CRIME PREVENTION IN SAUDI ARABIA [4].
1982 Publ. No. 20	A WORLD DIRECTORY OF CRIMINOLOGICAL INSTITUTES (3rd edition) [1].
1984 Publ. No. 21	COMBATTING DRUG ABUSE. *F. Bruno.*
1984 Publ. No. 22	JUVENILE SOCIAL MALADJUSTMENT AND HUMAN RIGHTS IN THE CONTEXT OF URBAN DEVELOPMENT [1].
1984 Publ. No. 23	THE PHENOMENOLOGY OF KIDNAPPINGS IN SARDINIA. *I.F. Caramazza, U. Leone.*

---

[1] Out of print.

[3] Available through The Architectural Press, 9 Queen Anne's Gate, London SW-H 9BY.

[4] At the request of the Government of the Kingdom of Saudi Arabia, UNSDRI published English, French and Spanish editions of this publication.

1984 Publ. No. 24   THE ROLE OF THE JUDGE IN CONTEMPORARY SOCIETY[5].

1985 Publ. No. 25   CRIME AND CRIMINAL POLICY. PAPERS IN HONOUR OF MANUEL LOPEZ-REY. *P. David* (ed.).

1985 Publ. No. 26   FIRST JOINT INTERNATIONAL CONFERENCE ON RESEARCH IN CRIME PREVENTION, Riyad, 23-25 January 1984[6].

1986 Publ. No. 27   ACTION-ORIENTED RESEARCH ON YOUTH CRIME: AN INTERNATIONAL PERSPECTIVE.[1] *U. Zvekić* (ed.).

1986 Publ. No. 28   A WORLD DIRECTORY OF CRIMINOLOGICAL INSTITUTES (4th edition). *C. Masotti Santoro* (ed.).

1987 Publ. No. 29   RESEARCH AND INTERNATIONAL CO-OPERATION IN CRIMINAL JUSTICE: Survey on Needs and Priorities of Developing Countries.[7] *U. Zvekić, A. Mattei.*

1988 Publ. No. 30   DRUGS AND PUNISHMENT[7]. *D. Cotič.*

1988 Publ. No. 31   ANALYSING (IN)FORMAL MECHANISMS OF CRIME CONTROL: A Cross-cultural Perspective[7]. *M. Findlay, U. Zvekić.*

1988   PRISON IN AFRICA: Acts of the Seminar for Heads of Penitentiary Administrations of the African Countries[8].

1988 Publ. No. 32   THE DEATH PENALTY: A bibliographical research[7].

---

[5] In collaboration with the International Association of Judges.

[6] In collaboration with the Arab Security Studies and Training Center.

[7] Available through United Nations Publications in Geneva (Palais des Nations, CH-1211 Geneva 10, Switzerland) or New York (United Nations Headquarters, Room A3315, New York, N.Y. 10017, USA).

[8] In collaboration with the Ministry of Justice of Italy and the International Centre for Sociological, Penal and Penitentiary Studies, Messina, Italy.

1990	Publ. No. 33	LA CRIMINOLOGIA EN AMERICA LATINA [7]. *L. Aniyar de Castro* (ed).
1990	Publ. No. 35	A WORLD DIRECTORY OF CRIMINOLOGICAL INSTITUTES (5th edition) [7] *C. Masotti Santoro* (ed.).
1990	Publ. No. 38	DIRITTI UMANI ED ISTRUZIONE PENALE. CORSO DI FORMAZIONE SULLE TECNICHE DI ISTRUZIONE ED INVESTIGAZIONE.
1990	Publ. No. 39	SOVIET CRIMINOLOGY UPDATE [7]. *V. N. Kudriavtzev* (ed.).

FORTHCOMING PUBLICATIONS

Publ. No. 34	CRIMINOLOGY IN LATIN AMERICA [9]. *L. Amiyar de Castro* (ed.).
Publ. No. 37	PRISON LABOUR [10].
Publ. No. 40	INFANCIA Y CONTROL PENAL EN AMERICA LATINA [11]. *E. Garcia Méndez, E. Carranza* (ed.).

---

[7] Available through United Nations Publications in Geneva (Palais des Nations, CH-1211 Geneva 10, Switzerland) or New York (United Nations Headquarters, Room A3315, New York, N.Y. 10017, USA).
[9] Publication deferred.
[10] Tentative title; publication deferred.
[11] Joint UNICRI/ILANUD publication.

كيفية الحصول على منشورات الأمم المتحدة

يمكن الحصول على منشورات الأمم المتحدة من المكتبات ودور التوزيع في جميع أنحاء العالم . استعلم عنها من المكتبة
التي تتعامل معها أو اكتب إلى : الأمم المتحدة . قسم البيع في نيويورك أو في جنيف

如何购取联合国出版物

联合国出版物在全世界各地的书店和经售处均有发售。请向书店询问或写信到纽约或日内瓦的
联合国销售组。

HOW TO OBTAIN UNITED NATIONS PUBLICATIONS

United Nations publications may be obtained from bookstores and distributors throughout the
world. Consult your bookstore or write to: United Nations, Sales Section, New York or Geneva.

COMMENT SE PROCURER LES PUBLICATIONS DES NATIONS UNIES

Les publications des Nations Unies sont en vente dans les librairies et les agences dépositaires
du monde entier. Informez-vous auprès de votre libraire ou adressez-vous à : Nations Unies,
Section des ventes, New York ou Genève.

КАК ПОЛУЧИТЬ ИЗДАНИЯ ОРГАНИЗАЦИИ ОБЪЕДИНЕННЫХ НАЦИЙ

Издания Организации Объединенных Наций можно купить в книжных магазинах
и агентствах во всех районах мира. Наводите справки об изданиях в вашем книжном
магазине или пишите по адресу: Организация Объединенных Наций, Секция по
продаже изданий, Нью-Йорк или Женева.

COMO CONSEGUIR PUBLICACIONES DE LAS NACIONES UNIDAS

Las publicaciones de las Naciones Unidas están en venta en librerías y casas distribuidoras en
todas partes del mundo. Consulte a su librero o diríjase a: Naciones Unidas, Sección de Ventas,
Nueva York o Ginebra.

Printed in Rome
Tipografia Poliglotta della
Pontificia Università Gregoriana,
Piazza della Pilotta, 4 - Roma
July 1990
ISBN 92-9078-010-X

Price: $US38.00
(or equivalent in other
currencies)

United Nations publication
Sales No. E.90.III.N.2